Cultural Analysis of Texts

Cultural Analysis of Texts

Mikko Lehtonen

Translated by
Aija-Leena Ahonen and Kris Clarke

SAGE Publications
London • Thousand Oaks • New Delhi

SAGE Publications Ltd
6 Bonhill Street
London EC2A 4PU

SAGE Publications Inc
2455 Teller Road
Thousand Oaks, California 91320

SAGE Publications India Pvt Ltd
32, M-Block Market
Greater Kailash – I
New Delhi 110 048

British Library Cataloguing in Publication Data

A catalogue record for this book is
available from the British Library

ISBN 0 7619 6550 5
ISBN 0 7619 6551 3 (pbk)

Library of Congress catalog card number available

Typeset by Keystroke, Jacaranda Lodge, Wolverhampton.
Printed in Great Britain by Biddles Ltd, Guildford, Surrey.

CONTENTS

We begin to think where we live. When I was writing this book I lived in Tampere, an industrial city that lies in between two lakes in southern Finland, which is often claimed to be the centre of Finnish literature, sometimes the mecca of Finnish rock, at other times the city of women, occasionally the red city, and not only the cradle of Finnish ice hockey but currently the cradle of Finnish cultural studies, as well. When I still lived in Helsinki, every time I visited Tampere I felt I was in Finland (Helsinki being a Finnish-Swedish-Russian-German city). But Tampere, too, was founded by a Swedish king and industrialized by a certain Scotsman with the kind assistance of the then Russian Tsar (at least the rapids are originally from Tampere). Moreover, currently Tampere is known not only for the sole Lenin Museum in existence in the world, but also for its many international conferences, for its bedrock that is among the most ancient in the world (of which the residents know nothing about, but which enthusiastic international tourists hurry to touch in vast crowds) and for the tiny neighbouring town called Nokia. A small Finnish locality has swiftly developed into a global city.

So, where did I live as I thought about and wrote this book? Here, but in a 'here' the locality of which is increasingly determined by its connection to other places. Besides, in the name of honesty I must confess that my work in Tampere would not have been possible had I not had the opportunity to spend time also in the famed reading room of the old British Library, the very place where Marx, Gandhi and other such personalities with a bit more renown than myself have tried to settle comfortably in their chairs.

Even Tampere globalizes, but different contexts – local, national and international – maintain their significance even in a globalized world. Hence, this book's context of birth has been not only the everyday of highly literate people of Tampere but also the ever-increasing community of researchers in the fields of culture, literature and media, to whose smorgasbord the book hopefully brings its zesty addition.

Excellent assistance in the process of recontextualizing the book was provided by the translators Kris Clarke and Aija-Leena Ahonen. Welcome help was also given by Pertti Alasuutari, Sari Elfving and Juha Koivisto of Tampere, as well as the North-Carolina-based Larry Grossberg, and Julia Hall and Seth Edwards in London. My warm thanks to you all!

Tampere

CHAPTER I

STOP THE WORLD, I WANT IN!

This is a book about the formation and study of meanings. In the following pages, I attempt to develop a notion of the *contextual* and *cultural* nature of textual meanings. In addition to being an introduction to its subject matter, this book contributes to the development of a theory of meaning that is based on a theory of articulation. Unlike many theories concerning meaning, I endeavour to go beyond the level of signs and texts to study how their meaning potentials are realized in their cultural contexts.

The meanings of the world decline to organize themselves into a serene landscape that is conveniently placed at a researcher's disposal. On the contrary, the researcher must construct an image of them piecemeal; an image which will largely resemble the cognitive and conceptual frameworks that were utilized in its production. In this sense, to research the meanings of the world is in itself to produce meanings.

It is not my objective to produce a general view of the world of meanings or to divide them into controllable segments, removing the components from their contexts or arranging them into neatly labelled patterns. On the one hand, my objective is more limited than the objective of one who produces overviews or a lepidopterist. On the other hand, it is perhaps more challenging. In the pages of this book I ask: where and how are meanings formed? I seek an answer by combining the tools of *the poetics of texts, the hermeneutics of contexts* and *notions concerning the subjectivity and identity of readers, viewers and listeners.*

As to the study of texts, my book is localized in the 'long revolution' that took place during the second half of the twentieth century, where the previously author- and production-centred views were substituted firstly by text-centred and later by increasingly context and reader-centred views.[1] *Radical contextualism* forms the basis of this book. All in all, I deal with six issues that are present in one way or another in the formation of meanings: culture, language, media, texts, contexts, and readers.

There are seven main chapters in this book:

- In the second chapter, 'The Meaningfulness of the World, the Worldliness of Meanings', I delineate the approach I have chosen.
- In the third chapter, 'Language as Human Being in the World', I study the historical and social nature of symbolic meanings.
- In the fourth chapter, 'The World of Sign Systems and Technologies', I consider the share of different material forms of texts (oral, literary, audiovisual and digital) in the formation of meanings.
- The focal point, the fifth chapter, is 'The World of Texts', which examines the formation of meanings on a textual level, and the action

of textual signifiers. In this chapter, which largely focuses on the printed text, I ask: *How do texts work?*

- In the sixth chapter, 'The World of Contexts', I analyse what happens when texts meet other texts. Now, in addition to text, the concept of context is introduced. It seeks to explain how the multiple meaning potentials of texts become or do not become realized. The central question of the chapter is: *What do texts mean?*
- In the seventh chapter, 'The World of Readers', I study the subjectivities, activities and cultural identities of the readers (and the spectators and listeners).
- In the eighth chapter, 'The World of Articulation', I weave the threads together and seek to develop a tool box based on the theory of articulation for cultural text analysis.

In this book I thus analyse the relationships between texts, contexts and readers in the formation of meanings. Correspondingly, I seek methods through which each of these three elements can be analysed in relationship to the other elements. This is necessary for the very reason that in the formation of meanings, none of these elements exists on its own, independent of the other elements. On the contrary, texts, contexts and readers do indeed obtain their identity in interaction with one another.

In spite of their mutual dependency, texts, contexts and readers are not identical and therefore cannot be studied in the same way. Hence, when it comes to texts, I attempt to develop a *poetics* whose objective is to analyse the different kinds of meaning potential that texts reveal. Where contexts are concerned, I develop a *hermeneutics* that would assist in analysing which of the meaning potentials opened up by texts can be realized in the actual readings. When it comes to readers, I outline the tools which it is possible to use to answer questions, not only 'what kinds of meanings are there and why do these people produce them from this particular text in this particular historical place and time?' but also 'what kinds of effects do texts have regarding the subjectivity, identity and empowerment or disempowerment of the readers?'

The organization of the chapters does not imply an order that starts from the most important subject and proceeds to the least important one – or the other way around. Though culture, symbols, technologies, symbol systems, texts, contexts and readers all relate to each other in the formation of meanings, the order in which they are presented does not represent any kind of a hierarchical mutual relationship. Had it been possible, I would have liked to present the subjects side by side.

Now, however, the context of the book defines the order of the chapters. Since the notion of meanings is generally solidly wound around texts not only in disciplines that study texts, but also in our culture in general, I must first criticize this text-centred view in order to progress to other elements that I find equally important: contexts and readers. Nevertheless, the book can freely be read in any other order. If the reader wants to know something about contexts, s/he can quite happily start from Chapter 6.

In the book, I lean on the discussion on the significatory nature of culture and the textuality of culture that has been going on for the last two decades in the various human sciences, particularly in literary studies, communications studies and cultural studies. Alas, among other things, my book is intended to be a suitable introductory textbook in the field of cultural text analysis, among others, for the above-mentioned fields. However, I have not attempted solely to write an introduction, but also to formulate a new methodology for cultural text analysis. To be on the safe side, it should also be mentioned that my intention is not to require everyone who practises the cultural study of texts to undertake a study concerning the triad of texts, contexts and readers within each and every one of the texts they analyse. As beneficial as this kind of comprehensive study can be, it usually demands a great deal of time and human resources. I content myself with emphasizing that the model I attempt to develop functions first and foremost as a research horizon, a necessary reminder of the fact that whether we enter more closely into texts, contexts or readers, we cannot presume that any of the three acquires its form on its own, independent of the other two.

Human beings are by their nature cultural

My book treats the subject of *cultural* text analysis. As I place stress on the cultural nature of texts, I want to emphasize two closely connected matters: the constitutive role of culture for human existence and the notion of the worldly nature of symbolic meanings that it opens up. Again, one can get a grip on these two by taking a moment to examine the concept of 'human nature'.

In these allegedly postmodern times, 'human nature' might not make it to the top ten list of popular concepts. Have we not just recently learned both in the social and human sciences that a human being is a thoroughly cultural being, *Homo significans*, to whose existence, which fluctuates from one place and time to another, meanings are fundamental and who, therefore, has no unchanging 'nature'? In spite of this – or perhaps for this very reason? – I begin with 'human nature'.

Naturally, nature is not very far from us. As human beings we all are close to nature in the sense of being physical creatures who would perish were we not in interaction with nature. Moreover, we are natural beings since we can be treated as objects. However, compared to other living beings we possess the extraordinary quality of not having a predetermined scope of activities and habits.

As physical beings humans are obviously part of nature, but they are part of a special nature; such a nature that while changing the material objects surrounding them, they can also change themselves. In this sense, the *specific nature* of human beings could be conceived of as not having a specific nature. Moreover, if human beings are actors that are able to change themselves, they are never identical with themselves in the same way as other animate or inanimate natural creatures are. We are formed in a creative relationship with our world.

In fact, the human body possesses the special ability to produce what reciprocally produces the human body. In this sense, the human body resembles another matter that, in addition to its physical nature, is fundamental to humanity: language. On the one hand, we encounter language as if it was already completed and learn to use it in a way that is comprehensible. On the other hand, however, we can also produce things in language that have never been done before. As linguistic beings we are astoundingly creative. Moreover, as physical creatures we encounter material reality as something already existing, yet we are able to produce something new from it.

From this perspective, humans are no more 'cultural' than 'natural' beings. We do not belong primarily to culture or to nature, but to both. We can think of ourselves as *cultural beings by our nature*.[2]

Nonetheless, we are not cultural beings only by nature, but also out of necessity. One of the great insights of psychoanalytical theory is that we are all born prematurely. It takes a great length of time before we are able to look after ourselves. Without immediate, long term care we would succumb to a very early death. This unusually long dependency on our parents is primarily connected to nurturing and caretaking, satisfying biologically determined needs such as nourishment, warmth and so on. Yet, beyond these biological needs of self-preservation, we are dependent on our parents for various other needs. We would not become humans without other humans.

Does this mean that as cultural and linguistic beings we are absolutely free to do whatever we please? Most certainly not. Though some philosophers have attempted to imagine such a thing, none of us is born in a vacuum. We function in conditions which are not of our own making. Yet this does not imply that we are absolutely unfree. The matters that determine us – body and language – are at the same time things that we, ourselves, can determine. In other words, being determined allows us autonomy to a certain extent. We are no more utterly predetermined than totally autonomous, but can to a certain extent determine ourselves, produce ourselves. This, however, is not a consequence of us being completely independent of our environment, but is due to the fact that self-determination is a necessity produced by our environment. Were we not able to determine ourselves, we probably would have become extinct as a species ages ago. In order to survive, human beings cannot trust only their instincts but must use their reflective resources as well. Humans are *preconceiving* creatures – preconceiving for we are so incomplete. As unfinished, naked, badly equipped creatures we must be able to preconceive dangers and foresee possibilities simply to survive. Therefore, our hunger is not merely crude hunger but, correspondingly, always contains longing, images, will and, finally – perhaps – also action. Were we not capable of crossing the borders of previous experience and customs to a certain degree, we would not make it as a species. *We are free for necessity's sake.*

The idea of people being naturally cultural, necessarily free beings has important consequences from the viewpoint of human culture and the studies of human meanings. It reminds us of the significant fact that *what is at stake in culture is never solely a question of only culture, but is always also a question of something else.* Contrary to an all-embracing culturalism, I want to stress the point that as we comprehend and interpret cultural symbols, the objective of comprehension and interpretation is always *something else.* We always comprehend something that we have perceived and that is never the same as the one who comprehends (this is also the case when we attempt to understand ourselves, for then we divide in two: the understander and the one to be understood). Likewise, our symbols always represent something that they themselves are not. The word 'symbol' is derived from the Greek verb *symballein,* which means 'throwing together' and 'bringing together'. Hence, symbolizing is always bringing together a symbol and something else. For which reason, besides being mere signs, there are always other things represented in symbols.

Cultural symbols are omnipresent precisely for the reason that they are essential for our survival. Culture is the *survival kit* of humankind. Being biologically defective, humans must resort to their reflective resources for survival.

Language and its meanings indeed mark the terrain of human beings, interpreting the reality and producing identities. They are an essential part of our common history, the making of us and our societies. Therefore, in this book I expressly attempt to practise worldly studies. It is also a part of this worldliness that I have attempted to compile a text that does not conceal its own intellectual operations, but that makes the methods and techniques it utilizes as comprehensible and useful as possible. It is my wish that my book offer something of a tool for other researchers of text to take hold of and brings delight to those who cast an inquiring eye on our world: the world of nature *and* culture.

Notes

1. Since there has been a discourse about 'the death of the author' for some decades already, I did not consider it necessary to return to it in this book. Important comments about the discourse can be found in Roland Barthes' essay 'The Death of the Author' (Barthes 1968/1986a) and Michel Foucault's essay 'What Is an Author?' (Foucault 1979).
2. See Eagleton 1996b, chapter 4, which I have used in this condensation.

CHAPTER 2

THE MEANINGFULNESS OF THE WORLD, THE WORLDLINESS OF MEANINGS

A few years ago, the side of a milk carton from Tine, a Norwegian dairy, featured the following *hjernegym* (mental exercise):

> A milk lorry from Trondheim begins its trip southwards. Another one drives north from Oslo. The lorry from Trondheim leaves two hours later than the one from Oslo, but drives at a speed of approximately 70 kilometres per hour. The lorry leaving from Oslo travels at an average speed of 50 kilometres per hour. The distance between Oslo and Trondheim is 500 kilometres. Which lorry is closer to Oslo when they meet?

As I happened upon this brain teaser, I tried to recollect similar exercises from my long-past school days. Thus, I began to calculate how many hours the lorry from Trondheim would spend on the journey, how many hours the lorry from Oslo would need, and at which point they would meet. Since I was having breakfast, I could not be bothered to complete the calculations but cheated and sneaked a peek at the correct answer on the other side of the milk carton, kindly provided by the dairy. It read:

> *Regardless of where the two lorries eventually do meet, they are naturally at an equal distance from Oslo!*

I had been fooled, just as the puzzler had intended. The textual form of the question and its connection to similar exercises in school mathematics had led me astray. Misled by the irrelevant details, I failed to notice the obvious clue to the correct answer which was included in the words *when they meet*.

In a Norwegian kitchen, the form, text and context of the exercise, as well as the reader's cultural location, all combined to contribute to the poor sleep-befuddled reader being cheated. Since the text was printed on the side of a milk carton, it could not be very long, and as a reader I also did not take it too seriously. The text was constructed in such a way that it provided information totally irrelevant to the solution, which led the victim on an erroneous path. However, it was not only the text and its form in and of itself that was enough to fool the reader; the process also involved contextual knowledge that was misleading on its part – the reader's experience of similar kinds of school exercises.

Moreover, the location of the reader made its own contribution. The puzzle caught my attention while I was on a summer holiday. I read it while sitting with my friends, amidst the other chatter at the breakfast table. My attitude – and my sharpness, I hope – might have been different had the same question been presented to me in another connection, say, at a mathematics examination at school.

The milk carton anecdote is not only embarrassing but trivial, if not banal. Yet, triviality and banality cannot be avoided as subjects, if one wishes to make any sense of the world of meanings. Indeed, it is precisely the trivial and the banal that must be the starting point of study. The well-known fact that that which is everywhere is usually not noticed at all also applies to meanings. It is often true that the most common is, at the same time, the most obscure. We live amidst meanings produced by other people, which we largely take at face value. We scarcely stop to contemplate such a peculiarity as, for example, the fact that in different contexts the colour red signifies Christmas, blood, leftism, love and prohibited driving to Western people. Moreover, while we are reading, we do not stop to marvel at the reality that in Western cultures, written texts are read from left to right and from up to down. The varying meanings of the colour red and the simplicity of our writing system conceal the fact from us that there is an enormous amount of human history as well as assumptions about our world encapsulated in them.

It is precisely this banal surface of 'common sense' that I want to break. Colour symbolism and writing systems are examples of special ways of producing meanings, which have their historical prerequisites and consequences. The point of departure of all research and creative thinking is wondering, fixing a searching look on matters that are seemingly obvious, and raising the question presented in the Brechtian spirit: 'Why is this so?'

The key questions of this book can be summarized by the milk carton anecdote: What happens when texts and readers meet? How are meanings produced? What roles do symbols, forms of symbols and texts have in this process, what is the role of contexts, and what is the role of the reader's cultural location?

At the same time, the milk carton anecdote is simple proof of the fact that we irreversibly live in a world of meanings. Meanings are 'here, there and everywhere', as the Beatles used to sing in their time. Still dazed with sleep, we don't make it past the breakfast coffee before we are already firmly embraced by the endless abundance of meanings. In even the most everyday and routine situations we are surrounded by a shoreless sea of signs comprised of imagery, sounds, writing and their combinations. We are the decathletes in the world of meanings – and more: while Daley Thompson and his chums can only concentrate on one sport at a time, we simultaneously read the morning paper, exchange words with our loved ones, glance at morning TV and go through the day's tasklist in our minds.

Humans are explanatory beings

In the second half of the twentieth century people have become the targets of an unparalleled flood of signs. Practically at every waking moment, different cultural signs speak to all our senses – to the extent that when I visited the woods with my then-three-year-old son, he asked: 'Doesn't it read anything in here?'[1]

Along with postmodernism, all traditional evaluation criteria are said to have been struck down. Since the public has diversified and different text forms appear side by side, everything in culture is in confusion and almost anything seems to go. The existence of different texts alongside each other does not, however, signify that no new criteria have been born or that all old criteria have vanished into thin air. Meanings are in an even more central position at the core of human life. Routines, rituals, traditions and myths are all an inseparable part of our everyday existence. With all their contradictions, they lay the foundation for the degree of stability we have. Signs directed at us are not so much an intrusion in our daily life, but rather maintain it. The morning paper, the favourite TV show and the novel by the bed produce a certain sense of order. These things participate in the construction of our everyday lives and ourselves in many ways that we tend to overlook for the very reason of their commonness.

The Swedish cultural researcher Johan Fornäs aptly describes the fundamental nature of meanings in our lives:

> Culture is everywhere in human life and society. We are human by understanding and interpreting what we perceive, that is, by constructing symbols where something stands for something else. Symbols make it possible to think of what is not present, and thus to reflect upon the past and plan the future, to explore the other(s) and speculate about the unknown. By collectively shaping such symbolic patterns we construct a world and give ourselves specific positions in it.[2]

However, the notion of the fundamental role of meanings in human life is not a twentieth-century discovery. Long before the birth of writing systems, people left marks which were intended to indicate something to others: grass and leaves piled at the start of a path marked that there was a reason to avoid that route; a twig stuck in the ground indicated the direction taken by the previous wanderer. Rocks piled on a graveside told passers-by that they were approaching a sacred place.

Likewise, shaping and decorating artefacts (carving, sculpting and painting) have been used in producing meanings. Australian Aboriginals have used wooden batons, sticks or boards engraved with marks, furrows and notches for messages. In Peru, even before the Incan Empire, beans marked with points and lines were used to send messages. The Iroquois' belts embroidered with pearls were used not only to convey messages, but also in rituals and as personal decorations. The colours of the belts each had their own meaning: dark shades marked solemnity and gravity, in addition to signifying danger, animosity, mourning and death. White was the colour of happiness; red of war. The belts were occasionally used when war was declared (a red tomahawk was embroidered in an otherwise black belt) or as signs of making peace (two dark hands on a white background).[3]

The decathlon in the world of meanings has not been limited to interpreting signs that are made for the express purpose of being signs. Throughout our existence, humans have been looking for causes, consequences and reasons behind everything. We make the world meaningful to ourselves by interpreting our experiences, telling ourselves and others stories, observing our environment and making assumptions about it. Wherever we go, we see meanings, patterns and analogies, and compare what we encounter to our earlier experiences. At all times we interpret the needs, motives, desires and abilities of ourselves and of others, and anticipate the reactions of others to our own actions. Without this perpetual signification that, for the most part, remains unnoticed by ourselves, reality would present itself as mere chaos to us.

In this general sense, producing meanings and reading them belong to the most frequently repeated human activities. To put it briefly, humans are *explanatory beings*.[4] We draw conclusions about reality, social situations and ourselves, and in this way produce conceptions of what this world really is and what our part in it is both for ourselves and others.

The cultural nature of meanings

This perpetual stream of meanings expanded into a real surge in the twentieth century in particular. The cultural revolution that took place in Western countries during the latter half of the century is perhaps best characterized as the disentanglement of the bonds that have traditionally joined people together and to their communities.[5] Consequently, traditional value systems as well as customs and habits have more or less disappeared. It is no coincidence that the question of identities was one of the most avidly discussed themes of the 1980s and 1990s. In all of this resounds the long-term crisis of meanings that are ready-made and appear relatively stable. Meanings have diversified – irreversibly, perhaps – and we all struggle to make some kind of sense of our lives.

As we produce the manuscripts of our lives we unavoidably use the words of others, and direct our words to others. In this very important sense, meanings are not of our own making. Even in the world of meaning, our freedom is by no means absolute. We may cruise from one TV channel to another, surf the net or spend hours in the book and music stores of big cities, but even then we are not sovereigns of the world of meanings. We certainly have freedom of choice, but our power to decide from which selection to choose is quite a bit more limited. (On the other hand, it is good to keep in mind that our choices always have an effect to some extent. Everything that is offered to consumers does not automatically 'make it'. Only every thirteenth recording, for example, recoups its production costs.)[6]

Meanings, values and views find their concrete forms in institutions, social relations, belief systems, customs and habits, and the usage of the material world and its objects. Together all these things form cultures. Cultures contain maps of meanings, which make the world comprehensible to their members. These maps of meanings are not located only in people's heads but also gain tangible material forms in those activity and behavioural models, the adoption of which we can prove as belonging to a certain culture. It is precisely through the networks of different maps of meanings and symbols that we enjoy, suffer, love, hate, know, evaluate and understand.[7]

Nobody is born in a vacuum. The time and place of our birth thrusts us into the midst of formations of meanings, with which we later learn to make sense of the world we are living in. Our growing into being a member of our community is first and foremost learning the maps of meanings of the culture we happened to have been born into. Thrown upon the world we do produce meanings, but as producers of meanings we ourselves are products of meanings, social relationships, customs – in short, culture.

Cultural phenomena are characteristically intersubjective. They require the consciousness of more than one subject. Cultural symbols transmit subjects by connecting them to each other through certain contents of meaning. It is also a part of intersubjectivity that meanings have their material dimension, that they also exist in a material form beyond the consciousness of subjects, in a textual form or otherwise.[8]

However, the intersubjectivity of meanings does not mean that they would be same to all people at all times and everywhere. To give an example: as offspring of Western culture, the desire to possess things runs in the blood of many of us. It is a habit in our culture to measure the happiness and success of a person by the amount of Mammon s/he has managed to pile up. In certain Native American cultures, however, possessing material things is considered a mark of misfortune. If someone has accumulated too many earthly things, it is considered a sign of a wretched person who lacks friends with whom to share his/her possessions.[9]

The worldliness of meanings

With the assistance of signs we are told and we tell ourselves what the reality is where we live, and who we are ourselves. For years now, advertisers have not sold us products by claiming them to be durable, inexpensive, practical or necessary. Instead they offer us their things on the pretext that by purchasing them we buy for ourselves certain identities.

Our decathlon in the world of meanings not only occurs in the arena of printed or audiovisual texts. It would be impossible for us to orienteer in the everyday were we not able to read and understand most of the different kinds of signs. Traffic lights, shop signs, and the garments and behaviour of our fellow beings are all signs we must be able to read and interpret.

Moreover, this is nowhere near all of it. There is an infinite number of symbols in our culture with which we are expected to be familiar. A fist symbolizes a readiness to fight, a skull with crossed bones is a sign of poison or signifies a violation of maritime law. Barbed wire symbolizes the lack of freedom and a dove is a symbol of peace; a length of thread wound around a finger is a reminder of something we are not to forget. A scale symbolizes justice, holding one's hand out to another person or raising it up in a greeting tells the other person that we do not have anything against him/her (the hand does not hold a weapon), and a ring is the sign of a union between two people. A cat symbolizes enigma, a dog faithfulness, a rooster France, and a cigar both wealth and gangsterism. An eye is a sign of providence and a fig leaf of modesty. Bearskin hats and double-deckers symbolize London, a harp Ireland, bees diligence; an hourglass is a symbol of the limited time a human being has on this earth, a house of cards symbolizes fragility and a Jack-in-the-box unexpectedness. A key is an emblem of the solution to a problem, a keyhole symbolizes voyeurism, the *Mona Lisa* is a symbol of the fine arts, a monkey of the worst features of a human being and the number seven infinity. An owl is a symbol of wisdom, a pipe of reliability, a marionette a lack of will, a road means life, a four-leaf clover is a symbol of good fortune, a snowman of winter, a tree symbolizes life and knowledge. Finally, a jungle symbolizes complexity – and the jungle of symbols is complex, indeed.

Our culture thus is dependent on the infinite mass of signs. Reading these signs is a focal part of our being in the world. There is a dimension linked to meanings in all human activities. Human reality can be approached through the metaphor of textuality: it is a weave of meanings, an entanglement of diverse ingredients. Our world is a world of meanings.

However, if our world is a world of meanings, the meanings we encounter are expressly *worldly meanings*. If human reality is a weave of meanings, these meanings possess a material and social, that is, worldly foundation. Texts are not stuck on top of the rest of the world, as messages detachable from it, but participate in a central way in the making of the reality as well as forming our image of it.

Obviously, there are other things in the world besides language. Since we humans are bodily creatures, there are important areas beyond language that are part of our experience. In spite of this, our *concepts* of reality are inevitably linguistic and textual by nature. Therefore, the meanings of language are also expressly worldly meanings.

The worldliness of meanings also becomes apparent in the many meanings of the words 'meaning' and 'to mean'. If something 'means' something – as the word 'chatterbox' means a particularly talkative person – the question is not only of the intention of the person who uses the word, but of a common significance connected with the word in our culture. Moreover, there is often a dimension of valuing connected to the 'meaning'.

For example, in the sentence: 'The traditions of my family mean a lot to me' meaning equals value which we attach to something.

The worldliness of meanings makes them essentially disputable. Self-evident meanings do not exist. The least commonsense meanings are the ones which pronounce themselves to be so. When we hear sayings such as 'It goes without saying' or 'Even a child knows that . . . ' we should prick up our ears and be even more alert than usual, since nothing is as suspect as 'common sense'. Because meanings are the creations of people, the same conditions apply to them as to any other human activity and their products: they are temporary, unstable and susceptible to change. Many of today's commonsense sayings will most probably be viewed as barbarism tomorrow. When talking about 'common sense' we should bear in mind that it is not so very long ago that 'common sense' told us to use corporal punishment to discipline our children, ordered young people to abstain from masturbation, firmly placed women in the kitchen and chained the representatives of the so-called black race into slavery.

The meanings I am talking about are public and accessible to anyone. However, from these very same meanings the private self of each of us is constructed – as far as, if at all, it is possible to separate the public and private from each other in the process of the formation of the self. Our personal and public experiences get mixed up when we construct our own life stories. The world of meanings also provides us with behavioural and role models. Many a little boy wanted to be Batman in the 1960s. Mark Chapman, the man who murdered John Lennon, had been influenced by J.D. Salinger's novel *The Catcher in the Rye*. One cannot but wonder how many computer hackers have sought inspiration in William Gibson's *Neuromancer*.

The effect of the world of meanings is certainly not limited to the level of representation. The significance of TV dramas, such as *Ally McBeal*, to their viewers is a good example of how it appears not only on the screen but also in the organization of their daily time economy. Fans of the Spice Girls and other immensely popular groups, for their part, do not merely listen to the music of their idols but at the same time construct and manifest their own identities. And how would boys learn to be boys if not from the cartoons and movies about superheroes?

The organizing of the world of meanings construes the daily life of entire communities and their concept of their own identities in an important way. In cultures where meanings are produced and transmitted orally for the main part, locale, individuality and tradition probably carry great weight; whereas in cultures where meanings are also produced and trans-mitted through printed materials, a national aspect rises up beside the local one, individuals who produce meanings are no longer necessarily known to the readers, and traditions have a tendency to diversify. Finally, producing and transmitting meanings electronically and digitally places globality next to the local and national levels, but also produces new local subcultures.

Meanings and power

The everyday life of people in our late modern culture includes not only oral, but written, printed, electronically and recently also digitally transmitted texts. Increasingly, many people work with these multifaceted texts. At the same time, the shortening of working hours has also come to mean that we have more time than previous generations to delve into the endless abundance of texts. Hence, in the world of meanings there are no such things as the green EXIT sign or the red OFF button.

The historian Eric Hobsbawm notes in his history of 'the short twentieth century' (1914–1991), *The Age of Extremes*, that at the beginning of the 1990s the stream of information and entertainment flooding every house was greater than that which the emperors were offered in 1914.[10] These meanings are not shadows of Platonic forms, a second-rate, lesser reality. On the one hand they are products of social reality, but on the other hand they are also participants in the production of this reality. As Johan Fornäs summarizes:

> Symbolic or cultural forms mirror, represent and thematize other parts and aspects of human life, society and the external world. This is no transparent reproduction but a symbolically coded reconstruction which is never the same as what it depicts or points at. And it does not imply that the whole cultural sphere is only a reflex of material, economic, political, social or subjective levels. Culture represents or refigures these other 'realities' while simultaneously opening an intersubjectively shared symbolic dimension of its own. Cultural texts mirror society but simultaneously take part in its formation.[11]

Therefore, meanings are 'realities' just as economics and politics are realities. Moreover, as economics and politics also have their own dimension of meanings, they, too, are areas of cultural practices and cultural production.

It also speaks for the reality of meanings that their raw material, texts, are today industrially produced. (As a matter of fact, the central cultural product of the modern time, the book, was the first merchandise produced for mass circulation.) Meanings have social influence, political consequences and cultural power. They have their politics.

Writing about meanings is never 'only' writing about meanings. This book does not concern itself solely with textual meanings or the symbolic values attached to different phenomena and activities, but attempts to get a grip on relationships between people – men and women, young and old, rich and poor, straights and the otherwise sexually oriented, 'us' and 'them' – through dealing with meanings. Meanings and social relationships are so tightly entwined with each other that it would be misleading to discuss one without discussing the other.[12]

Social relationships cannot be discussed without colliding with the question of power. Generally, power is understood as the ability to achieve various desired results: the power to buy and sell, the power to make other people obey one's orders, the power to reward and punish, give and take, do good to others or cause them emotional or physical harm. In all these forms of power language and its meanings have a central position.[13]

Power is not, however, created only through force. The functioning of power relations on both macro and micro levels is bound to the fact that certain meanings concerning reality are in a hegemonic position in relation to others. These hegemonic notions, valid ideologies in their respective societies and cultures, could be characterized as 'common sense' – groups of commonly accepted conceptions which in their self-evidence support the dominant power relations.

The aforementioned notions of children's corporal punishment, young people's abstinence from masturbation, tying women to the kitchen and forcing slaves into the field are good examples of this hegemony. Through corporal punishment, the parent attempts to root out the manifestations of the child's own will. By threatening blindness and the rotting of the spine as consequences of masturbation, adults try to prevent youngsters from becoming familiar with their own awakening sexuality. By chaining women to the stove, men shut them out of the arena of public matters. In each case, 'common sense' supported the dominant power relations and prevented the empowerment of the subordinate.

Even today, not all people have access to the world of meanings. At the dawn of the twenty-first century, there are still millions who cannot read written text. Cultural resources related to electronic and digital technology are even more unevenly distributed.

However, the lack of necessary skills or equipment is not the only reason for people to be excluded from the world of meanings. Dominant meanings can silence whole communities of people for long stretches of time. There are cultural situations in which deviants and dissidents simply do not have the words and meanings at their disposal with which they would be able to express their experiences and views in a form comprehensible to other people. In many countries gays and lesbians, for example, still either do not seem to exist to the mainstream media or the unmentioned but entrenched petty bourgeois morality, or they are not considered equal human beings on a par with the heterosexual population. In Western mainstream culture, a non-heterosexual orientation is still a taboo for which plain, matter-of-fact words are hard to find.

Different maps of meanings do not carry the same weight in every culture. Each map manifests the position and standpoint of the group that has formed it. Hence, the maps of meanings of the groups that are in a powerful position tend to become the valid ways of categorizing and arranging reality for the entire culture. However, this does not mean that the dominant map of meaning is the only accessible means to perceive and weigh reality in each respective culture. Along with the dominant maps there often exist residual maps, of which the royal houses of Great Britain, Sweden and many other countries are but one example. During the latter part of the twentieth century, the monarchy has been dented many times, particularly in Great Britain, but it still provides one way to construe reality and build national identity in these countries.

Next to dominant and residual meanings we can also talk about emergent meanings. This term refers to new meanings that challenge the dominant ones, in comparison to which they are either alternative or even contradictory in character.[14] Emergent meanings can also be liberating. The silenced can gain a voice, and experiences and consciousness previously excluded from the dominant culture can become visible. They can come forward and insults gain new meaning as the insulted adapt them to their own use (as the word 'nigger' is used nowadays by young African-Americans of themselves in certain contexts).

All in all, the existence of dominant, residual and emergent meanings implies that there is a continuous battle going on in the world of meanings regarding how reality is understood and what can be said about it.

The world of people

This book ardently participates in the battle of how the world of people should be understood. I do not take the dominant notions of the formation of meanings as given, but do my best to call them into question when it is necessary for my purposes. However, I do not see being 'critical' as searching for errors and being generally negative towards everything that exists. Radical criticism is rather like digging down to the root of things (*radix* in Latin) – observing how something works. A person who has adopted a critical attitude presents, for example, the following kinds of questions:

- Why is something or why does it happen?
- What is its purpose?
- Whose interests does it serve?
- Whose interests does it contradict?
- How does.it work?
- Can it be or work only in the way it is or does, or could it work better in some other way?[15]

To the one who digs into the roots, nothing – not even a milk carton – is so banal or trivial that the basis for its existence or its purpose and functions cannot be questioned. In this sense, a critical attitude means the strongly positive sense of considering everything human worthy of attention and significant and is not generally a negative attitude which wishes to strike everything down that exists.

Critical positivity, however, does not mean an uncritical acceptance of everything. It is rather a necessary point of departure in order to make sense of the phenomena of this complex world. In this book, a critical attitude manifests itself first and foremost in the attempt to get a textual meaning into motion. Meanings do not *be*, but *become*. Texts are not immobile objects but active agents which place themselves in relation to other active agents. Therefore, being critical is seeing how this functioning of texts takes place.

Producing new standpoints, points of view and meanings, and perceiving the world with fresh eyes, empowers us and improves our control over our own lives. This can be a dizzying experience. Years ago, a good friend of mine described an experience like this by saying: 'Having finished that book, I simply had to climb up to the roof to look at the stars.'

However, as the feminist poet Adrienne Rich has noted, perceiving with fresh eyes, entering old texts from a new direction, is more than mere cultural history – it is an essential part of what keeps us alive:

> Re-vision – the act of looking back, of seeing with fresh eyes, of entering an old text from a new critical direction – is for us more than a chapter of cultural history: it is an act of survival. Until we can understand the assumptions in which we are drenched we cannot know ourselves.[16]

As a feminist, Rich emphasizes that seeking self-knowledge is not just seeking an identity for women, but also stepping beyond the self-destructiveness of the society governed by men. For her, analysing meanings firstly means looking for clues to analyse how we live, how we have lived, how we have been taught to see ourselves, how our language has on the one hand imprisoned us and on the other hand freed us, and how we could see the world differently – and live differently.

The world of meanings interests me expressly as the world of human beings, as a world of conflicts and threats but also of potentials. It often appears as a desert of given and immutable meanings, but every once in a while one may happen upon an oasis of fresh outlooks which does not turn out to be a mirage, after all.

But let's get on with it: where and how do meanings form?

Notes

1. Had I and my son, Pyry, lived even one hundred years earlier, his question would most probably have never been asked. In all probability, I would then have been able to read nature's signs quite differently than now, and taught Pyry to read them as well.
2. Fornäs 1995, 1.
3. See Gaur 1992, 18.
4. I have borrowed the term from Donald A. Norman (see Norman 1993, 119).
5. Classical sociology positioned the beginning of the surge at the development of modern society that started in the sixteenth and seventeenth centuries.

However, it is the disentanglement of traditional communities at the end of the twentieth century that has reached phenomenal dimensions.

6. See Fiske 1989a, 29.
7. See Fornäs 1995, 134.
8. See ibid., 137–8.
9. See George 1992, 29.
10. Hobsbawm 1995, 12.
11. Fornäs 1995, 134.
12. See Lemke 1995, 1.
13. Ibid.
14. See Williams 1977, 121–7.
15. See Baynham 1995, 2.
16. Rich 1972, 18.

CHAPTER 3

LANGUAGE AS HUMAN BEING IN THE WORLD

While radical criticism is concerned with digging into the roots of things, as I said at the end of the previous chapter, there is good reason to start with the *radix* in studying meanings – namely, language, the oldest and most fundamental of all sign systems used by humans, and its part in the formation of meaning.

What is language? What an odd question, some people may think. Isn't it rather futile to contemplate such a thing – is this not work for children, the deranged or scatterbrained scholars? Whoever asks the question had better be prepared for having the shadow of suspicion cast upon him/her – the same one that inevitably smudges the wretched soul who begins to ask around for the right way to the station while standing on platform 3.[1]

We take it for granted that all of the people at the station know the way to get there. With regard to the rest of our being, it also applies to language that we do not expect or imagine that it could in some essential way be something other than as we understand it.[2] Language has intertwined with our lives in so many countless ways that it is nearly impossible to recall what an immense effort it once demanded from us to learn it.

Nevertheless, each one of us has become what we are at the station of language. Therefore, it is anything but self-evident that we should know the way that leads there. As subjects we are always already within language, which means (among other things) that language is about the only means we have to attempt to discover our position. Hence, even within language, we cannot ignore the question of what language is.

All views of human beings and their world embody some spoken or unspoken view of language. This applies particularly to views concerning meanings. So it is fitting to note at the outset what view of language this book is based on.

Language as practical consciousness

Perhaps it is precisely because of the complexity of language that many theories have attempted to make it into a one-dimensional object. The most common view of language in our time is probably the one that conceives of language as an instrument, which people use to send various messages. This concept can be summarized in the following way. Someone has a thought that s/he wishes to put in words. The thought in question is then sent through speech or writing to others, who receive it and decode it from words into a thought. At first glance, this model seems innocent enough. However, it conceals a large amount of preconceptions about people, language and meanings, which are anything but unproblematic. Firstly, the model presumes that thinking precedes producing words and speech. Secondly, the model expects that a message put into language is precisely the same as the message that is decoded into a thought. In other words, it presumes that communication can take place freely, without obstacles, and without loopholes for misunderstandings to creep in. Thirdly, the model assumes that linguistic activity is normally a bilateral, one-way activity in which one person is an active speaker and the other one a passive listener. A military model of language of this kind, however, is hardly ever realized. Fourthly, the model embodies the notion of the speaker as having total control over language and as able to express pretty much whatever s/he wants with it. Language in this model is considered to be little more than a transparent tool which has no influence on what can be conveyed through it.[3]

If we examine the idea of language more closely, we can see that the notion of language as an instrument is quite paradoxical. In fact, linguistic communication can only succeed if the 'sender' and the 'recipient' already share information by virtue of which each party is able to understand the other. Communication requires a certain degree of coherence between the participants at all times. The origin of the term 'communication' is the Latin adjective *communis*, which means 'common', in addition to conveyance, so communication is always 'community' as well.

This book does not approach language as an instrument. Instead, the point of departure is the idea of language as something much more fundamental than solely a means to communicate messages concerning 'reality'. Language is not a mere tool used when a message needs to be sent to a recipient, but is an inseparable part of being human. It is born within the interaction of people. It is practical and intersubjective consciousness. Language and its meanings are seizing reality, a changing but relatively clear-cut *presence* in the world.[4]

Reality is always both linguistic and non-linguistic, and has components which are signs and other items that do not function as signs. There are always entities and aspects in material reality which remain beyond our comprehension, language and meanings. It would be far too narcissistic to assume that these items on the exterior of culture and symbolizing do not exist at all or that they have no effect on us.[5]

Human reality is not composed of language *only*. There is a heart pounding in the chest cavity of each of us entirely independent of whether we give it a name in language or not. The continent of Asia and what has been for some centuries now called Europe were situated in their current places well before they were given the names by which we know them. The *existence* of reality is not dependent on language, nor is everything that exists derived from language.

However, one should not conclude from this that reality appears to us *per se*, without the intervention of language. Though the existence of hearts, continents or complex incidents in human reality does not necessarily depend on language, they can have *meanings* only within language.

Without linguistic signification, reality would probably be experienced as a uniform continuum. It is language that divides the world into entities. Linguistic activity can be compared with the game where one seeks different figures in the clouds passing above, while lying on the ground. Before ships, busts of old men and rabbits begin to take form, the clouds are a shapeless and insignificant mass. Similarly, language makes reality meaningful by dividing it into parts distinguishable from one another, by giving it shape, by lending it form.

The anthropologist Edmund Leach describes the central position of language in the perception of reality:

> I postulate that the physical and social environment of a young child is perceived as a continuum. It does not contain any intrinsically separate 'things'. The child, in due course, is taught to impose upon this environment a kind of discriminatory grid which serves to distinguish the world as being composed of a large number of separate things, each labeled with a name. This world is a representation of our language categories, not vice versa. Because my mother tongue is English, it seems self evident that *bushes* and *trees* are different kinds of things. I would not think this unless I had been taught that it was the case.[6]

In other words, reality does not divide within itself and by itself into meaningful parts – entities, phenomena, incidents, etc. – but it is divided into these parts by human signifying practices. Language does not passively reflect the reality that is outside language. Though we, as physical beings, can have *experiences* that are immediate and outside of language, knowledge is possible only through signification. The meanings of reality are not given, but they are *produced*. As the cultural studies researcher Stuart Hall notes:

> things and events in the real world do not contain or propose their own, integral, single and intrinsic meaning, which is then merely transferred through language. Meaning is a social production, a practice. The world has to be *made to mean*. Language and symbolization is the means by which meaning is produced.[7]

Hence, the 'transparency' and 'unproblematic nature' of language are illusions. Language does not name entities that exist independently of language, but signification actively produces meanings and makes the world meaningful in certain ways. In this sense, language always means representing the perceived reality in a certain way.

In our daily interaction with other people it seems that we are able to utilize language for our own personal purposes. Language seems to provide each of us as individuals with an opportunity to express ourselves and our needs. However, nobody creates language from a vacuum. The form in which language is given to us is already quite far advanced, full of tracks left by people throughout the centuries. In this way, language shapes us no less than we shape language.[8]

Yet, this does not mean that we are always prisoners of an already existing language. Language is the scene of continuous production. Greatly varying meanings can be attached to the same things and incidents. This intrinsic possibility of language to endlessly produce different meanings is the basis for the ongoing battle between the different linguistic possibilities to make reality signify (mean). In an essential way language is a battle-field where there are meanings that are dominant, but also alternative meanings that question those that are dominant. The term 'homosexual', for example, has outwardly remained the same. Yet, in recent decades, the content of its evaluation has gradually changed since it was introduced not so long ago. 'Homosexuals' were still castrated in many countries as freaks as late as in the 1960s, whereas 'gays' are perhaps more easily accepted amongst the mainstream at the turn of the millennium. (By this I certainly don't mean that old homophobic attitudes have vanished altogether or that homophobia has suffered a defeat in the war over the meanings of homosexuality.)

As an arena of producing many meanings, which are at times contra-dictory, language is part of our practical consciousness, of our being in the world. All social practices have their linguistic dimension. Moreover, all meaning-producing structures have their material, practical side.

The idea of language as practical consciousness, as a process of signifying the world and being in the world, is the point of departure of this book. This approach has far-reaching consequences for how I analyse the formation of linguistic and other meanings. Provisionally it can be said that in this book, meanings are seen as *worldly*. In other words they are *historical*, bound to time and place, and they change from one time and place to another. Meanings are also *social*, that is, intersubjective. If language is practical consciousness and activity, its meanings derive from human practices and activities. Thus, language signifies the world, makes it meaningful. Signification is a practical and material activity that occurs through the use of language and/or other formal signs, a special part of practical consciousness. Since it is a question of producing signs, signi-fication does not take place in, nor is it an activity of, 'consciousness', but it is expressly a material activity which is 'involved from the beginning in all other human social and material activity'.[9]

As practical consciousness, language has a crucial role in how we perceive reality, orienteer in it, and position ourselves in relations with other people. Therefore, linguistic concepts have a central position in the specification of our everyday realities.[10] As the sociologists Peter Berger and Thomas Luckmann argue:

> The language used in everyday life continuously provides me with the necessary objectifications and posits the order within which these make sense

and within which everyday life has meaning for me. I live in a place that is geographically designated; I employ tools from can-openers to sports cars, which are designated in the technical vocabulary of my society; I live within a web of human relationships . . . which are also ordered by means of vocabulary. In this manner language marks the coordinates of my life in society and fills that life with meaningful objects.[11]

Language participates in a central way in the formation of our conception of reality. In addition to routines, customs and other matters we take for granted, it lays the foundation for the certain degree of stability there is in our lives. The most demonstrative form of the influence of language on reality is found in concrete speech acts – we move from one marital status to another by simply uttering 'I do'. The effect of language, however, is much broader than the example above illustrates. In fact, only a part of everyday language transmits something that already exists. Expressions such as 'Hi', 'No Smoking', 'Sorry', 'Dinner is served' or 'Get lost' are insults, prohibitions, apologies, greetings or announcements, not descriptions of the reality that exists. In these, just as in countless other expressions such as warnings, complaints, comments or threats, it is a question of the direct or indirect interaction between people who linguistically relate to each other, which also includes determining the roles of oneself and others.

The examples above are *performatives*, utterances which, linguistically, perform the act to which they refer. The term 'performativity' was first used by J.L. Austin as a part of his speech act theory in the book *How to Do Things with Words* which was published in 1962.[12] Austin separated constative utterances, which express that something either is or is not something, and performative utterances, which are linguistic acts rather than true or untrue utterances. In quite an interesting manner from our viewpoint, Austin argued, however, that constatives are implicitly performative because they perform the act of expressing a statement. Hence, for Austin, even constatives are not straightforward descriptions of reality.

Language as interaction

Language is centrally an area of interaction between people. It can be considered a fundamental part of humanity. 'The world' and 'the language we use to talk about it', 'reality' and 'consciousness' cannot be practically distinguished from one another. Language is human being in the world, a practice. It is not a tool or an instrument which is picked up when people have the need to communicate with words, but 'a faculty that makes them not only able to relate and communicate, but in real terms to be practically conscious'.[13]

Language is an inseparable part of the existence and activity of human communities. It functions in all areas and levels of communal life from the simplest to the most complex ones. It both conditions this activity and is conditioned by it. As such, language can be compared to something which is simultaneously *a producer, an instrument* and *a product*.[14]

Thus, language is an *active* element of human interaction. It is not some kind of transparent and passive medium which transmits meanings of entities that exist outside language to people using language. On the contrary, language has an active role in the formation of meanings: it sets its own restrictions to meanings, determines human life through its own ways of sorting out what can be said of reality. Producing something new within language is always related to language that already is. We can only produce new meanings in some relation to already existing meanings.[15]

When a child learns language, s/he simultaneously learns a great deal more. S/he not only learns an entire image of the surrounding reality, but also an image of her/himself. In this process, perceiving reality cannot be distinguished from adopting the system of meanings with which reality is divided into meaningful parts. In this sense, language is simultaneously both part of experience and the intersubjective interpretation of experience.[16] The philologist and literary historian Roger Fowler describes this in the following way:

> The meanings of the words in a language are the community's established knowledge. A child learns the values and preoccupations of its culture largely by learning the language: language is the chief instrument of socialization, which is the process by which a person is, willy-nilly, moulded into conformity with the established systems of beliefs of the society in which s/he happens to be born.[17]

Similarly, Peter Berger and Thomas Luckmann emphasize that people see reality through those categories which each culture has in use to be able to perceive it. Symbolic systems hold a central position in this. Language produces labels for the objects that are considered important in each culture.[18] The existence of linguistic signs warrants the identity of different objects by distinguishing, for example, 'girls' from 'women' or 'power' from 'despotism'.

In addition to differences, language produces similarities. It organizes Chihuahuas, Dalmatians, Alsatians and other such creatures into the category of 'dogs', though in many ways Chihuahuas resemble cats more than Alsatians, and Alsatians look a lot more like wolves than Chihuahuas.

Similarities do not apply to nouns only. Language also categorizes human experiences and activities through verbs. For example, the verb 'to climb' can be used to describe many activities that may differ greatly. Climbing to the top of Mount Everest, climbing the social ladder and a runner of an ivy climbing up a wall are decidedly different phenomena. Nevertheless, the use of the same verb in all three cases posits them in a certain relationship to each other.

In addition to nouns and verbs, adjectives produce certain similarities. The adjective 'hard' can be connected to, say, booze, values, or not having money, though being hard up is not related to hard values, or to hard booze – linguistically speaking.[19]

The above-mentioned examples of the categorizing nature of language concern individual words. Still, linguistic categorizing is not only a lexical phenomenon. If we move from the 'spatial' relations of single words to the 'temporal' dimensions of language – narration – the category produced by language is equally clear.

Language as selection

Language is extremely selective as it organizes our perceptions concerning reality. Putting into language includes plenty of abstracting. In this context, it is useful to remember the etymology of the term 'to abstract'. The Latin preposition *ab* means 'away,' the verb *traho* means 'to pull, to draw'. Hence, abstracting is unfastening, pulling away. As abstracts, sentences are not verbal photographs or moving pictures which represent their objects as such. The one who produces a sentence must break away from the many different sides of the object and draw one or a few sides of it into sight. In practice, speakers never have enough time to take every single thing into account that might possibly have an effect on what is said – neither do they usually have an interest in this kind of beavering away at linguistics. Writers, on their part, are usually short of space in addition to time and interest. Thus, linguistic expression is always an outcome of choice. A child's complaint to his/her kindergarten teacher about an incident with words 'Axel hit me' reports only a fraction of what really happened. It does not reveal when the hitting took place, whether it appeared like a bolt out of the blue or was preceded by a provocation of some sort on the part of the child who was hit or as a result of another squabble. Furthermore, it does not tell us at exactly what part of the body and with how much force the accused directed the blow.

Besides choosing the elements of an expression, linguistic selection appears in the way the expression is organized. All languages include mechanisms through which certain elements can be emphasized and others faded into the background. The child who has been hit highlights certain elements in his/her message by intonation and stress: In '*Axel* hit me', the identity of the alleged hitter; in 'Axel *hit* me' the particularity of the deed; and in 'Axel hit *me*', the person of the poor victim is stressed.

In addition to stress, different sentence structures emphasize elements in different ways. The usual structure 'A dog bit a man' can be varied in several ways; for example, 'The man was bitten by a dog', 'It was a man that the dog bit' or 'It fell to the man's lot to be bitten by a dog'. Through the means of selection and organization the speaker's values, as well as his/her judgements relative to the speech situation, become one of the central foundations of linguistic expressions. If the speaker assumes that a listener knows in advance that a man was bitten, and the new information provided by him/her is related to the fact that the biter was expressly a dog, it is natural for the speaker to use a sentence 'The man was bitten by a dog.' Provided that the speaker assumes the listener to know that a dog has bitten something or somebody, s/he may well use the sentence 'It was a man that the dog bit.' In case the speaker wishes to make a more general philosophical statement about human fate in this sharp-fanged world, s/he might choose the third sentence, 'It fell to the man's lot to be bitten by a dog.'

These observations indicate that linguistic activity is always two-way in character. Every expression we produce is moulded not only by our own viewpoint on the issue in question, but also by our conception of what those we address know or think about that issue. In other words, we compose our expressions to function interactively with the information, presumptions, attitudes and other such things of relevance we expect our audience to have.[20] (I will return to this matter, which is central to my argument.)

In addition to the audience, certain institutional factors influence our expressions. An illustrative example of this is the widely known Finnish anecdote about Uncle Marcus, the immensely popular host of a 1930s children's radio show who allegedly forgot to turn his microphone off and proclaimed to every wide-eyed tot and nipper that 'now this feller is gonna take a crap'. Whether the anecdote is true or not, it is quite a different thing to address half the nation than to chuck an impromptu remark at a sound checker in an isolated studio. A medical doctor uses one language when discussing a case with a room full of colleagues, another one while examining a patient, and a third one during a family dinner. In neither of these examples does the language simply reflect the social situation; instead it participates in the formation of each social situation in an essential way. Professional jargon is the most expedient means of disseminating information to those who share its secrets; a less formal language tells others that there is no punctilious business going on here.

Language as production of the new

Besides being restrictive, language is a productive system within which new categories and viewpoints can be created. Metaphor is the central means in this process. A metaphor is a linguistic image which produces meanings through analogies, by explaining or interpreting one thing through another. Metaphor can be considered fundamental to the signification of reality. In a metaphor, something previously unknown is explained by drawing a parallel between it and something already known.

Let us take as an example of this metaphoric talk how a ship ploughs a sea. Navigation is described by extending a verb familiar to us from farm work to a different element. In this way, 'new' activity is signified through 'old' vocabulary. Additionally, the ploughing metaphor not only signifies a physical comparison, but also invites comparison of certain similarities between a plough and a ship's bow. 'Ploughing a sea' can be understood as bringing material wealth just as the cultivation of land does.

However, not all analogies are metaphorical. Drawing an analogy between France and Paris and Italy and Rome, for example, does not produce a metaphor. The elements of these analogies come from the same range (a country, a capital) and therefore are not metaphoric, but function as literal analogies. When two previously unconnected elements are joined together and an analogy is found where it did not exist before, that is when a metaphor is produced.[21] The term 'metaphor' has its origin in classical Greek and means 'to carry over'. Thus, it can be seen in the etymology of the term how the borders of the elements' 'own' ranges are surpassed in a metaphor.

The metaphors of languages are largely so-called 'fossilized metaphors', solidified and established forms of perception and comparison that used to be alive in their time but which are no longer necessarily recognized as metaphors. Nevertheless, their existence – as well as the existence of 'living' metaphors – is a good example of how central is the role of metaphors and analogies in human attempts to understand and interpret the world.

Metaphors are an essential form of language for several reasons. One of them is economy. If each of the above-mentioned examples about 'climbing' required its own verb, handling language would be much harder. However, metaphors also have their conceptual use. The ability to recognize similarities makes it easier to interpret the world. They assist us in adapting to new situations without having to learn every detail of every case from the very beginning. Our adaptation to the 'revolution of information technology' – a metaphor in itself – would be much more difficult without similarities: we 'save' files and 'surf' the net, while hard discs 'go down' and systems 'get stuck'. In all of these cases, metaphorical analogies serve our ability to orienteer in new terrains.[22]

According to the linguist George Lakoff, metaphors are focal in the process of understanding reality. He has encouraged us to pay attention not only to how an analogy is drawn between love and a journey, but also to how we tend to compare a debate to warfare between the parties. (This view has a long history: the classical Greek word *polemikós*, from which the term 'polemic' derives, has the meanings both of 'the art of war' and of 'enmity'.) The idea of debating as warfare becomes apparent in such common sayings as 'Tony seized the weak point in my argument' or 'I shot down all of Bill's arguments' or 'Hillary's critique hit the target'. Through such expressions, any intellectual or other kind of debate is interpreted as if it were an activity aimed at the physical destruction of the opponent or opponents. (I take note of having myself compared language to a 'battle-field' earlier in this text.) Hence, all possible expressions related to warfare can be harnessed to characterize debates. ('Tony's strategy was mostly that a good offence is the best defence'; 'my argument struck like a neutron bomb – it destroyed Bill's defences but left the man standing.') Instead of using such expressions, Lakoff urges us to imagine a culture where debates are not seen as battles which end up with winners and losers, where the opponents do not attack and defend and lose or win ground, but where the debate is seen as something like a dance in which participants are performers whose primary aim is to bring forth their argumentation in a balanced and aesthetically attractive way. In such a culture, 'people would view arguments differently, carry them out differently, and talk about them differently'.[23]

We have seen how metaphors participate in the understanding of the world. Different metaphors produce different interpretations of their object. When we talk about debating as warfare, the resulting conception is quite different than it would be if we drew an analogy between debating and trade, for example, or compared it to a game.

Similarly, the idea of life as a journey, which is the origin of several common expressions such as 'to go through an experience', and 'there is plenty to worry about ahead', is based on transforming physical space into an abstract area. Furthermore, the division into something that is 'up' or 'down' produces heaps of metaphors concerning moods ('Why are you so down?' 'I was on such a high').

For a long time, metaphors were considered to be a specific feature of poetic language. Later it was realized that metaphors characterize all use of language. They are no longer seen as a privilege of poetic geniuses; we common mortals have been granted a visa to their realm.

On closer inspection, the fundamental role of metaphors in language is quite understandable. Since people divide reality into comprehensible sections by means of language, it is easier to describe what is new and previously unknown via what is already known. If we know 'a leg', it is simple to employ the same word in other connections and talk about 'table legs', for instance. Similarly, the hold of a ship has lent its name to the hold of an aeroplane, which is a much more recent invention.

Metaphors are quite handy in producing descriptions of reality. Recognizing similarities (and differences) makes the world perceivable. Through metaphors we can readjust to new situations relatively fluently, as in the aforementioned example of adapting to the presence of computers. Every now and then, however, metaphors 'carry over' outdated meanings. They are not only vehicles to create something new, but also for building on to the old, as the example of metaphors of debates as warfare shows.

Language as representation

If I try to make a three-year-old child eat his breakfast by urging him 'not to disregard the most important meal of the day', most probably my message will not get through to him. The child might not know the verb 'to disregard', nor the old adage according to which 'breakfast is the most important meal of the day'. Linguistic expressions are not mere tools that transport meanings from a speaker to a listener. Rather, they can be seen as *producing* the meaning in an interaction with certain conceptual structures that the recipient has a command of. According to this notion, individual utterances are not so much instruments as mobilizers of the signification process, a certain kind of catalyst. Again, this metaphorical reference to a catalyst emphasizes the fact that the formation of meanings cannot be realized unless there are other elements present. In a communicative situation, these other elements must be sought out in the recipient's own knowledge and conceptual base (which in itself is also linguistic).[24]

A good commonplace example of this is spontaneous speech between two or more people. It is characterized by ellipsis, interruptions and quick transfers, among other things. Still, the listeners do not usually consider it particularly tangled, shapeless or incomplete. From their viewpoint, the cohesion of the speech is on equal level with the cohesion of written language, because they attempt – though they are not necessarily aware of doing that – to produce coherent meanings out of what they hear, fill the gaps and seek for logic between parts of speech which are seemingly disconnected and loose. Spoken language is the raw material for the formation of meanings, a catalyst which mobilizes the listener's mental exertion.[25]

Language enables us to talk with other people. Simultaneously language makes it possible to talk about something. Therefore, besides providing us with a means of interaction, it gives us the ability to represent the world, to make statements about it.

As is well known, the meanings of the word 'representation' are quite complicated. According to its etymology, 'representation' can be understood as causing something to be present again. From this point, however, we can proceed in two directions. Firstly, 'representation' can mean representing something physically. The parliament of Great Britain can be said to 'represent' the nation (in so far as you believe in representative democracy). Secondly, 'representation' can mean the symbolizing or picturing of something. In this sense, the term 'representation' can be briefly defined as 'presenting something as something'.

Producing meanings, namely, *signification*, means producing such signs as awaken meanings in other people. The notion of language as representation emphasizes that the symbols of language do not present the objects that are outside of it as such, but in accordance with the prefix, 're-'present it, or present it in another way. In fact it is a prerequisite to representation that the one that represents and the one being represented differ. A drawing of a pipe represents a pipe for the very reason that it is not that pipe. (René Magritte wrote in his well-known painting of a pipe: 'Ceci n'est pas une pipe': 'this is not a pipe.') If the drawing somehow produced the pipe in question in its 'pipey' materiality, it would no longer be a *re*presentation of the pipe.[26]

As with representation, language is always part of human activity. Language is produced and understood as part of the practices of the formation of meanings. Each linguistic statement, such as texts, symbolically refers to a whole body of meanings. Let an example enlighten us on this matter, too: On 1 June 1953, the whole of England was informed that the New Zealander Edmund Hillary and his Sherpa guide, Tensing Norgay, had climbed to the very top of the world's highest mountain, the Chomolungma. The British Isles, which was busily preparing for the coronation of Queen Elizabeth II, welcomed the news with joy. The next morning the *News Chronicle* announced on its front page:

THE CROWNING GLORY
EVEREST IS CLIMBED
TREMENDOUS NEWS FOR THE QUEEN
HILLARY DOES IT
Glorious Coronation Day news! Everest – Everest the unconquerable – has been conquered. And conquered by men of British blood.

The news came late last night. Edmund Hillary and the Sherpa guide, Tensing Norgay, of Colonel John Hunt's expedition, had climbed the summit of Earth's highest peak, 29,002 feet high.

New Zealand's deputy Premier announced it at a Coronation Day ceremony at Wellington – and within seconds it flashed around the world.

Queen Elizabeth the Second, resting on the eve of her crowning, was immediately told that this brightest jewel of courage and endurance had been added to the Crown of British endeavour. It is understood that a message of royal congratulation is being sent to the climbers . . .[27]

Newspaper language is customarily considered a means of communication that aims at objectivity by supplying readers with messages about reality. But as is apparent in the excerpt above, newspaper descriptions of reality are always produced from a certain perspective. Linguistic activity can never be the mere transparent duplication of reality, but always embodies the signification of the world in a certain way; in our example, for the advantage of the glory of the British Empire.

All incidents in reality can be signified in countless ways. In a Sherpan newspaper, the conquering of the mountain top might have been reported in the following way: 'TENSING NORGAY CLIMBS THE CHOMOLUNGMA ACCOMPANIED BY HIS NEW ZEALANDER PARTNER HILLARY.' Or: 'HILLARY VIOLATES THE SACRED MOUNTAIN. COERCED ONE OF US ALONG.'

In the light of the above example, we can conclude that representations mean making the object present, which takes place with the assistance of accessible means of expression and the conventions and norms intrinsic to them. Customs, norms and conventions restrict and mould what can be said and when about each matter. Besides, the object of representation is not necessarily 'reality in itself', but other representations of it – in our example, 'men of British blood' which (the British blood), strictly speaking, does not even exist in forms other than as a representation.[28]

A regrettably fresh example of language's power of representation is the way it has recently been employed in connection with various military actions. The 'smart bombs' used against 'Saddam Hussein' (read: the Iraqis) by the 'allies' were not so smart. The 'ethnic cleansing', as the Serbian leaders called the activity conducted by the Serbs in the former Yugoslavia, is simple genocide from the perspective of the victims and the international community. Much as the influence of news photographs and films on our conceptions of the state and events of the world is – quite justifiably – discussed these days, spoken and written language are anything but innocent in the competition for people's minds.

Moreover, representation is not actualized only on the level of individual words. Expressions also have their significance in the different ways of representing reality. When an activity is represented, *transitivity*, that is, who (or what) does what to whom, carries weight, as is very much the case in the debate over abortion: Is it 'the murder of an unborn infant' or 'the termination of an unwanted pregnancy'? These are obviously ways of 'presenting as something', namely, representing one and the same matter. However, they give us a reason to contemplate whether 'neutral' representations of abortion or any other human matter can exist at all. Doesn't the most detached scientific manner of speaking about abortion appear as a manifestation of moral irresponsibility from the standpoint of a fervent anti-abortionist? Hence, doesn't everyone who utters even one word concerning abortion necessarily, at least to a certain degree, choose their side on the issue? Isn't 'transparent' representation a sheer impossibility?

Language, identity and power

Language takes part in producing identities.[29] As a child learns her/his mother tongue, s/he becomes a part of a certain linguistic community. However, a human seedling who learns English or any other language does not learn the 'entire language', but the linguistic customs of his/her immediate community. The English language of a child who is growing up in Edinburgh is probably quite different from the way of speaking adopted by a child from Los Angeles.

In addition to local differences, social stratification produces different linguistic customs and identities. Though the everyday language of taxicab drivers or supermarket cashiers may differ greatly from Edinburgh to Los Angeles, clergy or university teachers from the two cities can use languages that are much more similar to one another. In the last two occupations, striving towards the use of standard language is in fact an important part of professional identity. Hence, 'dialects' can be seen as connected to the social status of the speakers at least to the same extent as to their geographical residence.

Gender, ethnicity, 'race', occupation and other factors can produce so-called social dialects, or, sociolects. The languages of men and women, for example, differ in various ways. In many cultures, the dissimilarities appear in the genders' different tendencies towards euphemisms, emotionally loaded adjectives, the rhetoric of hesitation, and adherence to 'correct' grammar.

Language is of great importance when people join together, but also in their distinction from each other. Language is a vital marker, as well as a means, of social and cultural stratification. This is well illustrated by the English historian Olivia Smith's characterization of the conceptions of the upper classes in the 1800s in relation to the speech of the common people:

> 'The vulgar and the refined', 'the particular and the general', 'the corrupt and the pure', 'the barbaric and the civilized', 'the primitive and the arbitrary' were socially pervasive terms that divided sensibility and culture according to linguistic categories. The baser forms of language were said to reveal the inability of the speaker to transcend the concerns of the present, an interest in material objects, and the dominance of the passions. Those who spoke the refined language were allegedly rational, moral, civilized, and capable of abstract thinking.[30]

Distinguishing the 'refined' and the 'vulgar', the 'corrupt' and the 'pure' from one another was a central factor in creating official languages. The new official languages – such as English and French – were also the languages of literature and the fine arts as well as of science. They became those authoritative languages of which Mikhail Bakhtin (1895–1975) writes:

> The authoritative word demands that we acknowledge it, that we make it our own, it binds us, quite independent of any power it might have to persuade us internally; we encounter it with its authority already fused to it. The authoritative word is located in a distanced zone, organically connected with a past that is felt to be hierarchically higher. It is, so to speak, the word of the fathers. Its authority was already *acknowledged* in the past. It is a *prior* discourse. It is therefore not a question of choosing it from among other possible discourses that are its equal. It is given (it sounds) in lofty spheres, not those of familiar contact. Its language is a special (as it were, hieratic) language. It can be profaned. It is akin to taboo, i.e., a name that must not be taken in vain.[31]

As such, language is a seedbed and instrument of power. Indeed, Valentin Voloshinov (1894–1936; more about his linguistic conceptions later on), a colleague of Mikhail Bakhtin, noted that linguistics has from the very start been associated with questions concerning power. When he defined 'a philologist' as a 'solver and teacher of "sacred foreign" writings and words,' he wrote:

> The first philologists and the first linguists were always and everywhere *priests*. History knows no nation whose sacred writings or oral tradition were not to some degree in a language foreign and incomprehensible to the profane. To decipher the mystery of sacred words was the task meant to be carried out by the priest-philologists.[32]

'Sacred writings and stories' have justified power in two ways. On the one hand, they have told about how power indeed belongs to those who already have it. On the other hand, the control over these writings is intrinsically a sign of power. The long-term power position of Latin as the language of West European scholars, for example, was expressly related to the attempt to keep the whole domain of learnedness as a monopoly of the Roman Catholic Church and Catholic universities.

Language had a central position in the birth of the current national states. During the nineteenth century, language and nationality were considered to be closely connected. However, the formation of nation states also included the standardization of language both in small and large countries. In fact, the rise of one language or dialect into a hegemonic position over others was an essential part of the formation of national states. This rise did not take place in isolation; new hierarchies were produced especially for the needs of the new elites. In England, for example, the formation of the so-called 'King's English' began in the fifteenth century. It had its origin in the dialects of London and the surrounding areas, and was the language form used in literature, administration and, in the course of time, in education as well. In turn, this language form gradually became the 'class dialect' of those who were privileged by birth or education. Later on it functioned as the foundation for the formation of the standards of English language.[33]

Correspondingly, in France, the language that rose to an official status was by origin the dialect of Paris and its surroundings, Île de France, called the *langue d'Oïl*. In 1539, the dialect was made into the official language of the multilingual kingdom. It was given priority over the *langue d'Oc*, Occitan, that was spoken in the southern parts of the country. This official French language became the official written language in southern France as early as in the seventeenth century, though *Provençal*, the successor of *langue d'Oc*, was primarily spoken there. French was the language of public speech and writings, whereas Provençal was spoken in an everyday context. However, French gradually replaced Provençal in everyday use first amongst the upper classes in the eighteenth century and, after the 1789 Revolution, also amongst the lower classes and in rural areas.[34]

Language and power fuse together not only in major historical events but also in everyday life. People actualize their power relations through their linguistic acts as they reinforce their own position and role in the community and transmit common information and values to each other. Let's take the example of a school class to enlighten us on this idea. Every day the teacher of the class reproduces his/her position as the teacher by speaking in front of the class to pupils, who, in turn, reinforce their own role as pupils by agreeing to – or being compelled to – speak in the way that is required of them by the teacher.

From this standpoint, some of the most essential questions concerning language are the ones raised by the French philosopher Michel Foucault (1926–1984) in his works. Who is entitled to speak a certain language? In what situations and places does s/he have the right to speak that language? How does s/he classify reality into the 'normal' and 'abnormal', the 'acceptable' and 'unacceptable' through the means of his/her language?[35]

However, language is also a terrain of resistance. In addition to external signs – gesticulation, ways of dressing, behaviour and so on – resistance is often manifested in the breaking of linguistic norms. In the case of the school class, students could choose to express their resistance by answering the teacher's questions correctly in content, but using the latest slang expressions, muttering or otherwise making themselves incomprehensible.

All in all it can be said that all people have more than one 'linguistic identity'. Each of us has contact with several speech communities in our everyday life. The use of language does not vary only according to who is speaking, but also to whom and in which situation one speaks. Charles V (1500–1558) is reported to have said: 'To God I speak Spanish, to women Italian, to men French, and to my horse – German.'[36]

Behind the Emperor's witticism is the idea that the forms of the language we use are tied to the context in which and the people to whom we speak. We choose between a dialect and standard language, as well as between different vocabularies, according to how we understand the speech situation. While an 11-year-old schoolboy might write in his assigned essay how 'during the summer vacation, I visited an exhibition of old automobiles', he may refer to the same event by telling his schoolmates during recess that he 'checked out these wheels and man they were way cool!' Different social roles produce different ways of using language – and vice versa.

The contextuality of language

I stated above that users of language do not possess a solid, predetermined and immutable identity, but that their identity varies in accordance with language situations. Moreover, we can conceive that the signs of language do not have defined and unchangeable meanings, but that 'in practice it [a sign] has a variable range, corresponding to the endless variety of situations within which it is actively used'.[37]

A fundamentally distinctive mark of language is polysemy.[38] As we speak or write, we can never be sure of whether our speech or writing will be understood in the way we mean it. Our linguistic output is not our private property, nor do we have the exclusive right to interpret it. Our every linguistic act enters the endless abundance of meanings and becomes interpreted in relation to other meanings of which we do not necessarily have any clue regarding the producers of the utterances.

This book, for example, faces innumerable interpretation frame-works, which in their distinctive ways determine the manner in which the content of the book is understood. The book's claims create different interpretations according to the knowledge and conceptions each reader already has of the subject at hand. Indeed, the 'senders' of language often come to realize that their linguistic acts have completely different consequences than they intended or wished them to have. The 'recipients' do not necessarily possess the same reserves of meanings as the 'senders', and they may understand speech or writing in quite a different way than was intended. This book too can be read in various ways, which need not have much to do with what the writer originally imagined they would be.

Language is irreversibly *heteroglottic*. This term, originally used by Mikhail Bakhtin, refers to the simultaneous existence of languages of many different groups of people – based on ethnicity, class, geography, sex and gender, age, occupation, and so on.[39] As heteroglottic, language is also an arena of conflicts. Every expression travelling from a speaker to a listener or a writer to a reader is inevitably a part of the net of manifold meanings.

Hence, language is always used in certain contexts. Language does not exist for us as an abstract system of phonetics or grammar and vocabulary, but always in relation to its use, to our ability to act linguistically. We know language in the sense that we know how to use it. We know how to communicate with our fellow human beings and how to choose the forms of language suitable to each respective situation of language use. Language to us means the ability to act, the skill to use language 'correctly'. This would be impossible if we did not also have knowledge of contexts. Hence, language never appears as mere grammar and vocabularies (in spite of the impression one might get from a school class or possibly the desk of a philologist). We do not use language in isolation, but always in relation to certain situations or contexts formed of people, activities and events, which give meaning to the matters expressed through language.[40]

The notion of the historical and social nature of language was preceded in an interesting way by a circle that surrounded Mikhail Bakhtin in the Soviet Union of the 1920s. Its other most renowned members were the aforementioned Valentin Voloshinov and Pavel Medvedev.

Voloshinov's work *Marxism and the Philosophy of Language* sum-marized certain essential features of the Bakhtin group's conception of language. Voloshinov's point of departure is that language is not a reflection, a shadow of reality, but 'also itself a material part of that very reality'.[41] Therefore, language is an inseparable part of reality, and more: understanding is possible in the first place only within certain sign material. In this way, according to Voloshinov, consciousness itself can only be actualized as it is realized in certain signs.[42]

Hence, language is as much a part of reality as is human consciousness. As it is realized in signs between people, it is expressly common social consciousness. Language and community inseparably belong together. There are no real meanings that exist only for one person. Entering the sphere of meanings always signifies entering the sphere of human interaction. Subjective consciousness is also dependent on intersubjective language:

> Consciousness takes shape and being in the material of signs created by an organized group in the process of its social intercourse. . . . Consciousness can harbor only in the image, the word, the meaningful gesture, and so forth.[43]

Consciousness is thus language, but as consciousness language is located in human practice. Hence language appears as a human being's practical consciousness, as his/her being in the world.

In order for Voloshinov to be able to develop his view, he simultaneously had to criticize two views that considered themselves as opposed to one another. On the one hand, he criticized views which considered language the subjective expression of an individual; on the other hand, he criticized views that regarded language as an objective system.

For Voloshinov, language is not merely the self-expression of an individual, because 'the reality of the inner psyche is the same reality as that of the sign. Outside the material of signs there is no psyche.'[44] An individual's inner self is constructed of sign material, which in turn is created by an organized community. From this standpoint, the self is never only or even primarily 'internal', but is intersubjective, social. Correspondingly, experiences exist only within signs to the one that has the experience. There is no leap between an 'internal' experience and its locution: an experience is not first experienced outside of language and then put into words; sign material is fundamental to the experience itself.[45] Falling in love cannot be separated from the abundance of linguistic material which already tells us in advance what falling in love 'must' be. Our notions of our 'internal' experiences cannot be separated from the 'external' language.

Next to 'individualistic subjectivism', Voloshinov targeted his criticism at 'abstract objectivism', which holds that language is 'a system of phonetical, grammatical and lexical forms'.[46] As the most lucid expression of abstract objectivism, Voloshinov mentions the founder of modern linguistics, Ferdinand de Saussure (1857–1913). Voloshinov noted the inability to study linguistic changes or the creation of the new within language as the problem of the trend represented by Saussure:

> From the point of view of [this] trend, meaningful language creativity on the speaker's part is simply out of the question. Language stands before the individual as an inviolable, incontestable norm which the individual, for his part, can only accept. . . . The individual acquires the system of language from his speech community completely ready-made. Any change within that system lies beyond the range of his individual consciousness.[47]

Hence, the image of language becomes one-dimensional and ahistorical:

> An overriding characteristic of [this] trend of thought in the philosophy of language is its assuming a special kind of discontinuity between the history of the language and the system of the language (i.e., language in its a-historical, synchronic dimension).[48]

Saussure opened up interesting visions for the study of meanings, but not all his views were as fruitful. When Saussure emphasized language as a system of differences, it was possible to proceed in two directions from that point: either to study linguistic practices or to study language as an abstract system. He chose the latter. Hence, Saussure can be compared to an engineer who can very discerningly solve the secrets of a certain mechanism (the engine of a car, for example) but whose field of vision does not cover the real purpose of its existence.

Saussure treated language as an abstract system by distinguishing two sides of language. *Langue* is a language system, whereas *parole* is actual speech, those speech acts which are made possible by language. *Langue* is what an individual adopts as s/he learns a language. *Parole* is its 'operative' side. According to Saussure, of these two it must be *langue* that is the primary object of linguistics. It is not the task of linguistics to study speech acts, but to determine the units and rules which comprise a linguistic system.

However, even Saussure himself emphasized that when language is studied, social facts are studied. By choosing the sign as an object of study, he simultaneously happened to make social conventions and facts the nucleus of linguistic study. In this connection, Saussure talked about the arbitrariness of signs: the spoken or written word 'dog' has no closer relation to the concept of 'dog' than the words 'chien', 'hund' or 'perro' do. Instead, the relation between the signifier and the signified is determined by a custom, rule or contract. It is specifically the arbitrariness of the sign that indicates how language is bound to social conventions. As Saussure said:

> The arbitrary nature of the sign explains in turn why the social fact alone can create a linguistic system. The community is necessary if values that owe their existence solely to usage and general acceptance are to be set up; by himself the individual is incapable of fixing a single value.[49]

However, at the same time, Saussure obscured this central emphasis by abandoning the study of *parole* and choosing *langue* as his object. To

Saussure, *parole* did not mean the dialogical activity which Voloshinov discussed and through which it is possible to study the *actualization* of a language system in speech acts, which also are not arbitrary or purely individual. Instead, *parole* appeared to Saussure as 'expressing the speaker's own thoughts' and 'psychophysical mechanisms', with which the speaker could 'externalize' his/her own internal productions.[50] Hence, Saussure did not attempt to seek the social in what was private, nor the communal in what was personal, which is Voloshinov's point of departure.

First and foremost, language to Saussure means *langue*, an abstract and solidified structure, whereas actual speech acts are the objects of study for the members of Bakhtin's circle. For them, words are ambiguous; they are always words of one human subject to another, and this practical context perpetually moulds their meanings. Linguistic activity is primarily defined in an immediate social situation:

> In point of fact, word is a two-sided act. It is determined equally by whose word it is and for whom it is meant. As word, it is precisely the product of the reciprocal relationship between the speaker and the listener, addresser and addressee. Each and every word expresses the 'one' in relation to the 'other'. I give myself verbal shape from another's point of view, ultimately from the point of view of the community to which I belong.[51]

Voloshinov does not consider the meanings of language to be born from the activity of an abstract system, but from human interaction. To him language is not an objective system, nor subjective expressions, but something else. It is no more an abstract system than it is internal psyche:

> In point of fact, the linguistic form . . . exists for the speaker only in the context of specific utterances, exists, consequently, only in a specific ideological context. In actuality, we never say or hear *words*, we say and hear what is true or false, good or bad, important or unimportant, pleasant or unpleasant, and so on. Words are always filled with content and meaning drawn from behavior or ideology. That is the way we understand words, and we can respond only to words that engage us behaviorally or ideologically.[52]

Hence, language is *activity*, *practical consciousness*, concrete being in the world. As such, to Voloshinov language is innately *dialogical*: comprehensible only through being inevitably directed to someone else. His description of the matter in a nutshell goes as follows:

> The meaning of a word is determined entirely by its context. In fact, there are as many meanings of a word as there are contexts of its usage.[53]

Voloshinov himself presents a splendid example of the words' link to context in his work that deals with Freudianism:

Two people are sitting in a room. They are both silent. Then one of them says, 'Well!' The other does not respond.

For us, as outsiders, this entire 'conversation' is utterly incomprehensible. Taken in isolation, the utterance 'Well!' is empty and unintelligible. Nevertheless, this peculiar colloquy of two persons, consisting of only one – although, to be sure, one expressively intoned – word, does make perfect sense, is fully meaningful and complete.

In order to disclose the sense and meaning of this colloquy, we must analyse it. But what is it exactly that we can subject to analysis? Whatever pains we take with the purely verbal part of the utterance, however subtly we define the phonetic, morphological, and semantic factors of the word *well*, we shall still not come a single step closer to an understanding of the whole sense of the colloquy.

Let us suppose that the intonation with which this word was pronounced is known to us: indignation and reproach moderated by a certain amount of humor. This intonation somewhat fills in the semantic void of the adverb *well* but still does not reveal the meaning of the whole.

What is it we lack, then? We lack the 'extraverbal context' that made the word *well* a meaningful locution for the listener. This *extraverbal context* of the utterance is comprised of three factors: (1) the *common spatial purview* of the interlocutors (the unity of visible – in this case the room, the window, and so on), (2) the interlocutors' *common knowledge and understanding of the situation*, and (3) their *common evaluation* of that situation.

At the time the colloquy took place, both interlocutors *looked up* at the window and *saw* that it had begun to snow; both *knew* that it was already May and that it was high time for spring to come; finally, *both* were *sick and tired* of the protracted winter – *they both were looking forward* to spring and *both were bitterly disappointed* by the late snowfall. On this 'jointly seen' (snowflakes outside the window), 'jointly known' (the time of the year – May) and 'unanimously evaluated' (winter wearied of, spring looked forward to) – on all this the utterance *directly depends*, all this is seized in its actual, living import – is its very sustenance. And yet all this remains without verbal specification or articulation. The snowflakes remain outside the window; the date, on the page of a calendar; the evaluation, in the psyche of the speaker; and, nevertheless, all this is *assumed* in the word *well*.[54]

Voloshinov's example stresses that meanings are necessarily contextual. They are bound to intersubjective social relationships. Therefore, the signs of language are also not internally restricted and immutable units, but active elements of speech, whose meaning changes depending on the social intonations, assessments and connotations they condense within themselves in each social situation. (The word 'well!' can also function as an exhortation to get going, a reminder of a previously given order to be quiet, or to express pleasure as the dessert is presented at the dinner table.) Since intonations, assessments and connotations continuously change and since linguistic communities are in fact heterogeneous communities that consist of contradicting interests, a sign is not so much a neutral element of a given structure as the focus of struggle and conflict. Instead of asking 'what does a sign mean?' we must study its multifaceted history, where different social groups, classes, individuals and the discourses of all of them attempt to take possession of the sign and use it for their own purposes.

So if meanings are the contents and results of social activity, studying texts separately from their contexts is not sufficient. Instead we must pay attention to contexts, those 'connections of use' in which the texts are posited and where they obtain their actual meanings. The basis of studying language – and therefore of texts – is specifically in *interaction*:

> The actual reality of language-speech is not the abstract system of linguistic forms, not the isolated monologic utterance, and not the psychophysiological act of its implementation, but the social event of verbal interaction implemented in an utterance or utterances.[55]

Language as a system of differences

From our point of view, part of what is interesting in Voloshinov is linked to his criticism of Saussure's conception of the formality of language. In many significant ways, Voloshinov's critique portended the transition from structuralism to post-structuralism approximately 50 years later. In order to be able to examine this transitional stage and its consequences, the main features of Saussure's language theory must be sketched out.

Saussure understood language as an abstract system, which is composed of sign chains. Each sign is formed of a signifier (a sound or a penned figure) and the signified (the image that is created within us as we hear or see the signifier). The two elements of a sign connect to each other arbitrarily, that is, artificially: there is no natural connection between the phonetic or visual appearance and the concept it identifies (i.e. the image it creates).

As Jonathan Culler notes in his monograph on Saussure, this idea does not differ all that much from the traditional views concerning language. After the perception of the arbitrariness of the signifier and the signified, it indeed would still be possible to think that language is mere nomen-clature: a body of names which have been arbitrarily selected and then linked to certain objects or concepts.[56] Nevertheless, this is not so.

If language were mere nomenclature whose only function was to name objects or concepts which exist by their own force, then each and every language would have to retain precisely corresponding vocabularies. However, an example of the contrary is the manner in which different cultures divide the spectrum of colours into different colour categories. The Cymric word *glas* covers an area which in English would be described as three different colours: 'aquamarine' (or bluish-green), 'blue' and 'blue-grey'. Similarly, the word *llwyd* covers the English concepts of 'grey' and 'greyish-brown'.

As the examples above illustrate, languages produce differences in different ways. Each language has its own manner in which to divide the world into concepts or categories. Since the languages of both Cymric and English work just as well with their own particular way of differentiating colours, it follows that the differences each of them makes are not natural, essential or inevitable, but synthetic – or, to use Saussure's vocabulary, artificial in the sense of arbitrary. (Yet, it must be added that arbitrariness does not necessarily mean high-handed, or accidental, selection. Differentiations may well have had their connections to the practical needs of the people who once chose to make them, which can be seen, for example, in the fact that Sami, the language of the Sami people who live in northern Norway, Sweden, Finland and Russia – for obvious reasons – has a markedly broader vocabulary to describe the shades of the colours of reindeer than either Finnish, Norwegian, Swedish or Russian. But it is also good to remember that even in these cases where the need for differentiation arises from the people's practical activities, the differences still exist in the language, not in reality.)

All languages describe colours in one way or another, but the conceptual differences thus made are not predetermined. They do not originate from a reality external to the language, but from the language. Concepts are not autonomous entities but acquire their meaning as a part of the system; they are determined in their relationship to the other members of the system in question. The speakers of the English language differentiate 'blue' and 'aquamarine' because in their language system these are two different concepts. However, in English it would not be possible to discern the Cymric *glas* and *llwyd*, since the language lacks the equivalent concepts. Therefore, colours are not autonomous concepts which determine certain features of reality, but each colour is one element in the system concerning colours and is determined through other, restrictive concepts. The most essential feature of each one is, according to Saussure himself, the fact that 'their most precise characteristic is in being what the others are not'.[57]

Another example of the linguistic structuring of the reality is the case where the English language recognizes two different animals, 'a mouse' and 'a rat,' whereas the speakers of classical Latin in their time only perceived one rodent, *mus*. Since the language did not distinguish a rat from a mouse, they were not two different species for the ancient Romans. Hence, the question is not the natural variances in the fauna but specifically cultural, dissimilar definitions.

These examples underline the fact that there are no natural similarities between languages' signifiers and signified; instead the meanings of words are tied to the established ways of using a language, that is, how language interferes with reality to give it meaning. Meanings are not born from innate differences in reality, but from the distinctions with which a language grasps reality.

Language as discourses

The views of Ferdinand de Saussure have been employed in many different ways and sometimes combined with other standpoints. They have most perceptively had an impact not only on linguistics, but also on semiotics (or semiology, as Saussure himself and the French still call the discipline), anthropology, psychoanalysis, Marxism and deconstructionism. After the 'linguistic turn' of the human sciences, it is nearly impossible to name an area in which Saussure's views have not left their mark. At this point, however, I am mostly interested in the manner in which Saussure's conceptions concerning language have been further developed among post-structuralists (e.g. Roland Barthes and Julia Kristeva) and cultural studies researchers (e.g. Raymond Williams and Stuart Hall). For it is here that the social character of language – and its *paroles* – (which Saussure lost sight of) expresses with its full force.

The post-structuralists and cultural materialists agree with Saussure on two significant matters. Firstly, language does not reflect the innate meanings of the reality outside of it; meanings are produced within language. Secondly, individual signs do not have their own, innate meanings, but they acquire their meanings through their position in the linguistic chain. Contrary to Saussure, however, they do not consider language to be an abstract system. Where for Saussure language meant solid and systematic facts, the post-structuralists and cultural materialists stress the polysemy and historical mutability of meanings.[58]

In recent years, the concept of 'discourse' has been used in the attempt to get a grip on the polysemy and mutability of language. Stuart Hall has presented a deft definition:

> A discourse is a group of statements which provide a language for talking about – i.e. a way of representing – a particular kind of knowledge about a topic. When statements about a topic are made within a particular discourse, the discourse makes it possible to construct the topic in a certain way. It also limits other ways in which the topic can be constructed.[59]

Hence, a discourse does not consist of a single statement, but of several statements, which together construct – to use Michel Foucault's term – 'a discursive formation'. Foucault writes:

> We shall call discourse a group of statements in so far as they belong to the same discursive formation; it does not form a rhetorical or formal unity, endlessly repeatable, whose appearance or use in history might be indicated (and if necessary, explained); it is made up of a limited number of statements for which a group of conditions of existence can be defined.[60]

Statements that form a discourse are regulated by a certain *discursive practice*. It creates a group of compelling unspoken historic rules, which in turn determine in a certain social, economic, geographic or linguistic area what can be said, how it can be expressed, who may speak, where, and under which dominant preconditions. A discursive practice oversees the distribution of knowledge and arranges certain ways of speaking into a hierarchy. As Stuart Hall reads into Foucault, he summarizes:

> Discursive formations [. . .] 'formulate' their own objects of knowledge and their own subjects; they have their own repetoire of concepts, are driven by their own logics, operate their own enunciative modality, constitute their own way of acknowledging what is true and excluding what is false within their own regime of truth. They establish through their regularities a 'space of formation' in which certain statements can be enunciated [. . .].[61]

Discourses can be either inclusive or exclusive of each other. As an example, we can examine all the discourses that can be used in talking about sexuality. There are biological, medical and psychoanalytical discourses available for discussing sexuality, but there are also religious, literary and pornographic discourses. These discourses are relatively common and public. The public and the more private types of discourse can be further mixed together, as for example in the Catholic faith where the religious discourse takes priority over the medical one. As a consequence, the only form of contraception permitted in people's own, private sexual activities is so-called 'rhythm method' (which, in turn, as a term is a part of a certain discourse on sexuality in which the criterion of 'real' sexual intercourse is a man's ejaculation into a woman's vagina).

As people produce meanings in discourses, the result may be texts (speech, writing, sound and/or visual images) similar to each other in the way that they share the central assumptions of the discourse. In this sense, the concepts of 'a text' and 'a discourse' are complementary, lending support to each other. If we want to focus our attention on a particular case of a speech, writing, TV programme or other equivalent textual phenomenon, we talk about 'texts'. Again, if we attempt to seek for more universal patterns and matters that link the texts to other texts and human practices, we talk about 'discourses'.[62]

The concept of 'a discourse' thus defined is in a critical relationship to the notion of language as communication, where language is seen as a somewhat transparent 'medium' of communication and where 'a subject' is understood as 'an individual'. The point of departure in the definition of 'a discourse' is that meanings are an outcome of signification, and that signification belongs inseparably to language. It is a consequence of this view that both the reality 'somewhere out there' and individual consciousness are comprehensible as such only as products of language and meanings, not as their origin. The definition of 'discourse' that I use contains the question of why certain meanings are experienced as right at certain times while others are considered to be wrong, how these meanings considered correct are born, and how they come to prevail.

The concept of 'discourse' has somewhat overtaken 'language' as a subject of study. Unlike 'language', which seems to refer to some static entity or condition, the term 'discourse' includes an idea of activity.[63] The term comes from the French word *discours* – meaning speech, presentation, conversation or chat. The French word in turn derives from the Latin *discursus*, which means running about. Hence, ' discourse' is a dualistic term. On the one hand, it means that interactive process in which meanings are produced. On the other hand, it means the outcome of that process.

The concept of 'discourse' includes the notion of meanings as never being abstract, that they are not based merely on abstract differences in a language system but produced in discourses which are social, historical and institutional processes. Though in principle an abstract language system is able to produce meanings infinitely, the meanings produced in reality are limited since they are regulated and stabilized by the web of social relationships that prevails in a certain time and place; a network that is itself represented through the means of various discourses.

Discourses, for their part, have their own regulations, and produce their own representations of reality. For example, discourses control the way ideas can be linked: what can be seen as a cause of a consequence, and vice versa. Hence, a discourse within itself sets restrictions to what can be said about relationships between the sexes, the status of a certain country or a nation in the world, or any topic.

Since all discourses include some notion of reality, they also produce a position for a speaking or writing subject from which the conception concerning the reality is assembled. Whether it is realized or not, when speaking or writing a discourse is always adopted which is experienced as more or less fitting for the treated topic, as well as for the situation where the speaking or writing takes place. In this way people provide themselves with a discursively specific position in the language, where they can present themselves as subjects of knowledge and represent the reality in a way it is represented in the discourse they use.[64]

However, discourses are not quite as solid and uniform as one might conclude from the above discussion. Michel Foucault laid stress on the notion that a discursive formation simultaneously steps on the terrain of several different relationships, and that it does not take the same place, nor fill the same function in all of them. Hence, general discourse theory is not of much benefit if, also and above all, the specific discourses in which the socially produced meanings are met and either accepted or contradicted are not discussed. These discourses, which stretch from the discourses of the media (TV, the press) to institutionalized discourses (such as literature and science), are characterized by the following features:

1 Discourses are social practices, which mould social reality (a discursive dimension).
2 Discourses do not mould reality by themselves, but are formulated in relation to other discourses (interdiscursive dimension).

3 Discourses are defined in relationship to 'external' relationships and
   forces, such as institutions, social processes and structures (extradis-
   cursive dimension).

These relationships are hierarchical: some discourses prevail and are more
self-evident than others. Others must struggle hard to be recognized at all
as possible ways of speaking, let alone to reach the position of the dominant
discourse.

Already Saussure emphasized that reality is divided or constituted as
objects only through creating signs. However, by means of the concept of
a discourse it is possible to proceed further and examine those concrete and
mutable ways in which people use language to signify the world.

Through examining discourses it is also possible to perceive that even
though individual signs are arbitrary, the signification system as a whole
is anything but accidental. Meanings are reciprocal and more or less
established. They are not so much products of the intentions of individual
persons as intelligibility between individuals. In other words, meanings
are socially produced and signification systems have a close relationship to
social formations: groups, communities and entire societies.[65]

For this reason, studying meanings separately from the spectrum
of human activity that is such an essential part of our being would lead us
astray. In human practice, we do not 'first' have texts which mean
something in their noble solitude, and 'then' readers who enter some
Olympian sphere to have a tête-à-tête with the text, leaving the rest of the
world behind. On the contrary, both the texts and the readers are worldly
beings which are positioned and produce meanings in the midst of the
complex everyday.

Language as signification

Are meanings formulated within language, then? Most certainly. It would
be absurd to claim that language has no significance in the formation of
meanings. At the same time, though, it would be rather useless to stay on
this general level. The notion of the formation of meanings in language
cannot be incorrect, but simultaneously it is far too general to be utilized
as a tool to grip the concept of the formation of meanings. We must be able
to split up the general question of how meanings are formulated in language
into smaller questions, through which we can approach the mystery of
meanings from several different directions.

These questions can be perceived by leaning on the views of the
language's polysemy and the context-bound character of meanings as
our traveller's staff. I return to the polysemy of language more closely
in Chapter 5, and contextuality is examined in more detail in Chapters 5
and 6.

In Chapter 4, I seize one side of contextuality and approach the formation of meanings through analysis of the forms of language. I ask: what role do the technologies of language, as well as the sign systems connected to them, have in the formation of meanings?

Notes

1. It is probably no surprise that the joke is not one of my own. I picked it up from Roy Harris (see Harris 1980, 1).
2. See Schutz 1973, 229.
3. Regarding the critique targeted to the language conception in question, see, for example, Mills 1995, 27.
4. Cf. Williams 1977, 77.
5. See Fornäs 1995, 202.
6. Leach 1964, 34.
7. Hall 1982, 67.
8. See Montgomery 1986, xxi.
9. Williams 1977, 38.
10. See Lakoff 1980, 3.
11. Berger and Luckmann 1981, 35–6.
12. See Austin 1975.
13. Williams 1977, 32.
14. See Rossi-Landi and Pesaresi 1981.
15. See Hall 1994, 260.
16. See, for example, Halliday 1978, 1–2.
17. Fowler 1996, 30.
18. See Berger and Luckmann 1981, 85–9.
19. See Lee 1992, 2.
20. Ibid., 11–12.
21. See Steen 1994, 12–13.
22. See Lee 1992, 68–70.
23. Lakoff 1980, 5.
24. See Lee 1992, 79–81.
25. The notion of the catalytic nature of language also applies to non-linguistic signs. Let us think, for example, of the way in which church bells are employed to give notification of the proceeding of time. The Turku Dom bells in Finland mark the first quarter of an hour with one toll, half an hour with two tolls, three-quarters of an hour with three tolls and a full hour with four tolls. After four tolls, the bells still notify the hour by the double tolling of its number. Were a listener not familiar with this system, s/he could think at the moment of one quarter to a full hour that it is three o'clock – is it not exactly three tolls s/he hears? (To further promote the opportunity for misunderstanding the listener could be well acquainted with a church bell that marks quarters with a double toll and full hours with one toll – as in Marylebone of London, which I once had the chance to hear.) Thus, the number of tolls of the Turku Dom do not notify as such what the actual time is. The signs provided by the bell are catalysts, which initiate an interpretation process in a listener. It is only the

listener's knowledge of the difference between one toll and a double toll that enables him/her to produce the intended meaning.
26. See Eagleton 1991, 213.
27. Borrowed from Tiffin and Lawson 1994, 1–2.
28. See Dyer 1993, 2.
29. Hall 1992b is a good introduction to the problematics of identity.
30. Smith 1984, 3.
31. Bakhtin 1981, 342.
32. Voloshinov 1971, 74.
33. Grillo 1989, 156.
34. Ibid., 65–9 and 162–8.
35. See Foucault 1972, 50–1.
36. Burke 1993, 16.
37. Williams 1977, 39.
38. Cf. Voloshinov 1971, 101.
39. See Bakhtin 1981, 291.
40. See Halliday 1978, 13 and 28.
41. Voloshinov 1971, 11.
42. Ibid.
43. Ibid.
44. Ibid., 25.
45. Ibid., 27.
46. Ibid., 52.
47. Ibid., 55.
48. Ibid., 54.
49. Saussure 1974, 113. By the term 'value,' Saussure means the relationship of a sign with other signs in the system.
50. Ibid., 14.
51. Voloshinov 1971, 85.
52. Ibid., 68.
53. Ibid., 79–80.
54. See ibid., 99.
55. ibid., 94.
56. Culler 1990, 20–1.
57. Saussure 1974, 117.
58. On the relationship between Saussure and the post-Saussureans see, for example, Weedon 1987, 21–7.
59. Hall 1992a, 291.
60. Foucault 1972, 117.
61. Hall 1988a, 345.
62. See Lemke 1995, 7.
63. In fact, as Michel Foucault spoke about 'discourse', he debated between discourse and 'language.' In *The Archaeology of Knowledge* he wrote that the task is no longer 'treating discourses as groups of signs (signifying elements referring to contents or representations) but as practices that systematically form the objects of which they speak. Of course, discourses are composed of signs; but what they do is more than use these signs to designate things. It is this *more* that renders them irreducible to the language (*langue*) and to speech. It is this "more" that we must reveal and describe' (Foucault 1972, 49) (author's emphasis).

64. In this sense, the concept of discourse comes close to the concept of 'ideology', by which there has been an attempt to describe largely similar types of matters as by the concept of 'discourse'. The viability of 'ideology' is linked to the fact that through using the term it is possible to distinguish battles that are either central or not so central to some social formation from one another. To turn to Terry Eagleton in this matter: 'A breakfast-time quarrel between husband and wife over who exactly allowed the toast to turn that grotesque shade of black need not be ideological; it becomes so when, for example, it begins to engage questions of sexual power, beliefs about gender roles and so on' (Eagleton 1991, 8).

   In this respect, it is possible to think that 'ideology' is a matter of a discourse, a consequence of certain discursive effects. There has been an ardent debate on the concept of 'ideology' during recent decades, but the concept still holds on to its value. All discursive use of language aims at producing certain effects and subject positions in the recipient. From this viewpoint, all language has its rhetorical dimension. However, it would be unanalytical to claim that all use of language is rhetorical to the same degree. By the concept of 'ideology' we can describe those areas of language use that deal with the interests of different groups and questions concerning power.

65. Belsey 1980, 42.

CHAPTER 4

THE WORLD OF SIGN SYSTEMS AND TECHNOLOGIES

In the previous chapter, I attempted to demonstrate that language is human being in the world. But in what ways do language and other systems of symbols exist in the world? And what is the significance of these ways to how meanings are made?

Language and other systems of symbols are not in the world abstractly, existing by their own virtue, as if some non-material force. Strictly speaking, language as such exists nowhere at all but as an abstraction. In practice, language exists as spoken, written, printed, electrical, digital or otherwise produced texts. We never encounter 'language as such', but a language that is produced through certain means and that is, in addition to being in certain material forms, moulded by specific sign systems.

As such, the concept of 'language' is not restricted only to spoken or written language. We may well think that language consists of all communications systems which utilize signs arranged in a certain specific way. Hence, the concept of 'language' expands to include, for example, pictures and music as well.

Correspondingly, 'text' can mean any form of signification: writings, photographs, movies, newspapers and magazines, advertisements and commercials; all and all, every kind of human signification practice. These, in turn, often combine spoken and written words, images and sounds. Indeed, categorizing texts is not always an easy task, and all categorizing has its own problematics. One way is to divide texts into verbal and non-verbal categories. Verbal texts, however, can be either written or spoken, just as non-verbal texts can be images or sounds. Another way is to make a distinction between visual and auditory texts (for example, between writing and speech, or image and sound). Brought together these divisions produce the following chart:

	auditory	visual
verbal	speech	writing
non-verbal	music	picture

As writing and speech are linked because of their verbalism, writing can also be considered as a type of visual text and speech as a type of auditory text. Moreover, the discussion about auditory and visual qualities emphasizes the fact that texts are always sensually perceptible by seeing eyes or hearing ears.[1]

These manifold forms of language have traditionally been studied through the concept of 'a medium'. The word *medius* in Latin meant 'average', 'mean' or 'something being in the middle'. Additionally, it included meanings such as 'transmitting', 'distinguishing', 'intrusive' and 'preventive'. The noun 'medium' is derived from the word meaning 'middle', 'publicity', 'common good' or 'public road'. All of these meanings are still apparent when we talk about 'a medium' or its plural form 'media'.

In a broad sense, 'medium' means some sort of transmitting organ that makes communication possible. In its more narrow sense, the term – particularly in its plural form, 'media' – refers to that technological development which expands the channels, range and speed of communications. Thus, 'media' expands physical human resources both in the production of meanings and in reading them. In the printed media, signs are reproduced and physically distributed. In the electronic media, signs are encoded into impulses which are sent forward through space via cables.

The fundamental symbolic forms – words, pictures and music – are not 'media' in themselves, though they hold a central position in each medium, such as books, photographs or recordings. Music, for example, is connected with several forms of the media in a symbolic form: vinyl records and CD discs, tapes, videos, etc.[2]

Speech, writing, facial expressions, body language and ways to dress can all, in a broad sense, be considered 'a medium' of communication. Today's established media are television, movies, videos, radio, recordings, magazines, books, telephones, telefaxes, the internet, e-mail, billboards and hoardings. A list of currently utilized media would be endless – besides, it would be getting longer as this was being written – since virtually everything, from a pencil, A4 sheet of paper or piece of clothing all the way to a CD disc or to schedules and timetables would be included in its range.

'A medium' or 'media' can therefore be understood as a social vehicle or institution of general communication. Media are essential elements in the formation of meanings. They are not merely instruments with which the 'senders' transmit something (words, pictures, sounds) to the 'recipients'. TV, radio, movies, recordings, newspapers and magazines, and books in themselves, contain meanings which leave their mark in the texts they transmit. So the notion of 'a medium' or 'media' as an organ which simply transmits one thing to another, and which exists regardless of the message, is quite problematic. How is it possible, for example, to distinguish such things as journalism or music videos from their media? Isn't the development of journalism linked with the development of the news and other press, and hasn't the video as a technical form enabled the development of the form of music videos and their content in an important way, rather than merely acted as their passive transmitter?

Speech as interaction and material activity

The technologies of language are nowadays more complex than ever before. Every single medium of language that has been developed in the history of humankind is at our disposal simultaneously, from speech to digital technology. In these conditions, it can even be difficult to fathom speech as a specific technology of language. However, if we perceive a 'technology' as an organized activity and an entity of special skills, it becomes clear that speech is one of the technologies of language.

In spite of its commonplaceness and prevalence – or, perhaps, because of it – speech is often considered incomplete, irregular, and even treacherous. It is claimed to be constituted of incomplete sentences, pauses, repetitions, hesitances, unfinished and otherwise muddled elements; altogether an entity of unclear material. Interestingly enough, not many people seem to pay a lot of attention to these shortcomings as they themselves hear a speech act. In order for speech to appear somehow deficient, one must first be detached from it. Often this happens when speech is examined through the criteria of written language.

Writing is considered a higher function than speaking. This is thought to have its roots in the notion of the sanctity of writing, a notion that originates from the long tradition of allowing only the members of the ruling classes to become literate. The holy books of the world's great religions have long been used as talismans: they have been touched and kissed, vows and pledges have been given on them. The ministers in the Finnish government, to give one example, usually still take the oath of office placing a hand on the Bible. Regarding the 'sanctity' of writing, the facts show that blasphemy in written form is considered to be far more dangerous than blasphemy when spoken, which the case of Salman Rushdie sadly proved.

As a 'real time' activity, speech – unlike writing – is most often spontaneous. Additionally, in speech methods are utilized which are not available to a writer: tones of voice, gestures, facial expressions and other such means.[3] If language is a fundamental form of human interaction and people's social activity, then the oft-scorned speech is this interaction *par excellence*.

Speech is decidedly more interactive than writing. Speech takes the listener into account in many ways, whether it means supporting the spoken word with appropriate facial expressions or children's common reiteration of 'do you know what' and 'guess what?' By addressing the listener with different phrases ('you know', 'isn't it?', 'n'est-ce pas?', 'tu comprends?' etc.) the speaker creates a contact, seeks reinforcement for his/her own words and attempts to direct the listener's process of comprehension.

In the light of current, complex technologies it may be not so easy to perceive speech as a material activity. At first glance, it might feel more comfortable to place speech in the area of physiology – aren't people equipped with organs of speech? Nevertheless, speech is not merely physio-logical, but first and foremost, a social skill: it is a well-known fact that young children kept in isolation from other people do not learn to speak.

Why is it that speech is not often thought of as a communications technology, but is considered instead as an automatic function of sorts? People learn to speak well before they struggle to acquire the skill to read and write. Speech is simultaneously the most informal way to communicate in our everyday life and the most fundamental form of communication on the whole.

Speech is a material activity. It is the physical production of currents of air and acoustic waves. As we speak, the physical qualities of the act are ever-present. We never produce 'pure' words or sentences that exist beyond their physical quality. Our speech is always produced through recognizable means that are characteristic to us, that bring to our speech 'non-linguistic' dimensions capable of creating their own possibilities of meaning. Neither do we speak in face-to-face speech situations without also producing meanings by gesturing, facial expressions and other symbolic ways with which we wish to emphasize certain sides of our message and hence assist in becoming 'correctly understood'.[4] So 'language as such' does not exist at all external to its physical nature and materiality, but materiality and worldliness mark it in its most immediate form, speech.

Besides immediate speech, we can meet with recorded speech in forms such as messages on the telephone answering machine, voice mail, recorded literature, speeches and radio plays. Moreover, a large part of audiovisual texts contain recorded speech as one of their meaning-producing elements. Where recorded speech is concerned, the material nature of language is more obvious than with respect to immediate speech.

Writing as a sign system

The material nature of language and its worldliness are even more apparent in writing than in recorded speech. Even though writing usually conceals its own production processes and presents itself as a final product, the matters considered faulty in speech – hesitations, discardings, difficulties in producing coherent presentations – belong to writing, as well. Without them there would be no erasers or delete buttons, nor wastepaper baskets. It is precisely the use of these material auxiliaries that prevents the imprint of the working process from being seen in the finished text.[5]

Thus, not even in writing do thoughts freely flow onto a sheet of paper without material intermediary phases. We cannot write without using a visual communications system, whose signs and symbols always have a dimension of their own which goes beyond its linguistic meaning. The use of capital letters as a sign of the start of a new sentence is one example. Writing from left to right and in lines from up to down is also familiar to us as a part of a visual communications system, which would be Greek to people who read Chinese or Hebrew, for example – the former read vertical lines of signs, whereas the latter write from right to left.

The foremost sin of writers throughout time has been their lack of gratitude to their editors, typesetters, printers, booksellers and other participants in the technology of writing. There has been a persistent aim to keep texts 'pure': apart from their material and practical nature. For example, literary studies have remained nearly free from any ponderings concerning the technological history of writing.[6]

Associated with this, there has been little concern to discuss the general effects of arranging texts into pages in a certain way. Dividing novels into chapters, for example, directs reading by joining certain parts of the text closer to certain other parts of the text (the end of a chapter is linked to the beginning of the same chapter) than to others (in this example, to the beginning of the next chapter, to which the end of the previous one is, in fact, closer). The division of a novel into chapters is a convention born in the mid-1700s. As a genre, the novel does not have any inner compulsion to separate into parts such as chapters. Nevertheless, the division into chapters has functioned in the practical life of the novel as an unquestioned norm for a couple of hundred years.[7]

The rejection of the material quality of writing has been possible on the basis that writing appears to be more independent than speech due to its material outlook, which seems detached from its makers. It seems as if writing exists by its own virtue: ready, finished in form and without contexts.[8] The objectified existence of written texts as tangible, seemingly autonomous material entities makes us, almost inadvertently, consider them as autonomous in a semiotic sense as well.

However, it is expressly the material nature of texts, the being of language as writing, that links texts together with a group of contexts that form meanings. Different forms of typesetting alone raise a number of historical and social connotations for us. Our upper case letters originate in the Roman alphabet, whereas the lower case letters were picked from the manuscripts of tenth-century monasteries. We regard these forms of lettering as natural, even beautiful.[9] Then, when we bump into a 'deviant' type, the Gothic type, for example, we are unusually conscious of the existence of typesetting and the connotations of the particular one in question – regarding Gothic type, the connotation currently would possibly be 'German', even 'Fascism'. (However, in Finland in the early 1900s Gothic type was considered the national type.)

The pitch and volume of voice that occur in speech, as well as the speed of speech, all of which support the production of meanings are called *prosody*. Written and/or printed texts also have their own prosodic means. Writing can be enhanced with **bold type** or *italics*, <u>underlining</u> or CAPITAL LETTERS. Different typesets and point sizes, for their part, separate parts of the text from each other. This book, for example, is typeset in ten on twelve point size and in Sabon typeface, and its subheadings are letterspaced, in Gill san roman. Furthermore, the signs must be laid out on the pages in a certain way. The use of colours, graphics and illustrations further creates a number of new possibilities to enhance certain meanings more than others. Text dominancy, black-and-whiteness and the sparing use of pictures – as in this book – produce a certain identity linked to 'matter-of-factness', 'seriousness' and 'scholarship'.

Hence, written and/or printed text does not simply repeat spoken language in a visual form. Letters do represent certain sounds at least to a certain extent, but there is plenty of such material present in the written and/or printed form of language that spoken language does not have – even if it equally lacks many such elements that mark spoken language.

Literacy

In the history of humanity, writing is a much later acquisition than speaking. For Western citizens at the turn of the millennium, reading and writing seem the most natural activities in life, but thinking in global and historical terms they are anything but natural. As recently as 1985, nearly 30 per cent of all the people on earth could not comprehend a written text. In the same year, almost 900 million of the entire global adult population of over-15-year-olds were illiterate. Reading and writing skills that are considered natural are totally dependent on intentional training and conscious learning. They are not among the natural abilities of human beings, but are special skills acquired only through serious exertion.

As a matter of fact, literacy can consist of a wide range of activities. On top of printed texts, the objects of reading can include, for example, a barometer, tea leaves or facial expressions. In this connection, there are also various kinds of reading skills. A person with fluent reading skills can have inadequate skill in reading movies, or may well be musically illiterate.

Literacy is a social activity by character. It can best be described as practices on which people draw in different reading situations. People have various kinds of reading skills, which they utilize in different ways in different areas of life. However, all forms of literacy include the ability to control different systems of symbols through which reality is represented to readers.

As individuals, all of us have developed literacy through various phases and experiences.[10] The ability to comprehend a scientific text, for example, requires different training than reading a literary text, and it must be learned separately. Acquiring literacy means transferring from one world to another – in more ways than one. In reading and writing skills, a more methodical and formal way of interaction emerges than in spontaneous and informal linguistic interaction. The rules of language gain more importance than before, and simultaneously a transfer from private to public spheres takes place.[11]

From the historical point of view the spread of literacy can also be thought to have had an impact on the changing conception of the human self. In oral cultures, the self is not necessarily conceived an entity, as in a literary culture. Even the matter of not being aware of one's birthday, where it is not a custom to mark it down, contributes to a different notion of the self from that of our own culture, where the attention paid to birthdays from the very beginning of life brings about the idea of the uniqueness of the birthday boy/girl. Moreover, such habits as reading by oneself and keeping a diary have been significant in the creation of notions about a solid self. Converting the self into texts also means that the self can be submitted to examination and it can be experienced as a permanent unity. Therefore, the birth of the modern self can be thought to be tied not only to the development of the realm of the private self, but also to the creation of more or less public language applying to it, such as in diaries and autobiographies.[12]

The diversity of writing

Writing and reading require a command of certain sign systems. These sign systems are anything but natural, as is shown by the mere fact that the same task is served by many different writing systems (such as Latin, Cyrillic, Greek and Arabic alphabets, and Chinese and Japanese ideograms). Nor do different languages have their own writing systems which are naturally linked to them. For example, the Karelian language, spoken near the northwestern border of Russia, has been written, depending on political fluctuations, sometimes in the Cyrillic alphabet, sometimes in the Latin one. In Tanzania, the principal language, Swahili, is even today written in both the Arabic and Latin systems. This phenomenon, called 'bigraphism', has been more the rule than the exception in the history of languages.[13]

Each one of these sign systems is an outcome of long development. Historically, writing is closely connected to drawing, engraving and painting.[14] This also becomes apparent in the etymologies of the word 'writing' in different languages: the English word 'write' corresponds to the old Norse verb *rita* (to engrave). The Greek *graphein* was originally linked with carving and engraving. The Slavic verb *pisati*, in turn, originally meant painting.

According to Raymond Williams, the history of writing can be divided into four principal stages:

The first stage is connected with societies where oral knowledge and tradition prevailed. Writing functioned as a supporting and recording tool of these traditions (in the areas of the Mediterranean and the Middle East approximately before classical antiquity).

In *the second stage*, this recording function was complemented by writing for oral presentation (such as the tragedies and court speeches of ancient Greece and Rome).

In *the third stage*, written texts began to be produced also to be read privately, though even then they were frequently read aloud (for example, in Southern and Central European monasteries in the Middle Ages).

In *the fourth stage*, familiar to all of us, the major part of – or practically all – writing is intended to be read quietly alone.[15]

Even though the technique of writing has been known for a relatively long time, in the three early phases the existence of the alphabetical sign system was not sufficient in itself to cause the spread of writing tools or literacy. Only in the fourth phase were such social relations and forms developed as a result of which the majority of people were able to learn to command an alphabetical sign system. Hence, technologies, forms and the sign systems of language have never existed in isolation from society and culture.

Still, the development of writing is shadowed by the underdeveloped stage of literacy. Only during the last 150 years have there been any cultures at all where the majority of people have had even the minimum of resources to comprehend written texts.

Meanings and power

The above does not mean that the 500-year-long history of printing and books – nor the couple of hundred years' briefer history of the press – was a peaceful and conflict-free evolution. Throughout time, the development of written sign languages has incorporated a struggle over who is allowed to use these systems and for what purposes.

Moreover, since their birth, writing systems have been closely connected to economic activities; to money in particular. It is generally presumed that writing was first created to mark down trading contracts. The introduction of coins made out of metal placed signs and money in a close relationship to each other. Questions concerning meaning and money have never moved very far apart.[16]

Thus, the production of meanings always includes the question of cultural power. Modern information technologies not only help us to have a view of the whole world; through them we also become objects in power's cross-hairs in many new ways. Those who carry a mobile phone are within reach at all times. If I pay for my purchase with a credit card or draw money from a cash machine, my location at that particular moment is recorded. Surveillance cameras placed on streets or in malls may increase the safety of the people attending to their business at those places, but the cameras also mean that there is trace of every passer-by in the authorities' video archives. Such technologies may ease our everyday lives, but simultaneously they make it easier to control our lives.[17] Big Brother might be present in a fitting-room in the form of a device the size of a matchbox. It is small wonder that the term 'electronic civil disobedience' has been added to our vocabulary.

The technical devices and systems important in our everyday lives can be utilized in various ways. Their use is the object of an ongoing battle. The use which prevails has its own effect on our work, communications and travelling, as well as patterns of consumption. On one side of the battle over the usage of these devices and systems are the authorities and educators who emphasize their instrumental and educational significance; on the other side are commercial interest groups to whom the entertaining and self-expressing ways of using the equipment are of the utmost importance.[18]

What about pictures?

Without scruples, I made a leap straight from speech to writing. However, from the perspective of the history of sign systems this kind of leap has no basis – after all, all of the writing systems currently in use have developed on the basis of pictorial expression.

The visual world, the world of pictures, has a central role in modern and late modern cultures. Industrialization, the capitalist tendency to make everything into a marketable good, as well as urbanization, have made our daily life pictorial in an essential way. Pictures have become 'reality'.

In the current culture that is imbued with mechanically, electronically and digitally duplicated sounds and pictures, the term 'text' covers all the products that make the formation of meanings possible. However, this does not mean that spoken, written and visual texts can be studied with exactly the same methods. As mentioned in the previous chapter, in spoken and written language the relationship between the signifier and the signified is conventional, even arbitrary. Where pictures are concerned, the situation is dissimilar to a certain extent, since pictures are able to signify something principally on the basis that they, in some respect, resemble the thing they signify.

Pictures differ from spoken and written language in certain significant ways. Firstly, pictures are said to be *indexed* signs. By index is meant that a sign is in a concrete relationship with its referent. An arrow or a finger pointing at a place or an object is indexical. Moreover, various symptoms, marks and tracks are indexical. A classic example of indexicality is smoke as a sign of fire. The signs of spoken and written language – such as 'a dog' – on their part are not necessarily in any relationship whatsoever to their referent. Secondly, pictures are said to resemble their object; they are iconic signs. By *iconic* is meant that the sign represents its referent by bearing some kind of resemblance to it or having certain similar features. Photographs are typical examples of iconic signs. Yet, the signs of spoken or written language do not usually resemble their referents in any way.

Fictive pictures may have a concrete relationship to their object, but no referent at all in reality. Not even documentary photographs are faithful copies of their objects 'as they really are'; they are always portrayals produced from a certain angle of vision with certain means. The iconography of pictures appears unproblematic, but mimetics, that is pictures that mimic their object, can function as special allegories – a picture of a snake can symbolize deviousness and treachery in the same way as the equivalent verbal sign.[19]

Therefore, it should be emphasized that pictures and forms also have a language of their own.[20] As with other languages, they have their own vocabulary, grammar, syntax and rhetoric. Unlike spoken and written language, pictures cross cultural borders relatively effortlessly. From this standpoint, the fact that the globalization and visualization of culture occur in the same era is by no means a coincidence.

Pictures are a text of their own. They lean on a certain visual language which has its own spatial rules, as well as rules regarding colours and forms. Like other texts, they are not uncomplicated representations of their objects 'as they are in reality'. Visual signs are not based on similarity, but represent the three-dimensional world in two-dimensional way. Visual representation is also narration, presenting stories.[21]

Hence, there are a number of similarities between visual and verbal texts. Yet there are also significant differences between them. In verbal narration, it is possible to construct temporal relations by using tenses. In visual narration, a special narrative means must be used in order to do so. Where a novelist can transfer to the past from the time in which the novel takes place by simply switching from the present tense into the perfect tense, or the past tense into the past perfect tense, a movie director must resort to flashbacks and the taker of an individual photograph must either resign him/herself to silence or develop tricky forms of visual narration. On the other hand, in a movie it is possible to utilize a substantial number of other effects, such as lighting and music, of which a novelist can only daydream.

Technologies and meanings

A text can exist in many material forms. It can be auditory (as in speech or recording), written (as in printed matter) or pictorial (as in paintings, photographs or traffic signs). In audiovisual texts, all three forms can appear at the same time (such as in 'foreign' films where speech and images have been supplemented with subtitled translation).

In each of these forms, meanings are produced in different ways. The meanings of oral texts are produced, for example, with the assistance of the speech rhythm, pauses and tones of voice. If the speaker and the listener(s) see each other, the gestures of the body and the face also matter. The meaning of written texts is made up of totally different elements, into which we will delve in more detail in the next chapter. So we can say that the forms of texts are anything but innocent. It would be naive to think that if someone wants to tell a story, it is of no consequence whether s/he presents it as an oral narrative, a novel or a movie. Expression through these different media is never an uncomplicated transmission: the form of the performance always leaves its distinct mark on it.[22]

This claim can be weighed by pondering on how reading the news in a daily paper differs from seeing the news on the television. In the former case, the reading starts by glancing through the headlines, after which the reader can concentrate more on certain pieces of the news. Of these, s/he can pick some to read faithfully word by word, whereas some can be given a quick overview. The reader can also stop to chew on certain things that s/he has just read, go back to certain parts, and so forth.

A spectator of TV news is tied to the temporally linear presentation of the news. A spectator, led by news anchors and journalists, is not free to decide what and what not to read, unlike the reader of a newspaper. In individual TV news broadcasts, the supply of news is also more scarce than in a whole newspaper, due to the limited amount of time available. News stories that provide broader background information are usually broadcast in other current affairs programmes rather than in actual news shows.

The forms of texts produce different attitudes towards them. It is fairly safe to say that in modern Western cultures printed texts are considered to be more reliable than oral ones. However, the notion of published books as being something other than more or less worthless versions of stories known by everybody but subtly and deliciously varied by skilful narrators is a novel notion in some African communities where the traditions of transmitting meanings are primarily oral.[23]

Hence we can conclude that technologies of language are not neutral. They have effects which cross the borders of a clean technological sphere. In a significant way they set limits to what can be said to whom, and what the reactions will be. Visual media, for example, are considered more realistic than others, and within the visual forms of texts, a photograph is considered to be more realistic than a drawing.

However, the study of the role of technologies in the formation of meanings is made difficult by the polysemy of the term 'technology'. It is anything but clear in its meaning, and its similarities to and differences from 'science', 'skill' and 'economy' are vague. On a certain, basic level, the term refers to physical objects, such as cars, lathes, vacuum cleaners or computers. Not many people, though, would limit the term to the level of devices. Cars or vacuum cleaners are technology only through being a part of human activity. If there were no programs in a computer, it would be no more than a useless piece of metal, plastic and silicon. So 'technology' refers not only to objects, but also to human activity. In addition to objects and activity, 'technology' can mean what people know and are able to achieve when they are doing something. Thus, technology is knowledge. Technological devices can be quite worthless without knowledge and skill in their utilization and maintenance.[24]

When I emphasize the contribution of technology to the formation of meanings, I certainly do not mean that technologies themselves are capable of determining the course of development – they do not determine even their own development. Hence, they should be studied less as reasons than as consequences in themselves, among other consequences. In other words, technologies do not exist in isolation from the social and cultural institutions which produce and consume them. Technologies are both symbolic and material objects and processes.[25]

Only when someone invests in product research and development (R and D) and, finally, in the actual production – that is, when technical innovations become technology – do novelties start to have significance and effects. Choices, investment and R and D are not so much technical as social and economic processes. Therefore, technical innovations in themselves do not lay the grounds for social and cultural changes; rather it is the social and cultural processes that direct which of the technical innovations transform into technological practices.[26]

The telegraph is a good example. Transmitting messages electrically was proposed as early as 1753. At the beginning of the nineteenth century, it was proven in many quarters that the technical system in question was not only possible, but also worked. Nevertheless, the British Ministry of the Navy quite harshly announced to a certain hopeful inventor that they were not the least bit interested in the telegraph. In fact, it was only the development of the railway system, which began in the 1830s, that made it clear that the telegraph was certainly worth looking into. Hence, it was other changes that created a 'social demand' for the telegraph. At the start of the 1860s, a telegraph cable connecting the old and the new worlds had already been laid under the North Atlantic, and in the 1870s the telegraph was in general use in Western cultures.[27]

Technologies themselves do not determine their usage. They are not static, or isolated from other human activities. The television, for example, has developed from a box broadcasting flickering black-and-white pictures into an ever-flattening colour and stereo set, which still receives broadcasts but also functions as the medium for watching text TV and videos, and for playing video games. Transformations that from one viewpoint can be seen as purely technological have revolutionized the cultural place of the television. The era of the whole communications centre, with its videophone, world-wide information network, CD-ROM stations, telefax machines and other such gadgets, is not all that far in the future.[28]

The reproduction of texts

Technologies are a significant part of the reproduction of texts. As a matter of fact, language itself, as well as all the systems of linguistic and non-verbal communication, can only exist to the extent to which it can be reproduced.[29]

The concept of 'reproduction' refers to the fact that texts acquire meanings only through their production, dissemination and consumption, that is, through reading. Earlier in history, the relationship between the producers of texts and their readers was relatively uncomplicated. The copiers of books who worked in medieval monasteries knew precisely for whom they produced the texts. Previous to the development of modern printing techniques, the production of texts was tied primarily to the immediate use of human physical resources. As examples of this, we can think of Homer reciting his epics, or singing and dancing. But in contemporary culture the reading of texts has escaped from the hands of the producers, so to speak. Texts can be read in many different ways and for various different purposes. The readership can be situated both temporally and locally quite far from the producers.

The reproduction of texts developed very slowly. The existence of technologies themselves did not mean their mass consumption. In the Middle Ages, cultural production was still a handicraft-like production of individual and unique cultural artefacts. Only the few woodcuts and the manuscripts produced by the copiers of monasteries, universities and courts were an exception. At first, the discovery of printing techniques, the development of copper engraving, and the introduction of lithography; and then the development of the recording techniques of the photograph, cinematography and sound contributed to further transformations in cultural reproduction.[30]

The technical reproduction of texts can be divided into three different forms: *the mechanical reproduction* of texts, when the most central technology is the printing technique; *the electronic reproduction* of texts, where the electronic transmission of texts moves into the foreground; and *the digital reproduction* of texts. All these forms are simultaneously present in our current culture. Through them, cultural texts are produced and distributed to diverse audiences of different sizes.

The introduction of printing in the late Middle Ages was the opening shot in the age of *mechanical reproduction*. During that time, book culture was fundamentally religious and supported papal power. However, new, quicker and cheaper papermaking techniques, the growth in the numbers of manuscript producers, and the vast changes that took place in the publication system (the shift from the universities, which were then in the sphere of influence of the monasteries and the Church, to guilds as the central producers of texts) together with the expansion of the significance of the urban merchants and manufacturers changed the situation. Though the Church still attempted to regulate the production of books, it was no longer capable of upholding direct censorship through a monopoly of production facilities.[31]

Hence, cultural products were able to function more freely from their production context. Printed texts were no longer necessarily read where they were produced. The volume of book production took a leap and the prices of books dropped, as a result of which the availability of books essentially improved.[32] Yet, the reading audience remained relatively small in numbers. Reading books required special skills, which could only be acquired through appropriate education. Mere technical innovations *per se* did not guarantee the spread of book culture. It was only the expansion of urbanization and the trade market that brought about the progressive spread of literacy.[33]

The expansion of the reading audience also changed the position of writers, as well as conceptions regarding writing. Whereas writing in the late Middle Ages was seen as a handicraft-like activity with its technical skills, apprenticeship years and patrons, the new concept of 'authorship' gradually substituted for this the image of the 'writer'. Authors were thought to be relatively free from social or artistic rules, as well as patrons and the audiences who later replaced them. The previous dependency on the patronage system was now replaced with a dependency on audiences – and quite soon also on publishers. Publishers were no longer mere printers, but also the middlemen between writers and markets. A troop of capitalist producers and agents – publishers, printers and booksellers, but also critics – all left their own mark in the preconditions of producing texts, and were elevated to take the place of upper-class patrons.[34]

For a long time still, reading audiences were small in numbers. The products were still pricey, literacy was limited, and free time scarce. Even the lighting in homes left a lot to be desired if one was to be able to read. However, the reading audience rapidly expanded in the nineteenth century along with the introduction of the steam printing press and the birth of popular literary serials.[35]

Strictly speaking, the birth of the so-called mass audiences is connected to *the electronic reproduction of texts*. Electronic reproduction was developed in the first place in close connection with the needs of the military and trade market. The telegraph, the telephone and, in the early stages of its development, the radio were utilized to transmit messages from one hierarchical level to another in the military and for industrial-commercial purposes. It was much later that the radio began to be used to reach larger audiences; as a 'general broadcasting' medium.[36]

Since electronic reproduction demanded quite a large amount of capital and a command of technical matters, few were able to send messages and the majority of people had to content themselves with the role of recipient. Reception itself required little skill compared to the mechanical reproduction of texts – as is well known, listening to the radio as such is not too demanding for any person with normal hearing.

Hence, the attempt to reach a mass audience was, from the very start, one of the focal determining features of radio and television. Advertisers (North American ones in particular) regarded radio and television as a means to break the borders of privacy; penetrate the market and bring new, mass-produced commodities to the central consuming unit of the modern world: the family.[37]

The masses were the target of activity for national radio and television broadcasting. The new cultural elites (above all in Europe) believed they acted for the benefit and on behalf of the masses. Commercial and national radio and television broadcasting share, after all, a number of common features: among other things, they must both be able to produce a large quantity of programmes to secure the profitability of production, for which reason, series have become the primary programme form.[38]

Digital reproduction, in turn, is said to be characteristic of the so-called information society. In the information society, ever increasing areas of human life are technologized and brought under supervision. Cash machines and surveillance cameras alone are information technology at its best, or worst. The technology in question aims at working on, recording and transmitting spoken or written words, drawings and pictures. Computers and semiconductors, as well as digital languages and codes that information technologies utilize, also form their nucleus. The advantage of digital forms lies in the fact that all signals – sounds as well as pictures – can be transmitted and worked on through the same means. Therefore, all information can be brought into the same digital form.[39] (In fact, digital technologies obscure the line between technologies and sign systems. They are no longer gadgets and devices, but rather code systems.)

'The information society' signifies the demise of the traditional borders between 'economy', 'society' and 'culture'. In a way never seen before, economic activities become penetrated by cultural forms. In the planning and marketing of products, the display value often exceeds the use value. Moreover, simultaneously the sphere of 'culture' becomes thoroughly commodified. Certainly a pencil and paper, just like musical instruments or books, are commodities in capitalism, but information technology, with its computers, internets, videos and CD-players, brings all our cultural activities into the sphere of the monetary economy. At the same time, the traditional views and practices regarding copyrights and originality reach a crisis. Computers have been manufactured to copy everything that moves. In order to read a computer, one first has to copy or write something into it. In this respect, digital technology is in conflict with all copyright demands.[40]

At times it is claimed that the book culture that once replaced oral culture is now, in turn, being derailed from its position of power by the new visual culture of our time. However, this argument contains an excessive simplification. Though it has indeed been characteristic of the latter half of the twentieth century that visual culture has expanded, the forms of this culture have not demolished book culture any more than book culture demolished oral interaction in its time. Late modern culture does not replace words with visual images *per se*, but rather broadens the stream of all words, images and sounds.[41]

Since technically, electronically and digitally reproduced texts are all available side by side, modern culture is characterized by a phenomenal volume and segmentation. Under these circumstances, the relationship between the cultural industry and the audiences of its products is neither established nor simply flows in one direction. Markets are always quite receptive to novelties. As a matter of fact, they essentially need novelties in order to be able to continue their existence as markets. Yet, novelties must not be too novel. They must not fluctuate too far from the expectations of the audiences: they must have a certain juxtaposition with the dominant standards. Novelties must be novel, but not too original. Hence, the daily tightrope dance of the mass producers of cultural texts consists of the search for the precisely balanced concoction of novelty and repetition.

High and low

In Western European cultures, the 'low' and 'high' pair of opposites has played a fundamental role in the interpretation and evaluation of social and cultural reality. However, like most other fundamental pairs of opposites, this one is also not symmetrical. If we talk about 'high' institutions – literature, philosophy, the Church, university – and juxtapose them with different subcultures, marginal cultures or the 'low' culture of people in the ex-colonies, we are immediately dealing with two different kinds of 'high' and 'low'.

Cultures examined from above and below are different. 'High' looks different in the eyes of a 'high' than in the eyes of a 'low', and, correspondingly, 'low' is two different things depending on whether it is viewed from up 'high' or down 'low'. It is nevertheless true that this asymmetry is easily obscured by the fact that 'high' discourses, due to their power position, are usually privileged in determining what can be considered 'low' and what is seen as 'high'.[42]

However, this asymmetry simultaneously refers to the fact that 'high' and 'low' are always in a relationship to each other. 'High' can only be 'high' by excluding 'low' from itself – defining itself as the opposite of 'low'. 'Low' is 'low' not only as something beyond 'high', outside of it, but also as something closely connected to 'high'. It is an image of what 'high' is not, and therefore an essential reminder of what 'high' is. This is why 'high' needs 'low'.

This train of thought could be continued even further. Perhaps 'low' is a sign of something that still exists within 'high'. It may be something that 'high' must repress and exile from its own being – safely transfer it to a foreign area, somewhere outside of 'high's' own, accurately determined borders. Perhaps something that is outside 'high' is simultaneously inside it in some way. Perhaps what is alien, is actually innate.

Moreover, hasn't 'low' always produced the raw material from which it has been possible to cultivate high culture? The rise of jazz within the high culture of our time provides an illustrative example of this. Another, more current example of the indistinctness of the line between 'high' and 'low' and how it is increasingly easy to cross borders is the rise of music videos into the category of art, with *auteurs* like the Indian-born Tarsem.[43]

Therefore, 'high' can be thought to be more or less an eclectic collection, which seizes material from 'low' for its own use. On the other hand, it can be thought that 'low' also frequently snatches material from 'high' for its own repertoire. Albinoni's *Adagio*'s descent to the background muzak of supermarkets provides an audible example of this.

Whenever the audiences of culture have expanded, the crossing of swords on the relations between 'low' and 'high' has become most fierce. The term 'popular' came into use in reference to certain forms of literature in England at the beginning of the nineteenth century, when the reading audience was rapidly broadening along with the spread of literacy, and when the introduction of the steam printing press made it possible to reproduce texts inexpensively.

Cultural texts and practices external to high culture have continued to interest representatives of high culture ever since. However, a large part of the discussion revolving around popular culture has reflected the state of the dominant culture rather than popular culture itself. This becomes apparent in the fact that throughout the ages, popular culture has been discussed as if it were something 'other'. Those analysing popular culture have usually attempted to place themselves outside of their object.[44]

Moreover, the discussion on popular culture has often been wound around the theme of 'the degeneration of culture'. The mid-nineteenth-century discussion of popular culture, for example, was largely linked to the 'problem' of how the inexpensiveness and easy accessibility of the new popular literature would corrupt the people.[45]

When first introduced, newspapers, cheap magazines, cartoons, movies, radio, TV, pocket books, videos and personal computers were all declared the heralds of the downfall of culture, if not the very embodiment of this downfall. Ultimately, doomsayers have envisioned the prospect of ardent internet users who find it cosy to surf the various sites and chat groups as losing all capacity to cope outside the virtual world. Nevertheless, one by one, each of these forms of culture has turned out – and will continue to do so – to be an established cultural form, which again will be considered threatened by new forms.

The expansion of media culture is often seen as a menace to culture's authenticity. Yet we should remember that the notion of immediate originality is mythical. Various media and culturally modified images have had an impact on the formation of human identity for hundreds, if not thousands of years. Long before computer discs and modems were invented, people told stories and drew pictures which assisted them in determining who they are. In this respect, media culture does not mean that much of a change, but it has certainly made us more aware of the formation of cultures and identities expressly in symbolic interaction.[46]

The current discussion of popular culture takes place in cultural circumstances in which the entire Western population can be thought to be within one and the same standard culture: media culture. In 'developed' Western countries, 'culture' is no longer a decorative element in the 'hard' world of production and commodities, the icing on the cake of the material world. On the one hand, commodity aesthetics penetrate the world of consumption. On the other hand, works of art have become commodities among other commodities. At the same time, reality and the images concerning it have become harder and harder to distinguish from each other since reality arranges itself symbolically in a certain, significant way through signs and meanings. Moreover, an increasingly large number of people utilize objects as tools in a game where they communicate who they are, when society is culture and culture is society.[47]

In this connection, Terry Eagleton has stressed the point that 'culture is now palpably part of the problem rather than the solution; it is the very medium in which battle is engaged, rather than some Olympian terrain on which our differences can be recomposed.'[48] According to Eagleton, culture is not innocent in questions concerning power, but has entwined its manifold threads in and around the problematics of power. This can be complemented by noting that within culture, questions that expressly concern 'low' and 'high' are most explicitly in contact with power-related matters.

By the term 'culture,' however, things other than high culture are also referred to. Culture is no longer a uniform and solid category, but a decentralized and fragmented collage of contradictory and even conflicting voices and institutions. Connected to this, forms of art and popular culture have not existed separately as autonomous terrains for quite a long time. The arts, popular culture and everyday life have thoroughly intermingled. In fact, at times it is hard to distinguish what is *not* popular culture, for the mass media and cultural industries participate in an increasing amount of cultural practice. This development characteristic of late modern culture has been described as 'mediatization'. By this is meant that culture is increasingly tied to communications media.[49] The traditional division into 'high' and 'low', or 'holy' and 'commonplace', is ever more foreign to this cultural reality – even if the divisions in question still have real influence.

Media and media texts, for their part, form the scene of continuous battle. The media are part of political and economic power machinery, but simultaneously they are part of their users' meaning production. They contain, at the same time, aspects that are either subjugating or empowering. In significant respects, popular media culture is harnessed

by market mechanisms for its own uses. The above-mentioned commodification of culture means that, among other things, cultural products are
always also instruments for the cultural industry to pursue profits.[50]

In this book, the mingling of 'high' and 'low' is seen in the way that
they are discussed side by side in the formation of meanings. By doing
this, though, I wish not to create new preconceived bases for value
construction to replace the old ones. If it was previously thought that 'high'
is unquestionably better than 'low', I am not about to propose substituting
the notion with a new, equally unanalytical model in which popular culture
would always be considered a true and real culture. In both high and
popular cultures there is an ongoing tug-of-war between the needs and
supply of the cultural industry and institutions and people's own needs
and actions. In this struggle, the question of values never disappears. It
would be insane to refuse to discuss which texts are good and which are
not – particularly since a large part of our talks consists of precisely these
sorts of ponderings. After all, the discourse should be specified when
it comes to the criteria by which we weigh the quality of texts. Since
everything in culture is topsy-turvy, there cannot be any predisposed
and immutable grounds. Yet, perhaps it is precisely the abandonment
of unwarranted universality that leads into us being able to present
assessments tied to a certain time, place and set of values, which attain
their value exactly from this positioning.[51]

Where does reading start?

Language is a material and practical activity. In speech, only immediate
physical resources are used in this activity. Writing, in turn, is material
production where non-physical resources are also used. Sign languages
written for reading exist in a material form in systems of signs, which are
fundamentally tied to those cultural systems where they are valid.[52]

Hence, technologies and sign systems always require interactivity, a
mutual command of certain signs. So all technologies of language – be it a
book as a physical object or a movie seen in a cinema – are also meaningful.

For centuries, textual theories in the Western tradition have focused on
published texts, as well as different versions of manuscripts. Various studies
have delved into the development of texts from 'primitive' raw versions all
the way to the finished 'masterpiece'. In the final analysis, though, sticking
to the inside of an individual text is impossible since texts are always read
in different contexts. Moreover, texts never have a meaning in their lordly
solitude: reading them requires that the reader already possesses knowledge
of culture's conventions.

An example may illustrate the matter. When do we start reading a book?
Just as we open it? Or perhaps it is when we reach the first actual page of
text? In fact, reading starts much earlier. As objects, books have many

qualities, which include the type of binding, the size of the text, the type, the layout of the pages, and the age of the book. These material qualities of objectified texts are anything but secondary to the formation of meanings. Actually nothing about the book is innocent: everything means something. Even the book's immediate physical qualities communicate something to the reader (is it a hardback or a pocket book, thin or thick, illustrated or not?). The thickness of pages and the smallness of its font may convey that the book is so-called serious, whereas its large size may signify that it is a reference book (or a children's picture book). These external signs form a language of their own, through which something about the nature of the book, its function and other such things can be communicated.[53]

These kinds of conventions concerning the appearance of books are socially produced, and they change from one time or place to another. What is essential in them is that the conventions create certain kinds of expectations in a reader who has a command of these conventions when s/he takes the book in hand.

Being a physical object, a book tells us that someone has approved of it for it to have been published. The name of the publisher, in turn, gives more detailed information about the kind of quarters in which the book has been considered worthy of being published. If the publisher were Sage, it would raise different expectations than if the book were published by Reader's Digest or some religiously oriented publishing house. All of these matters direct our choices and raise certain expectations concerning the contents of the book.

The expectations created by the reader's knowledge and value basis are also connected to how we know how to use the book: we know where to seek possible dedications, where the index and the table of contents are (in Nordic and Anglo-Saxon books the table of contents is currently usually at the beginning of the book, in French ones usually at the back). This kind of reading skill is not natural but obtained through training.

Moreover, inside the texts themselves are often places that require a certain reading skill, such as diagrams and tables, photographs and references to other places in the book. Each of these conventions which in a sense move on to the macro level of the book, produce along the previously mentioned micro level conventions inside texts – their own additional meanings in the text.

Thus, the different physical qualities of a text have an effect on how we read. They draw our attention to certain parts of the text rather than others and hence demonstrate how the writer considers some parts of the text as being more important than others. Reading written texts is not only a skill in forming words out of the alphabet and sentences out of the words, but also a skill in reading the many other qualities of a material text.

Hence texts are always part of a certain system of social relationships and characteristics. Besides being individual, texts are also social creations, since their existence is based on a common sign language. We never meet a text by its own virtue; before beginning to read it we always already have a number of expectations of the text produced by the above-mentioned social relationships and characteristics.

To illustrate the matter we might think how reading a telephone book and reading a novel differ from each other. The user of a telephone book must be informed about how to find what s/he is looking for, which in turn is only possible if the user is familiar with the alphabetical order in advance. It would be rather a waste of the user's time to begin looking for the desired number from the very first one in the book and work his/her way onwards. Reading a novel, on the other hand, requires being acquainted with the twists and turns of narrative prose. The reader is not trying to find a certain spot as fast as possible and then discard the book (unless s/he is the type that reads only the very middle of a whodunnit, because it is more fun to try to guess both the end and the beginning). On the contrary, novels tend to lure their readers to wade through them cover to cover.

Certainly, deviant reading styles are possible. A wag who is a friend of mine once wrote a book review of a telephone book for a minor magazine in his best literary critic's style. The cast of characters, in his opinion, was excellent in abundance; the juxtaposition of commercial businesses and private citizens he found ponderously significant. However, he could not but regret the unfortunate weakness of the plot.

Nevertheless, most commonly, ways of reading are in a certain relationship to the declared function of the text. These types of matter concerning context (which will be treated in more detail in Chapter 6) set limits to the ways texts are read.

Instrument and content

In the 1960s, Marshall McLuhan hurled his (in)famous slogan 'The Media is the Message' to the world. With this sentence, McLuhan referred to the notion that the effects of the new technological media in themselves are more important than the messages they transmit. From this viewpoint, the existence of the WorldWideWeb *per se* would be a more significant matter than all the contents that are transmitted via it.

One might think that as I accentuate the role of technologies and sign systems in the formation of meanings I agree with McLuhan's views. However, there are strong reasons to criticize his standpoint. McLuhan seems to base his argument on the assumption that media command the *entire* communications situation – in other words, not only the transmitted contents, but also those social relationships that the communication is an essential part of. There is reason to emphasize the significance of media, but they do not consequently need to be elevated to an autocratic status in the formation of meanings. An alternative slogan to McLuhan's could be: 'The Message is in the Media', to underline the fact that 'pure' contents do not exist.

Nevertheless, instruments do matter. Each medium has its own distinguishing textual features which require its own reading skill. Technologies also have an impact on each other. The introduction of the TV, for example, meant that movie-makers had to stop and reconsider the basis for their existence, and more clearly than before, direct movies for specific audiences. Moreover, periodicals and magazines moved on to a phase of specializing. Perhaps the most significant influence that the advent of the TV had, though, was on radio[54], which has specialized quite extensively with its channel divisions and local broadcasting.

In late modern culture, besides individual media, the discussion should focus on a media system that crosses media borders, as well as intermedial relations between texts in different media. The growing mediatization, commodification, globalization and digitalization of culture shake the customary borders between media. The media historian Anthony Smith describes this development in the following way:

> In respect to newspapers, we are used to a system that involves both mutual competition and competition with radio and television. We are used to cinema and television existing in a state of mutual tension, but also in joint competition with video. We think of newspapers, magazines and book publishing as completely different businesses. We think of the newspaper as a lightly or entirely un-regulated medium, but of television as highly regulated. . . . But we are moving into an era in which the distinction between corporations and institutions that own and manage these different media entities is becoming impossible to draw. The processes of the new technologies and the pressures generated in the new regulatory environment are beginning to suggest to managers of these enterprises that survival and further growth depend upon mergers and alliances across the divides that were so carefully contrived in the past.[55]

Smith talks about crossing media borders in the production of cultural texts. On the receiving end of texts, this border crossing has been an everyday occurrence for some time – are we ever readers of 'just' literature or an audience of movies or television, or do we not bring resources into our interaction with texts in different media that originate from our interaction with texts in some other media forms? Hence, the hybridization of late modern culture and the dissolving of the customary divisions (also divisions between different media) also reaches into the media system in a way that should have far-reaching consequences for the study of cultural texts (which, thus far, has been arranged on the basis of the media division).

All in all, the discussion about technologies and sign systems brings forth the notion that language never exists as such. In speaking, writing and producing audiovisual texts we always combine linguistic possibilities with other human resources. So it would be, or rather it is, insufficient to study the meanings of language without taking the inevitable material and physical quality of language into account.

Meanings do not, though, derive from technologies and sign systems alone. Content and those social relationships where material forms and sign systems function have their role in the formation of meanings. Therefore, we move on next to the world of texts.

Notes

1. See Fornäs 1995, 154–6.
2. Ibid., 156–7.
3. See Kress 1979, 45–8.
4. See Lemke 1995, 7.
5. See Kress 1979, 9.
6. See Hunter 1994, 41.
7. See ibid., 51–2 and Couturier 1991, Chapter 2.
8. See Barton 1994, 84.
9. See Swann 1991, 55.
10. See Barton 1994, 34–5.
11. See Baynham 1995, 117, on this transition.
12. See Porter 1991, 12. Régnier-Bohler 1988 and Duby and Braunstein 1988 are interesting presentations of the creation of 'the self'.
13. Mengham 1995, 40.
14. In the miniature history of writing I rely on the splendid introduction by Albertine Gaur (1992) and on the presentation by Jack Goody (1981). On the history of printing books, see Couturier 1991, Chapters 2 and 3 in particular.
15. Williams 1981b, 94. This history also becomes apparent in words signifying reading. The Latin word *lector* primarily means a reader who reads aloud – once a slave or a servant who read to his master. *Lector* is akin to the Latin word *lex* which means law. The roots of the words go back to the Indo-European root 'leg-' or 'lig-', which means tying together. Equivalently, the Latin verbs *ligere* and *legere* mean gathering and selecting, as well as reading. (See Docherty 1987, 3–4.)
16. See Mengham 1995, 143–58.
17. See Norman 1993, 12–13.
18. See Murdock et al. 1992, 146.
19. The terms 'icon' and 'index' originate in C.S. Peirce's semiotics.
20. See Kress and van Leeuwen 1996, 199.
21. Palmer 1991, 9–10. For more information about visual language see Mitchell 1994 and Saint-Martin 1990.
22. See Durant and Fabb 1990, 54.
23. See Still and Worton 1993, 2.
24. See MacKenzie and Wajcman 1985, 4.
25. See Silverstone 1994, 80–1.
26. See Williams 1983, 129–31.
27. See Williams 1990, 16.

28. See, for example, Barwise and Hammond 1998.
29. Williams 1981b, 184.
30. Lury 1993, 18.
31. Ibid., 99.
32. Ibid., page 100 onwards.
33. Ibid., 102.
34. Ibid., 108–9.
35. See, for example, Williams 1961, 156–72.
36. Lury 1993, 121–2.
37. Ibid., 121–5.
38. Ibid., 12.
39. Ibid., 156–7.
40. Ibid., 165.
41. See Fornäs 1995, 162.
42. See Stallybrass and White 1986.
43. Tarsem is known as a director of, for example, the band REM's music video 'Losing My Religion' and the Levi's jeans commercial 'The Swimmer'.
44. A good introduction to the field is Ross 1989.
45. See Schiach 1989.
46. See Fornäs 1995, 218.
47. See Hall 1988b, 24–9.
48. Eagleton 1992, 34.
49. Fornäs 1995, 145 and 210.
50. See, for example, ibid., 219.
51. On positioning, see also chapter 8 in this book.
52. See Williams 1977, 188–9.
53. Durant and Fabb 1990, 57–8.
54. See Crane 1992, 3.
55. Smith 1991, 17.

CHAPTER 5

THE WORLD OF TEXTS

What is text? Does the word equal a number of signs on a paper, television or wide screen, or is it something that we ourselves form on the basis of those signs? Do we talk about text as a physical material, such as ink, paper and what have you? Or is it a question of text as semiotic material, namely words, pictures or tunes? And what might be the relationship of these two dimensions of text – the physical and the semiotic?

Texts as physical beings

As often is the case with regard to two-sided questions, it is useful to study text from both angles at this point; as both physical and semiotic material. Moreover, the fact that physical and semiotic qualities are intertwined in texts argues for doing so. Texts are surely physical beings, but they exist in such forms in order to be semiotic beings. Conversely, texts can be semiotic beings only when they have some physical form.

With regard to their physical side we can think that texts are communicative artefacts, in other words, human-produced instruments of communication. As artefacts, texts have been produced through the assistance of various technologies. The material forms of texts reflect the nature of these. Early technologies that aimed at producing written texts were connected to axes and knives, with which signs were engraved in wood or stone. Such tools were not good for producing texts on a large scale, either in terms of length or in quantity. The use of feather and parchment in time created new types of artefact (long scrolls), as well as different writing styles. Later on, printing techniques gave birth to a new generation of books that differed from the previous ones in every respect. It then became possible to produce innumerable volumes of lengthy texts.

Texts created by these technologies have also left their mark on the conceptions of 'text' that prevail in our culture. Newer technologies, though, have rendered it possible to have other kinds of texts than those which consist of printed marks on paper. Libraries preserve texts on microfilm. Electronic mail messages are texts produced by the keyboard of a computer, and are visible on monitors and displays. The *Oxford English Dictionary* and the *Collected Works of William Shakespeare* are available in the form of CD-ROM and the *Encyclopaedia Britannica* can be read on the internet. None of these forms entail paper or ink. Each one of them demands specific skills and knowledge that go beyond regular literacy.[1]

There is not one minuscule bit that is natural in these manifold texts. They are indeed the most unnatural beings. As became apparent in the previous chapter's survey into the relationships between the physical forms of texts and the technologies that produced them, even the most seemingly innocent and simple of texts conceals an immeasurable amount of human history. All texts have their own production history. Certain people have produced them under certain historical and material preconditions. These preconditions reach from the language used to genres, assumed readership, distribution channels of texts and other such things.[2]

Texts as semiotic beings

Texts can be in the form of writing, speech, pictures, music or any other symbol. The essential point is that they are organized and there are relatively solid symbolic combinations that appear to be somewhat clearly defined. In all their forms, texts are characterized by three features: materiality, formal relations and meaningfulness. Firstly, the signs of texts are physical and material. Their physical existence and sensual perceptivity always have a material basis, be it the granite used in a sculpture or the airwaves emitted during the act of speech. Secondly, there are certain formal relationships between the signs contained in texts. Signs are positioned in certain temporal and local relationships with other signs, where they form different organized units on different hierarchical levels – such as letters, words, sentences or entire texts. Thirdly, signs have a semantic meaning. They refer to something external to themselves, whether it belongs to the sphere of the natural world or culture, or whether it is a non-textual or textual phenomenon. A piece of pop music, for example, works on all of the three levels: through the sound energy it contains, through the musical form it embodies and through the meanings it implies. All of these are connected, but for analytical purposes, they can also be temporarily examined as separate.[3]

The notion that materiality, formal relationships and meaningfulness are all connected to each other brings to mind the fact that as semiotic beings (in their meaningfulness), texts are not 'natural' but produced by effort; that is, fabricated. Frequently, texts – novels and TV series, for example – are read as if they were 'a window on the world', or as if they themselves produced some 'imaginary world'. In this case, attention is paid to such things as the themes of texts or their characters. The fact that texts do not *imitate* reality but, on the contrary, textually *produce* it often remains unnoticed.

In order to get a grip on this 'semiotic productivity' of texts, let us recall the ideas discussed in the second chapter. It is customary to call the language conception outlined in the second chapter *post*-Saussurean, since, in a certain decisive respect, it exceeds the limits of Ferdinand de Saussure's language conception. Above all, Saussure's interests lay in the language system, rather than language's relationship with the world or its different meanings to its various users. First and foremost, Saussure studied the relationship between the signifier and the signified within the sign – not the sign's relationship to its referent in the reality outside language. In other words, the object of his attention was the most generally accepted, therefore the most clear, meanings of sign, namely, their *denotations*. To summarize, we could say that Saussure paid attention to the immediate dictionarial meanings of words.

According to Saussure, a linguistic sign could be analytically divided into two inseparable parts: *the signifier* and *the signified*. The reference of the sign, namely, what the sign refers to, remained outside of those two:

> The linguistic sign is then a two-sided psychological entity that can be presented by the drawing:

> The two elements are intimately united, and each recalls the other.[4]

On the one hand, a sign according to Saussure was arbitrary, referring to communities and people practicsing linguistic activity. However, on the other hand, 'the only real object of linguistics is the normal, regular life of an existing idiom'.[5] In their arbitrariness, signs were relatively stable, which left little room for the contribution of those people who practised linguistic activity.

After Saussure, Roland Barthes (1915–1980) in particular raised the question of the formation of meanings in the interaction of signs and readers. (I use the word 'reader' in as extensive a meaning as the word 'text': 'readers' are all users who form meanings of texts in various forms.) Above all, the object of Saussure's interest was denotation, whereas Barthes described the interaction which is created when a sign meets the experiences and cultural resources of its users with the term *connotation*.

The terms 'denotation' and 'connotation' have a long history, through-out which they have been given various meanings. Usually, the 'primary' meaning of a word is meant by denotation, whereas connotation is understood as a number of qualities linked to a word's referent, such as contexts and emotional reactions. However, Barthes saw – inspired by the conceptions of the Dane Louis Hjelmslev (1899–1965) – that all of the derivative meanings that certain codes connect with denotative meanings were connotations. The denotation of a skull pictured on the label of a bottle, for example, is 'poison' and its connotation is 'danger' or 'Do not drink'.

Barthes criticized the sign that he termed 'classic', which 'is a sealed unit, whose closure arrests meaning, prevents it from trembling or becoming double, or wandering'. Instead, he talked about signifying practices as *activity* which did not occur on the level of abstract language, but *in the encounter of text, context and reader*. To Barthes, linguistic texts were productivity, stages of production, where producers of texts and their readers met each other.[6] As Barthes noted:

> it is necessary to cast off the monological, legal status of significaton, and to pluralise it. It was for this liberation that the concept of connotation was used: the volume of secondary or derived, associated senses, the semantic 'vibrations' grafted on to the denoted message.[7]

From Barthes' point of view, *denotation* is 'the literary meaning' conveyed by a sign, whereas Barthes uses the term 'connotation' to describe those cultural meanings that are linked with signs as well as units that are broader in significance – such as metaphors or entire texts. The term goes back to the Latin verb *connotare*, meaning something along with something. Hence, connotations are all about those historical, symbolic, emotional or other matters that some significatory unit can activate.[8]

So there is a notable difference in Saussure's and Barthes' conceptions of language and meanings. Where language to Saussure was a system which itself defined its meanings, Barthes saw the role of the people who practised linguistic activity as also being central in the formation of meanings. In his essay, 'The Death of the Author', Barthes wrote:

> We know now that a text consists not of a line of words, releasing a single 'theological' meaning (the 'message' of the Author-God), but of a multi-dimensional space in which are married and contested several writings, none of which is original: the text is a fabric of quotations, resulting from a thousand sources of culture.[9]

According to Barthes, then, the author is not an absolutely free agent in the production of meanings. As a writer operates within language, his/her activity is regulated by – either as conscious or unconscious factors – the limits of language, textual predecessors, literary and other conventions, of which none are of his/her own making. Literary and other currents of the time are also important. All of these factors set their own limits to writing and lead it into certain directions. To top it all, a writer is not a writer previous to the act of writing, but takes shape as one while writing. As the protagonist of a story by the Danish writer Peter Høeg ponders:

> Am I a man writing about what once happened to him? Or does this account add something to my life, in which case it would have to be said that I only come into being as I write; that, in a sense, this account makes me what I am?[10]

The author, therefore, is a figure that is simultaneous with writing, even taking shape within it, rather than preceding it.

To finish 'The Death of the Author', Barthes did indeed declare the death of the author, simultaneously signifying *the birth of the reader*. The reader ascended to the nucleus of the formation of meanings, and reading became the place where meanings belonged.

Barthes' views on connotation refer to the productivity of the signifiers of language. In traditional views about meanings, each signifier was understood to define itself in rather an uncomplicated relationship to what it signified. So, the signifier 'rain', for example, could be thought to signify the 'condensed moisture of atmosphere falling visibly in separate drops', 'falling liquid or solid particles or bodies' and still 'events that usually occur in multiples'. However, these definitions alone imply that when the word 'rain' is used in different contexts, the contexts call us to pay specific attention to some aspect of the word. The saying 'I hate rain' draws our attention to certain limited qualities of rain – above all to how raindrops feel as they fall on top of the speaker. When the speaker then continues by remarking that 'I guess the country people are pleased', our attention shifts to other matters connected with rain (such as how it fosters growth).[11] In each case, the context produces different meanings for the words.

Provided that the notion of the context-bound nature of meanings is valid with respect to words, it is at least equally plausible to claim that this is true also with respect to texts. According to this notion, texts as semiotic beings do not have natural meanings: they too acquire their meanings depending on their context.

Where do meanings lurk?

The meanings of texts as semiotic beings can be and also have been sought from many different directions. Most commonly, the point of departure has been the attempt to stabilize the multiplicity of the meanings of a text into a relatively limited object, 'the text in itself'. In this case, the text has been treated as a complex, though fairly solid and distinct object, which contains several layers of meanings that can be peeled off one by one in order to get a grip on the nucleus of the text, namely, its 'utmost meaning'. In this kind of a *text-immanent* (remaining within the text) conception, the starting point is that the meanings produced by readers indeed lie 'in the text itself'. Meanwhile, the notion of 'texts in themselves' signifies the disengaging of them from all their contexts, that is, *decontextualizing* them.

In different times, there have been different approaches to getting a hold of the meaning of a text that is disengaged from its contexts and solidified into a fixed object. The question of what the author of the text meant by it may have been asked. However, with regard to, for example, Shakespeare's *Hamlet* or Chaplin's *Monsieur Verdoux*, which is about a gentleman killer of wealthy ladies, speculating on the intentions of the author would be quite impossible. There is no way that Shakespeare or Chaplin could have anticipated all the contexts in which their texts have settled throughout time. We, for our part, can but feebly attempt to guess what was the intended significance of any of the lines, scenes or stage directions to the English of the early seventeenth century, nor could we know what the meanings were that Chaplin thought his film would contain as he was making it right after World War II and before feminism gained a foothold. Moreover, whatever the intentions of the makers, language and other symbol systems are always nimble and agile enough to produce totally unforeseen and unintentionally contradictory meanings that shake or even undermine the devised one.

As we study meanings, the figure of the author should be positioned in context instead of text – after all, the author functions first and foremost as an aid in categorizing the text, a little as genre does. It is the *name* of the author under which the texts written by him or her are grouped, and they are usually presented as an *oeuvre* forming a whole. The other texts written by the same person are then used to assist in the interpretation of each one of them. Therefore, the author (and all that the readers know of her/him) as a party in the formation of meanings does not in actual readings reside in the text but, on the contrary, in its context.

Thus it is not surprising that during the last few decades the search for the text's 'own' meaning has largely replaced the hunt for the author's intentions. Here, the point of departure is the notion that the features of the text itself direct their reading: the words and structures, as well as the imagery and notions guide the reader towards a certain meaning. From this angle, attention is paid to the details of the language, the style, and the manner of presentation. An attempt is then usually made to abstract some 'text in itself', which would embody the abstract system 'behind texts'. The task is to reveal the universal laws that lie behind texts (as semiotic beings). Certainly one can ask whether it is possible to keep within the limits of 'texts themselves' any more in this manner.

'The work itself' is an abstract produced from a concrete text by a researcher. Often, another equivalent construction 'the qualified reader' sets to reading it. 'Qualified' readers, in turn, appear to be those who attempt to obey the instructions formed by the system of unchanging qualities that the text contains. Therefore, 'a qualified reader' is able to see what 'the work itself' is. Again, the touchstone of qualification is expressly this ability to see 'behind' the text. When a reader is capable of recognizing the being of some text, s/he becomes 'qualified'. The circle is complete: a qualified reader defines 'the work itself', which in turn defines the qualified reader.

These ideas of the 'real' meaning lurking 'in the text itself' leave readers (and viewers and listeners) incredibly little room for manoeuvre. Readers – even 'qualified' readers – seem to be reduced to being a mere function of the text. They are some sort of meek slave of the text, striving to listen as attentively as possible to what the master text deigns to utter to them. When it comes to being a 'qualified' reader, only those can graduate who love their shackles the best and become the most faithful interpreters for their master.

There is one sensible focal point in the idea of 'the text itself', namely, that texts have their own dispositions, which have an impact on how they become read. However, in the search for 'the work itself' it is not taken into account – or it is considered marginal – that texts can be read in many different ways, that texts are never watertight entities and they can also be *consciously* read against the grain. Instead of studying the encounter of 'pure' texts and 'qualified' readers, we should study the actual production and the actual reading of texts, which cannot be separated from those cultural practices and relations where producers and readers act. Meaning is never written as if ready-made inside the text, but is formed within the reading of the text, which is affected by the position of the reader in contexts and cultural practices in addition to the text itself. By its nature meaning is processual, and therefore as a process it should be studied.

In the analysis of texts as semiotic beings it should not be a question of asking after one and only one meaning. The perspective could rather be what opportunities of meaning a certain text opens up. From this viewpoint, 'the text is productivity', as Roland Barthes aptly summed up. It is 'the very theatre of a production where the producer and reader of the text meet'.[12]

Text as productivity and an arena of production can be characterized by the term originating from classic Greek, *poiesis*, that is, 'doing' or 'making'. Studying texts as *poiesis* can therefore be called 'poetics'. This name has been used and is used about several different approaches. Customarily, it is used to mean studying the general features of some text type (lyrics, movies, or any other). As a theory, it means the study of the special features of different text types – language, forms, genres and suchlike. Here, I use 'poetics' in a somewhat more limited (though, simultanously, more extensive) sense: to describe the study of texts as *meaning potentials*. I call this study *the poetics of texts*. This use returns to the meaning of the Greek verb *poiein*. In the light of its etymology, poetics studies how texts are made, and what kinds of potentials for meanings they contain. Unlike the traditional study of texts, the central problematics in the poetics of texts are not *which* and *what*, but *why* and *how*. The task of this kind of poetics is to study what things texts are capable of signifying and by what means.

The linguistic and cultural comprehensibility of texts

As semiotic beings, texts are characterized by their potential multiplicity of meanings. However, with respect to different types of written and other texts, the preconditions for the formation of meanings differ. As an example, a natural science report and a modernist poem have been produced in markedly different ways. The former is written in an attempt to follow conventions, the aim of which is to act in as unambiguous a way as possible, whereas the latter is usually written in such a way as to leave ample room for the reader's connotations. Similarly, an episode of a television soap opera and an avant-garde music video diverge greatly. In the former, it is essential that the viewers can fairly effortlessly understand the turns of the plot and the relationships between the characters, whereas in the latter the prerequisites for comprehensibility are constructed on the assumption that the text is not explicit.

All in all, usually all texts manage to mean something. This, though, is not so much a result of the texts' comprehensibility as such, but due to the fact that they activate knowledge and skills in the reader that produce comprehensibility because they are connected to the raw material of meaning that the text contains. Texts' ability to function as the raw material for meanings, on its part, is linked to relying on certain linguistic or other features (in spoken and written texts on vocabulary and grammatical choices, in audiovisual texts on angles of view, the relationship between pictures and music and other such factors). These features do not exist automatically but acquire their meaning above all from their connection to the texts the readers know in advance (a reader's knowledge about the cultural position of newspaper articles guides him/her to read them as if they are 'factual' reporting on some incidents or circumstances, whereas a reader's knowledge about novels directs him/her to read them as 'fictional'). This kind of textual knowledge of readers is both material (being familiar with typographical features of texts, for example) and semiotic (the skill to recognize certain ideological views that are either concealed or revealed in texts).

Regarding our topic, it is of anything but secondary importance that *all stated linguistic or other features*, which texts rely on to mean something to their readers, *are bound to the readers' advance information*. Readers form a relatively coherent conception of texts only on the basis of what they already know. The readability of texts is therefore not only an 'internal' matter, but bound to certain factors that are 'external' to texts.

Let us take a moment to consider fables and assume for experimental purposes that there exists a reader who is not familiar with the convention of humanizing animals that is characteristic of the stories, but reads them as if they were meant to be factual reports of the humorous carryings-on of our biped or quadruped friends. For this reader, for example, the fairy tale of the ugly duckling by Hans Christian Andersen would merely be an account of a fortuitous swapping of eggs, and the consequential confusion.[13]

The world of stories

As semiotic beings, texts are united by a certain quite essential factor – they are all *representations*. Now we can complement the passage in the third chapter that dealt with representation by examining the representative nature of texts through the notion that they present stories about reality. Narration brings a temporal dimension to the spatial features of language discussed earlier.

Stories are an important part of our venture to interpret the world; to shape our courses in life. Storytelling indeed has been a part – so they say – of all known cultures. We do not bump into stories merely when reading novels or watching television series or feature films, but also, let us say, in reflecting on some incident in our lives or contemplating what to do next weekend. We present stories to our fellow workers, occasional acquaintances on a train, mates in a pub, judges in a courtroom – to whomever takes an interest in or has to listen to us. Fairly often we talk about ourselves: our exploits and mishaps, our cogitations and sentiments.

As Roland Barthes wrote, narration occurs at all times, in all places and societies. Storytelling is born in the encounter of our experiences concerning the world around us and their linguistic practices. Barthes stressed that stories are not clean and simple copies of our experiences, but signification of those experiences in a certain way.[14] Transforming life into stories produces beginnings and ends in the chain of events that otherwise appears infinite. Narration casts our experiences in certain moulds, and by doing so it lends shape and order to the world we live in. Apart from this, though, stories have nothing 'natural' about them. Selecting beginnings and ends, choosing some material for the narrative and leaving the rest out are tied to currently valid modes of narration.[15]

As a matter of fact, narration and evaluation are rather closely connected. When narrated, the material is arranged according to certain models to express and explain human experiences. Narration means an arranging of spatial and temporal material in chains of cause and effect. These chains have their beginnings, middles and ends. They contain value judgements about the nature of the events, as well as information about how the narrator knows the events of his/her narrative and is thus able to narrate them.[16]

Our culture is bound to an innumerable amount of stories. One simply cannot escape them. In addition to everyday stories, this inexhaustible mass includes novels, short stories, news, movies, television series, myths, jokes, songs, music videos, cartoons, paintings, advertisements and auto-biographies, among all the others.

In practice, narration leaves its stamp on an infinite amount of human activities. However, narration does not mean exhaustive describing. It can only be built on choice. There is not one story in which 'everything' can be told. A film a couple of hours long or a novel of a few hundred pages can cover several decades in time, in which case narration must be constructed on selection. This selection, in turn, always takes place from a certain point of view and for certain purposes; but even the most hair-splittingly accurate news story is inevitably a product of a selection of the material and a certain way of organizing it. Thus, since it is technically impossible to repeat everything connected to the subject in a narrative, and since narratives consequently are full of gaps, their readers are required to be active. Narrations merely create a framework within which the reader must complete the actual story itself. Tzvetan Todorov describes this in the following way:

> [W]e do not stop constructing because of insufficient or erroneous information. On the contrary, defects such as these only intensify the construction process.[17]

In other words, the less information narratives provide, the more actively readers attempt to produce some sense for them.

A mere list of descriptive sentences would not be a narrative anyhow. A telephone directory may be thought of as forming this kind of a list; after all, it does tell where each person listed lives and what their phone number is. Yet, nobody seriously reads a phone book as a narrative. A narrative cannot consist merely of circumstances. The fact that somebody has an address and a phone number is not a narrative. However, if the phone number and address of a certain person changes, we can speak about an elementary form of a narrative: *first* so-and-so lived there and the phone number was such-and-such, but *then* what's-his-name moved to this other place where the phone number was different. A narrative must contain events; it must have a temporal dimension. Additionally, the events must have some connection to each other. When Snoopy from *Peanuts* writes something like 'It was a dark and stormy night' and continues, 'At the same time a boy was growing up in a farm in Kansas', the reader is allowed to expect that in some later stage these two storylines will be linked one way or another. Finally, a narrative also must have its narrator. Stories do not merely exist, they are told. And they are always told from a certain point of view.

The point of view is the choice of the narrator. Narrative means exercising power, as Ross Chambers has stressed, yet it is not absolute power:

> To tell a story is to exercise power. . . . But, in this instance as in all others, authority is not an absolute, something inherent in a specific individual or in that individual's discourse; it is relational, the result of an act of authorization on the part of those subject to the power, and hence something to be earned.[18]

The limits of stories

The function of stories always relies on the fact that the listeners and/or readers possess information on the basis of which the stories become comprehensible to them. In presenting both factual and fictional narratives it can be assumed that the readers know certain established modes of narration. In each culture there are a number of narrative types that are characteristic of it, on which the producers of news, novels, television series and other current forms of narration can draw – and in doing so, can be fairly certain that other members of the same culture will understand them 'correctly'. When, let us say, a writer begins to work on his/her maiden work, or a copywriter starts to design a new blue jeans advertisement, they have at their disposal a large number of 'valid' means to narrate, to give meaning to things. Hence authors, copywriters, anyone who produces meanings – including the author of the present book – apply more or less consciously the generic and discursive modes of narration in their work. In this respect, writing can actually be considered critical reading, where the writer dives into the reserve of already existing texts and revises it with a view to the future, as Jonathan Culler has remarked.[19]

One aspect of the 'valid' discourses of our culture is that there is often an attempt to read fictional texts – and perhaps other kinds – through their characters. The characters are perceived as if they were real people. Their qualities and deeds are evaluated in the light of the readers' own experiences and values.[20] Characters' central status to readers can be thought to be linked not only to the fact that cultural texts are utilized as mirrors of a kind, through which it is possible to examine one's own life experiences, but also to accentuate individual beings and individuality, which is one of the basic tendencies in our culture.[21] No dilemma is readily considered true in our culture unless it is personified – a fact of which the tabloid editors are well aware.

In the eyes of writers themselves, matters concerning forms of narration and narrative types may seem relatively innocent 'techniques'. However, in regard to readers, they carry out an important role in the formation of meanings. As Stuart Hall sums up:

> If you tell a story in a particular way you often activate meanings which seem almost to belong to the stock of stories themselves. I mean you could tell the most dramatic story, the most graphic and terrific account of an event; but if you construct it as a children's story you have to fight very hard not to wind up with a good ending. In that sense those meanings are already concealed or held within the forms of the stories themselves. Form is much more important than the old distinction between form and content. We used to think form was like an empty box, and it's really what you put into it that matters. But we are aware now that the form is actually a part of the content of what you are saying.[22]

Where narratives are concerned too, it is in practice impossible to distinguish 'text' and its 'context', in a word, everything that the writer expects his/her audience to know, from one another. Narratives are actually 'contextual' in form, which means that they require readers to be familiar with their forms of presentation. When a storyteller starts by uttering the words 'once upon a time', s/he does not expect the listeners to take the opening at face value and stop to ponder when the stated 'time' was or why it was only 'once' and not twice or even more often. Correspondingly, the final words of many a children's story 'And they lived happily ever after' are generally understood conventionally, and the listeners or readers do not insist on getting answers to questions such as how long the protagonists lived, or doubt their happiness – let alone contemplating the nature of happiness *per se*.

Moreover, the notion that texts – at least any that awaken interest in their audience – cannot be insignificant, speaks for the obscurity of the line between text and context. William Labov, who has studied urban colloquial language in the USA, states:

> There are many ways to tell the same story, to make very different points, or to make no point at all. Pointless stories are met (in English) with the withering rejoinder, 'So what?' Every good narrator is continually warding off this question; when his [*sic*] narrative is over, it should be unthinkable to bystander to say, 'So what?' Instead, the appropriate remark would be, 'He did?' or similar means of registering the reportable character of the events of the narrative.[23]

In the light of Labov's observation, narration thus always appears to include a question of value. Trivial matters are not worth telling – at any rate, not if one wishes to keep one's reputation as a good storyteller. When it comes to fictional texts, the demand for non-triviality is even stricter. Ross Chambers has, indeed, compared narration with seduction. The maintenance of narrative authority requires that narration arouse interest and enchantment in readers.[24]

Fact and fiction

In many connections it is essential to be able to distinguish 'fact' from 'fiction'. However, there is one problematic result of what has been stated here about narratives: 'factual' and 'fictional' matters cannot be distinguished from each other on the basis of whether they have been told or not. Naturally, not all narratives are 'true', but in the final analysis, neither is any 'fact' disconnected from having been narrated; produced in a certain way. That is actually indicated in the etymology of the word 'fact'. The term goes back to the Latin word *factus*, which means 'fashioned', 'manufactured' and 'cultivated'. Hence, facts are always 'made'; someone has revised them and represented them in a certain way.

Customarily, 'fiction' is distinguished from 'fact' on the basis that the former is made up, whereas the latter is not. In the light of its etymology, though, 'fiction' is not very far from *fact*. 'Fiction' originates from the Latin verb *fingo*, which includes such meanings as 'to form', 'to frame (in words)', 'to arrange', 'to make', 'to develop' and 'to make up'. The first five of these meanings seem to indicate that in the light of their etymologies, 'fact' and 'fiction' are actually synonyms. It is only the last meaning of the verb *fingo*, 'to make something up', that brings forth the familiar conception of 'fiction' as something which does not claim to be concerned with events that have actually taken place in reality.

The division into fact and fiction is fairly fresh in the form familiar to us – which is approximately 200 years of age.[25] Nevertheless, during this time fiction has participated in a significant way in the formation of people's comprehension of non-fictional reality. In Finland, for example, the writer Väinö Linna's novels *The Unknown Soldier* (1954) and *Under the Northern Star* (1959–1962) have given shape to national self-understanding in a momentous way. The former demolished the dominant idealistically nationalistic and unrealistic image of the reality of World War II. The latter novel, if not quite restoring full civil rights to the insurgents, the Reds, of the 1918 Finnish Civil War, at any rate made them historical figures much easier to understand. Whether fictional texts are 'true' or not, they are part of the linguistic activity by which we produce representations that have influences on our understanding of reality.

In fact we could say that the difference between 'fact' and 'fiction' is not so much textual as contextual in nature. For example, the events in the novel *The Liar* by Stephen Fry take place in England, which is a place that exists 'factually'. Since the novel in question is called 'a novel', readers do not necessarily assume that it refers to any people who really lived or concerns events that took place in reality. Instead, Fry's autobiographical work *Moab Is My Washpot* is probably read as if it dealt with a person who really lived and events that really happened. In these texts, not necessarily dissimilar means of narrative have been used (apart from the fact that in biographies dialogue between characters does not usually occur to such an extent as in novels). Reading *The Liar* as fiction and the autobiographical work as fact is due to contextual factors: naming the former a fictional novel and the latter a factual autobiography.

The polyphony of texts

The example of the texts by Stephen Fry points out that not one text is a unity, comprehensible only within its own limits and according to its own conditions. As emphatically as authors have attempted to restrain this inevitable polyphony (which, by the way, does not apply to Fry – as a writer of comic texts polysemy is a necessity to him), alien tones invade the productions of their pen or typewriter. To be convinced of this there is no need to read James Joyce's *Finnegans Wake*, which is considered the embodiment of polyphony. It is quite enough to examine something like the first sentences of the novel *A Harlot High and Low* by Honoré de Balzac, who is generally considered a realist:

> In 1824, at the last opera ball, a number of maskers were taken with the
> good looks of a young man walking about the corridors and the crush-room,

with the air of somebody waiting for a woman kept at home by unforeseen circumstances.[26]

In what way are these sentences 'polyphonic' or 'dialogic'? At first glance, the first sentence of the novel seems a relatively uncomplicated account of the reactions that a young man's looks arouse in the rest of the present company. However, it is not a question of a straightforward report, since the narrator clearly presumes that the readers possess certain cultural knowledge. Since the narrator does not clarify in detail what the 'opera' or 'a ball' is, or what in particular is 'the last opera ball', he must be assumed to be speaking to a reader to whom these matters are just as obvious as they are to himself.[27]

As the narrator further describes the reactions of many maskers, he does not directly quote their own words or thoughts but presents a particular interpretation, according to which these people 'were taken'. Here, also, the narrator must presume his reader to be well aware of what 'to be taken' means, and how it differs from 'to be astonished'.

The narrator continues his account: '[he was] walking about the corridors and the crush-room'. Again, the narrator assumes that it is part of his reader's cultural competence to possess not only knowledge of the fact that there are corridors and crush-rooms in an opera house, but also what these are and what kinds of activities are conducted in them.

All of the above-mentioned assumptions of the narrator are so-called silent assumptions. However, at the end of the sentence ('with the air of somebody waiting for a woman kept at home by unforeseen circumstances') the narrator pronounces certain presumptions. Firstly, he presumes that the object of the young man's search is a woman; secondly, that the woman is absent for reasons that could not have been anticipated; and thirdly, that the woman is staying at home. These voiced assumptions, on their part, only make sense to a reader if s/he is familiar with the same discourses as the narrator – the priority of heterosexuality in this society, the capriciousness of women, and the privacy of the home as the rightful place for a woman to be.

There is an abundance of people in the first two sentences of the novel *A Harlot High and Low*. These sentences are crowded with 'a number of maskers', 'a young man' and 'a woman', as well as the entire attendance of the last opera ball. In a similar fashion, the sentences are filled with voices of different people. Besides 'a number of maskers' (who are not allowed to talk for themselves, though) there are the narrator and the readers he wrote for, and via their persons there are a number of ways of speaking that concern cultural knowledge and reality – certain discourses. These ingredients participate in the formation of meanings most conspicuously in regard to matters that the narrator takes for granted and which are therefore also self-evident to the reader ('opera', 'ball', 'crush-room').

Moreover, the ingredients in question are also active in the sense that the narrator calls the reader to join him in his presumptions. When 'a man is on the lookout for a woman', the narrator invites the reader to enter into a discourse where heterosexuality is an obvious norm: a man is on the lookout for a woman, not for another man. Again, when a woman is 'at home', the narrator invites the reader into another discourse in which the private sphere is the terrain of women. Had a man been looking for a man, the reason for the desired person's absence might well have been that he was spending time somewhere else in the sphere of public life, such as his club or a restaurant.

Thus, even the study of the first two sentences of a realist text arbitrarily chosen, picked randomly from my bookshelf, suffices to show that texts in themselves are not comprehensible as such, by their own virtue. Sentences that at first sight may appear pure accounts of a state of affairs are crowded with alien voices.

Paradigm

Earlier I spent a fair amount of time proving that cultural texts as such do not contain finished and fixed meanings, but that they are *meaning potentials*. Provided that there is a foundation to my allegations, the natural course to take next is to tackle the question of how, then, these meaning potentials are produced in texts.

Here we return to the linguistic theory of Ferdinand de Saussure. For Saussure, everything in the realm of language is founded on relations. The relations and differences, in turn, are divided into two divergent groups. In situations where language is used, words are in a linear relationship since they are bound together. The elements of language are arranged into a continuum in the chain of speech. Combinations produced by linear relationships Saussure calls by the name *syntagm*. Syntagm is always formed from two or more units that succeed each other. In a syntagm, each word obtains its value through its relationship to other signs, by differing from everything that either precedes and/or succeeds it. Syntagmatic relationships are present relationships of the nature of the here and now.

However, according to Saussure, words settle in different kinds of relationships outside of situations where language is used. These relationships are not determined by linearity, but are as if in a language reserve: potential and absent.[28] These relationships Saussure calls associative, though later they have generally been called *paradigmatic* relationships.

According to Saussure, the entire function of language can be explained with the aid of syntagmatic and paradigmatic relationships. The former determine what the combination potentials of language are, whereas the latter define which elements can substitute for each other.

Paradigms locate a sign in a language system by producing relationships between similarities and dissimilarities. For example, the English-language word 'tale' has the same phonetic signifier as the word 'tail', but a different signified. Correspondingly, it has the same signified as does the word 'story', but a different signifier. Therefore 'tale' is a sign of its own distinction from others.[29]

Paradigms maintain the conventions of language as stable and recognizable to its users. Phonology, syntax and semantics are important entities of paradigmatic relationships which categorize groups of signs that are alike (nouns versus verbs, interrogatives versus declaratives, fauna versus flora and so forth) and distinguish individual signs from each other.

Semantic paradigms distinguish meanings on the level of the signified. In order to be able to understand the meaning of the word 'tale' it must be perceived that it means something that differs from the meanings of the words 'history' or 'fairy tale'. Despite this, 'tale' can mean various things, such as 'a narrative' that relates the details of some 'real or imaginary event', 'a falsehood, a lie', or 'a rumour or gossip, often malicious or untrue' (examples are taken from *Webster's Encyclopedic Unabridged Dictionary*).

Syntagm

In addition to paradigms, language produces meanings through syntagms which set signs in chains with other signs. As noted earlier, in a syntagm each word gets its meaning, that is value, from being different from anything that precedes and/or succeeds it. Hence, a sign gets its particular meaning partially from its paradigmatic position in a language; partially from which syntagmatic position it receives in speech, writing, etc.[30]

To summarize, it could be said that paradigms organize vertical relationships of *similarity* (or difference) between signs on the systemic level of linguistic activity, whereas syntagms organize horizontal relationships of *proximity* in actual situations of language use.

Steven Cohan and Linda Shires illustrate this by using the rules of chess as an example. The paradigms of chess determine the principal value of each piece. A queen is *in principle* markedly more valuable than a pawn, but in an actual game of chess, let us say, after 40 moves, the *practical* value of each piece also depends on its syntagmatic position on the board: is it capable of moving, is it threatened, what other pieces does the player have left? and so forth.[31] Correspondingly, in principle linguistic signs can be thought to have their own paradigmatic, that is dictionarial, meaning, but the meanings each sign receives in practice are also affected by the other signs with which they occur.

Most clearly syntagms are apparent on the level of syntax as they determine the relationships of its elements to each other. Still, syntagms have an influence on all levels of actual language use. They place signs in mutual interaction, which forms the foundation of meanings. When a noun is qualified by an adjective ('black cat') or a verb is modified by an adverb ('purrs softly'), the position of one sign in relationship to another determines the signified syntagmatically, which neither one of the words could have done on its own. In the same fashion, coordinate and subordinate clauses, participle structures, explanatory remarks, coordinate and subordinate sentence structures and different metaphors organize signs into syntagmatic continuums. Since in each case paradigms enable the basic structure of the continuum, the value of an individual sign is determined by those signs that surround it (e.g. 'black' determining 'cat' in the example above).[32]

If we open a dictionary we perceive that there are a number of possible meanings listed next to each word. However, these meanings have been linked to each word precisely by their disengagement from contexts. In their concrete contexts, the words do not have all of their dictionary meanings: their meaning is restricted by the other words in connection with which they occur.[33] For example the word 'rain' probably never has all of the meanings the *Oxford English Dictionary* provides it with in actual use. Let us assume that we are planning to go to a picnic with our spouse and have promised to pick up Uncle Oswald to go along. However, as we glance out of the window we announce that 'it seems like it is starting to rain'. The word 'rain' refers in our utterance not only to 'condensed moisture of atmosphere falling visibly in separate drops', but also to the concrete, approaching rain that we can see from our window. To top it all, it gains either positive or negative additional meanings depending on how chummy we actually are with Uncle Oswald.

Thus, the polyphony and the context-bound nature of meanings are already very apparent with regard to individual words. So there is reason to say that the signs of a language in themselves are not units of meaning; that they do not possess a fixed and immutable meaning. They are raw material for meanings, part of the vocabulary and grammatical resources which we exploit as we produce meanings. There is not one word that means anything 'in itself', outside of its contexts, as if in a stage of pure paradigm. The meaning of an individual word is always determined by other words surrounding it.

As we then begin to analyse cultural texts, the first question cannot be what is the real and true meaning of some text, since symbolic deeds in themselves are just meaning potentials. Instead of searching for one meaning that is fixed and solidified from the very beginning, we must begin precisely from this potentiality, and ask *how can texts have meaning and how and by the effect of which factors do the meaning potentials of texts actualize?*

Text and analysis

The point of departure in the previously stated notion of symbols is not that meaning equals some 'content', which is presented in words, pictures or sounds. Instead, the point of departure is the idea that different symbolic systems produce meaning potentials. This happens by producing *differences* (on the level of the paradigm) and *positions* (on the level of the syntagm). The sign's position in a language system can be pinpointed through the kinds of similarities it has on the level of the signifier and the signified in relation to other signs. The place of a sign in actual speech situations, in turn, can be determined by how signs relate to each other in them. Paradigms position signs as if in their correct places in the reserve of the language system, whereas syntagms position signs in relationships with each other, and these relationships form the foundation of complex meanings. The grasping of the meaning potential of texts requires the analysis of texts, that is, dividing them into sections in order to reveal the elements of the sign level, the paradigmatic level and the syntagmatic level which produce the relationships of similarities and position.[34]

The term 'analysis' describes this activity well. It is a direct loan from the classical Greek, where the word 'analysis' contains meanings such as releasing, dissolving or disbanding, dissecting a problem (as an antonym of synthesis), as well as returning and departing. In the light of the etymological meanings of 'analysis', it could be said that it means releasing a text from its shackles, making its polyphonic voice heard.

Analysis also means dismantling, which nicely corresponds with the etymology of the word 'text'. The word 'text' has been imported into the English language from classical Latin. Its root word is the Latin verb, *texo*, which means (1) weaving, (2) entwining and (3) constructing a complex entity such as a ship. The Latin noun *textum* that is derived from the verb used to mean (1) a woven fabric, cloth; and (2) a construction which is produced by intercrossing timbers, framework (especially of a ship).

Analysis of a text can be thought of as disentangling a weave, or looking into what its symbolic construction is composed of. Here, the old meanings of 'analysis' as returning and withdrawing are quite suitable; analysis is returning to the roots of text's symbolic construction, to what it is composed of, and simultaneously withdrawing from text, detaching from 'the text itself' and going to contextual elements.

Differentiating the elements of sign, paradigm and syntagm produces different tensions and emphases to text. Differentiating elements always means that certain signifiers receive a heavier stress than others. Analysis questions what seems to be the 'natural' and solid relationship between signifiers and the signified. It can change the reader's angle of vision to the text and make him/her ask what a word, phrase or sentence, which at first glance appears 'natural' and 'self-evident', really means. Differentiating the elements and their mutual relationships means taking the *textuality* of the text into account; in other words, studying language as output, the production of manifold significatory effects.[35]

Roland Barthes calls taking textuality into account a transition from the work into the text. 'A work' to him is a finished, countable object, whereas 'text' is not an object but a methodological field which is only experienced while working on it, in production.[36] 'A work' is something solidified and final; text is like a process. As a work closes around one signified, text is characteristically pluralistic. 'This does not mean that it has several meanings, but that it fulfils the very plurality of meaning: an irreducible (not just acceptable) plurality.'[37]

'A work' can be seen as a kind of a container for meanings. If a text is studied as a work, it is considered to exist *per se* and to contain meanings which, when being read, are either found or remain hidden. From this point of view, meanings are *text immanent*, that is, they are inside the text and remain there, too. The task of the reader is only to perceive these meanings already existing in the text.

The notion of 'text' breaks this static conception. There are no ready-made meanings in a text. There are only meanings that must be produced, that are an outcome of the encounter and negotiation between the text and the reader's (con)textual knowledge and placing. Text does not provide its reader with meanings, but meanings are born in the interaction where text, context and reader all have their say.

Metaphor and metonymy

In the formation of meanings, the question is always of the encounter of old (previously known) and new (not yet known). Interpreting what is previously unknown on the basis of what is already known is actually one of the fundamental features of human thinking, which is apparent in the central role that metaphor and metonymy have in all language use.

Some preliminary notions about metaphor were outlined in Chapter 3. Metaphors are figures of speech, which produce meanings through analogies, by explaining or interpreting some matter with the aid of another. In a metaphor some being, notion or deed is referred to with a word or an expression that usually denotes another being, notion or deed. Through this the idea is presented that these two items have something or certain similar features in common. The word 'metaphor' is a metaphor in itself. Literally, it means 'carrying over'. Besides its figurative meaning, it still has its literary meaning in modern Greek. The word *metaphoréas*, that is, 'a transporter' or 'carrier', can for example refer to an airline – air carrier – or a porter at a railway station.[38]

Metaphor works like paradigmatic comparison. However, it differs from comparison by diminishing its own comparative nature and presenting itself as a realistic statement. To say 'that man is a pig' is a metaphor, whereas to say 'that man is like a pig' is a mere comparison, that is, a simile. Metaphors can also occur as verbs (someone's talent can 'burst into bloom'), as adjectives (the Green Party can be 'green' as a governmental party) or as longer idiomatic phrases (e.g. 'to throw the baby out with the bathwater').[39]

Metonymy, for its part, is a figure of speech in which meanings are produced by combination. Where metaphor transfers features from one place to another, metonymy combines meanings that are close to each other. It originates from the Greek word *meta* (which can mean, according to the case of the noun it occurs with, 'in the middle', 'among', 'with', 'after', 'during' and 'behind') and *onoma* ('name'). In metonymy, the name of one item is replaced with something that is closely connected to it. Here one term identifies with another term, either on the basis of their actual closeness or according to some generally accepted convention, to such an extent that it comes to mean it. 'The White House' in American politics signifies the presidential institution, just as '10 Downing Street' equals the Prime Minister of Great Britain. In this manner, metonymy works similarly as a syntagmatic combination.

An important form of metonymy is *synecdoche*, in which one part represents the totality of something (for example, in the phrase 'to beat swords into ploughshares', 'swords' represents the entire armaments industry and 'ploughshares', in turn, portrays all peacetime activities) or a totality represents one of its parts (e.g. the stance of 'Great Britain' on some current issue most often equals the standpoint of the Prime Minister in office).

All this is further complicated by the fact that metaphors and metonymies often overlap. Hence, the phrase about beating swords into ploughshares contains not only the stated metonyms, but also a metaphor: the 'beating' refers to a conversion; altering arms for civilian use.

Work and text

In the following, I attempt to concretize the relatively abstract notions presented earlier by applying them to an analysis of one (literary) text. I study textuality by analysing the poem 'The Day Lady Died' by the American poet Frank O'Hara, first as 'a work' and then as ' text.'

The Day Lady Died

It is 12:20 in New York a Friday
three days after Bastille day, yes
it is 1959 and I go get a shoeshine
because I will get off the 4:19 in Easthampton
at 7:15 and then go straight to dinner
and I don't know the people who will feed me

I walk up the muggy street beginning to sun
and have a hamburger and a malted and buy
an ugly NEW WORLD WRITING to see what the poets
in Ghana are doing these days
                I go on to the bank
and Miss Stillwagon (first name Linda I once heard)
doesn't even look up my balance for once in her life
and in the GOLDEN GRIFFIN I get a little Verlaine
for Patsy with drawings by Bonnard although I do think of Hesiod, trans.
Richard Lattimore or
Brendan Behan's new play or *Le Balcon* or *Les Nègres*
of Genet, but I don't, I stick with Verlaine
after practically going to sleep with quandariness

and for Mike I just stroll into the PARK LANE
Liquor Store and ask for a bottle of Strega and
then I go back where I came from to 6th Avenue
and the tobacconist in the Ziegfeld Theater and
casually ask for a carton of Gauloises and a carton
of Picayunes, and a NEW YORK POST with her face on it

and I am sweating a lot by now and thinking of
leaning on the john door in the 5 SPOT
while she whispered a song along the keyboard
to Mal Waldron and everyone and I stopped breathing

Reading the poem as a work, a product final in its meaning, would be to examine it as a special case of language, as poetry that requires literary competence in reading it.[40] According to Jonathan Culler, literary competence is a number of learned conventions that are used when it is known that it is 'literature' that is being read.

Culler divides these conventions into a tripartite schema. Firstly, into the presumption of the significance of the work, namely that the work expresses something important about some problem concerning human beings and their world. Secondly, into the supposition of the consistency of the work, that is, into the notion that the means of presentation of the work (metaphors, alliteration, rhythm, etc.) make it consistent on the levels of both the signifier and the signified. Thirdly, into the supposition of the work's thematic unity, which means that the linguistic features of the work, which have been brought out by reading it on the basis of the previously mentioned supposition, demonstrate that there is a consistent structure of form in the work, which in turn settles the author's intended meaning that is presupposed on the basis of the first supposition.[41]

A traditional analysis of the poem 'The Day Lady Died' as a work would follow these three expectations. Assuming that the poem expresses something important about the poet's experience in particular and human nature in general, the reader would strive to perceive those poetic conventions that are behind certain metaphors in the poem. Next, the reader would arrange these features into a consistent unity. From this point of view, the following matters in particular would be focal:

- Exact points in time (12.20, Friday; 17 July 1959; the 4.19 p.m. train; at 7.15 p.m.), locations (New York, Easthampton, Golden Griffin, Park Lane, 6th Avenue, the Ziegfeld Theater, the 5 Spot), the names of characters (Miss Linda Stillwagon, Patsy, Mike, Mal Waldron) and other people (the poets in Ghana, Pierre Bonnard, Paul Verlaine, Hesiod, Richard Lattimore, Brendan Behan, Jean Genet), as well as the details of commodities (a hamburger, a malted, *New World Writing*, Strega, Gauloises, Picayunes, the *New York Post*);
- the speaking subject of the poem, the 'I';
- the poem's language form, which follows the wanderings of the speaking subject and resembles an objective account ('and then'); and
- the title of the poem.

In this type of analysis, the aim would be to interpret the poem, to make it 'comprehensible'. The exact points of time, locations and names contained in the poem could then be interpreted as symbols which convey something that is generally applicable about a human being and his/her condition in the modern world. In this case, for example, points where the alienation of people living in a metropolis becomes apparent and catches the reader's attention ('and I don't know the people who will feed me', 'first name Linda I once heard') or points where the poem's *flâneur*ish self, as he, while drifting around an area of a couple of blocks in Manhattan, gathers all sorts of things into his possession from hamburgers to the philosophy of antiquity could be interpreted as symbols.

However, perhaps the most central task of interpretation would concern the title of the poem: who is the lady in question? For this, the answer could be found, besides the indirectly expressed day of her death (three days after Bastille Day: 17 July 1959), also in lines 25 and 28–9 ('with her face on it' and 'she whispered a song along the keyboard / to Mal Waldron and everyone and I stopped breathing'), and above all, in the title of the poem. This 'Day Lady' or 'Lady Day', who gets her picture in the evening edition of the *New York Post* after having died the same day and sings in the memories of the poem's speaking subject accompanied by the jazz pianist Mal Waldron, is naturally no one other than Billie Holiday. Hence, the wordplay 'The Day Lady Died' in the title could be used as the key for the reading of the whole poem. In one direction there would be the exact points and the names of the people as symbols of the alienation of modern people, in another direction there would be 'Lady Day' whose singing causes everybody to 'stop breathing'. In this respect, the last lines of the poem could be thought to position themselves in opposition to all the other lines, in which case it would be a question of a certain kind of inverse metaphor or oxymoron, that is, a parallel drawn between two unrelated elements: Billie Holiday is something other than everything mentioned in lines 1–25.

Thus, the poem could be read as a melancholic elegy on how the alienated everyday kills Billie Holiday. Consequently, spiritual reality is a touch poorer and people in the infinite hustle and bustle of their daily lives are doomed to drift even further apart from each other now, when the fine strand that connected them – Lady Day – has snapped. Even if the poem's speaking subject seems to be totally immersed in the terrain of mass production and global culture, according to the interpretation above, he still would nostalgically long to be back in some lost, authentic reality which Lady Day's singing symbolizes.[42]

However, the reading strategies corresponding with the 'literary competence' that Jonathan Culler distinguished – the suppositions about the significance, consistency and thematic unity of the text – are not qualities that are inherent in the poem's language, but conventions that are connected to the reading of the language in a specific way, that is, as a literary work. If the poem is studied in another way – as *text* – the stated qualities do not produce consistency in the poem, but break it apart, open innumerable holes in it.

The manifold everyday activities of the poem's speaking subject and the singing of Lady Day have not in fact been placed as in opposition, but in succession to each other. The meaning of the poem does not exhaust itself in this inverse metaphor – in so far as there are any inverse metaphors in the poem's text 'itself' at all. Instead, there are quite a number of metonymic relationships in the poem. Actually, the poem's Lady Day can be seen as metonymically equated with all of the other matters and people that the cultivated citizen of the metropolis meets – shoe shiners, trains, dinner invitations, hamburger sellers, literary magazines, bank clerks, Ghanaian poets, bookstores, de luxe editions, liquor, cigarettes and jazz clubs. On the level of textuality, Lady Day is not discernible from the rest of the poem, but she is united with all the sides of the miscellaneous everyday life of the metropolis.

In this respect, the reader can juxtapose any matter at all that is mentioned in the poem, in which case there is practically an infinite amount of ways of reading. For example, drawing a parallel between Ghanaian poets and Miss Stillwagon in fact obscures the difference between them: these two are placed side by side in the poem just as they exist in Manhattan's cultural melting pot. In this way, the poem can be read as a large metonymy, where everything mentioned in it means its title, 'The Day Lady Died', and through it, the day when the events in the poem took place.

A number of the poem's textual features support this way of reading. In it, the whole world and the entire history are as if side by side, simultaneously available, to be purchased piece by piece. All differences have been shattered. Even the free metre of the poem's language is as 'transparent' as possible (there is only one rhyme in it; nine – shine in line three). The word 'and' occurs a total of 19 times in the poem, often connecting things to each other as if arbitrarily (for example at the beginning of lines 14 and 20). This obviously intentional unpolished quality and banality pulls the rug from under the elegiac nature of the poem. When the theme of death is at last brought out, even that is referred to through a commonplace recollection of the sweaty and bothered speaking subject of the poem ('leaning on the john door').

In this way the poem can be studied essentially as an open text. There is nothing in the text itself that would establish the meaning of its different features. The poem is thoroughly imbued with cultural references, but the connotations of these references are not found in the text, but in the reader's cultural knowledge. For example, the significance of 'Easthampton' to the reader is largely dependent on whether s/he happens to know to what kind of a community the text makes a reference (to my knowledge, it is a wealthy community on Long Island, but I may well be wrong). With regard to other references, such as 'Strega' or 'Picayunes cigarettes', the case is similar. The reference to the *New York Post* works differently for a reader who knows that the newspaper in question is read particularly by the lower middle classes. Moreover, the reference to 'Mal Waldron' at the end of the text has different meanings according to whether the reader is aware of the fact that he was a jazz pianist, or if s/he knows during which period of time (1957–1959) he worked together with Lady Day.

Furthermore, the poem receives different meanings according to how much the reader knows about the life and other works of its author, Frank O'Hara (1926–1966). 'Patsy' and 'Mike'(who, according to Marjorie Perloff, refer to O'Hara's friends Patsy Southgate and Mike Kanemitsu[43]) can stand as a lover and a friend of the narrator in two different ways depending on whether the reader assumes that the narrating subject of the poem is, as its writer was, a homosexual man or not. The reference to 'Bonnard' raises novel connotations if the reader happens to know that O'Hara worked in the New York Museum of Modern Art (MoMa), where he organized several touring exhibitions. A reader very familiar with O'Hara can finally also ponder on how come a joint like the '5 Spot' jazz club pops out of his text, and maybe even end up with the notion that for this writer, who felt comfortable in places like Carnegie Hall or the Metropolitan Opera, this reference to the jazz club in question might have been irony directed towards stereotypical beat poets.

Finally, familiarity with Billie Holiday's biography may produce different connotations in the reader. The well-known fact, for example, that in her youth Holiday was coerced to work as a prostitute links her to a text abundant with commodities and certainly does not detach her from it.

Both textual and contextual matters interfere with the contrariness presented by the inverse metaphor, and as a matter of fact, destroy it. There is no contrariness in the text, but everything is adjacent in it. No inverse metaphor exists in the language of the text, but it is brought out in the learned conventions of the reader.[44]

Irony, jokes, exaggeration

_____

Naturally, a modernistic poem uses a special language, but polysemy is not by any means limited to poetic texts. Any text can be read in several ways if desired. As Terry Eagleton jestingly notes:

> Consider a prosaic, quite unambiguous statement like the one sometimes seen in the London Underground system: 'Dogs must be carried on the escalator.' This is not perhaps quite as unambiguous as it seems at first sight: does it mean that you *must* carry a dog on the escalator? Are you likely to be banned from the escalator unless you can find some stray mongrel to clutch in your arms on the way up?[45]

In addition to unintentional polysemy, there is also intentional polysemy aplenty in everyday language. One of the central producers of polysemy is irony. In an ironic utterance, the user of the language seems to be saying one thing, but in fact means something else. As a rhetorical device irony is always ambiguous, that is, polysemic language, and at first glance open to topsy-turvy readings, since it places meanings in opposition to each other. A user of irony usually holds the knowledge of which meaning s/he considers primary, but irony itself cannot convey that knowledge to others. Irony always leaves plenty of room for its recipients. As Linda Hutcheon remarks:

> Because irony . . . happens in something called 'discourse', its semantic and syntactic dimensions cannot be considered separately from the social, historical and cultural aspects of its contexts of deployment and attribution.[46]

In other words, irony is always bound to the interpretational resources of the people who become objects of ironical address. Necessarily, there is nothing in irony as such that would guarantee that it really is recognized as irony (as many a language user aspiring to be successfully ironic has had to discover).

Similar to irony, many jokes also work through making meanings collide. As an illustrative example, let us look at the joke about an American, a Brit and a Chinese who ended up shipwrecked on a desert island. The American declares himself 'the Leader of the Island'. The Brit, in turn, is appointed the 'Secretary of Foreign Relations', whereas the Chinese is left to be responsible for provisions, 'the Head of Supplies'. For a day or two all seems to go well, camp is pitched, a reed hut is put up and provisions are acquired, until all of a sudden the Chinese vanishes into thin air. The American and the Brit wait until late afternoon, but then decide to organize a search party. They scour the little island till sunset, but have to return to the camp empty-handed. Then the Chinese man leaps out of the reed hut and hollers: 'Supplies! Supplies!'

What is it that makes us laugh in this joke? First of all, probably the notion that the phonetic signifier of the word 'supplies' is mixed up with the phonetic signifier of 'surprise' in the mouth of the Chinese, and consequently he has understood his job in the party in his own way. However, there is also another comical matter involved: it is amusing if and when linguistic confusion leads to mix-ups in the real world. Thirdly, the form of the joke – an American, a Brit and a Chinese do this and that – already attunes us to be open to laughter: haven't we all our lives heard more or less amusing stories in the same form about the comical mishaps of representatives of different nations? The reading could be taken even further, but already making two languages collide with each other creates such polysemy of meanings that we react to it by laughing.

In addition to irony and jokes, we bump into polysemy in the matter of *exaggeration*. One of the forms of exaggeration is hyperbole, which means an emphasis on one thing in such a way that it is not intended to be understood literally. A common example of hyperbole is the situation where someone complains: 'It takes you a million years to get ready!' This kind of exaggeration can also be self-conscious, where it can include parody targeted on oneself (as often is the case in Madonna's music videos, for example). Intentional exaggeration makes it possible for matters that seem focal at first glance to totter, when the reader can simultaneously enjoy both the meaning that seems primary and the meanings that shake it.

Semiotic abundance works in a similar fashion. There is always 'too much' meaning in texts for them to be tied only to a one-time reading. Texts through their own structure attempt to limit the meanings read into them, but never quite succeed in this ambition. A familiar situation is the case when one begins to explain what one in fact meant by something said earlier. This further clarification contains even more possibilities for misunderstanding, which again perhaps must be resisted with new clarifications – and so forth, all the way to the gates of despair.

One meaning or several meanings?

Classic realist literary texts are lucid examples of texts which attempt to restrict the readings targeted on them. However, realism is not a privilege of literature only, but even today has a strong influence on mainstream feature films and television series. It is characteristic of realism to perceive individuals as the source of meanings, knowledge and action. In realist texts, the role of language and other symbols in the formation of an individual are passed over and the individual him/herself is studied as a whole entity that determines him/herself. The source of the meanings of text is their *maker*.

Catherine Belsey defines these kinds of realist text in the following way: 'Classic realism is characterized by *illusionism*, narrative which leads to *closure*, and a *hierarchy of discourses* which establishes the "truth" of the story.'[47]

By illusionism, Belsey means that a classic realist text presents the author as the authentic source of the text's meaning, and the reader as an autonomous subject who is 'free' to read the text the way the author intended it to be read. By the narrative leading to closure, Belsey refers to the following:

A realist narrative aims at producing a riddle by creating a state of disorder. The most common sources for disorder in plots of realist narrative are murder, war, journey or love. However, the story inevitably progresses towards closure. Simultaneously, though, the closure can be considered *an opening*, the solving of the riddle through the return to the original order.

Closure means that moment when the events of the narration become completely evident to the reader. The most clear example of this is a detective story. In the final pages of the story, the murderer is exposed as well as his/her motives, and the motives of other characters are also brought into daylight. Before the closure, the comprehensibility of the text depends on the fact that a hierarchy prevails between the different discourses of the text. This hierarchy works most perceptibly as that privileged discourse which places other discourses into a subordinate position in relation to itself by putting them between quotation marks. What is presented in quotation marks is the dialogue of the characters. It is subordinate to the narrator's accounting, which can explain the characters' speech, present their motives, penetrate into their psyche, reveal that they lie, and so forth. The voice of the narrator in a realist text is always the voice of an author. Correspondingly, a realist text strives to have the reader unite with the omniscient narrator, to perceive things from his/her point of view; to go and stand with him/her on the top of the discursive hierarchy.[48]

As such, a realist text appears to be a closed work, in which all meanings are padlocked. However, it can also be read as an open text, examined as a construction produced in a very specific way. From this viewpoint, it can be asked firstly, by what means the text is capable of meaning expressly what it claims to be meaning; and secondly, what kinds of problems the attempt to achieve this one and only meaning causes within the text itself. In other words, it is a question of a study of the work's production process – not an examination of the author's individual consciousness, but examining the text with regard to what materials are utilized in the text and how. With respect to realism, it is thus possible to seek the text's own internal inconsistencies where it breaks the boundaries within which it has been constructed; where it, so to speak, breaks its own realism. Now it is not a question of an attempt to fix for good the one way of reading the text that smooths out its contradictions and smothers other ways of reading as an 'interpretation' of it, but of studying which ingredients the text utilizes in its construction.

Let us study the first two paragraphs of a classic realist novel, Jane Austen's *Pride and Prejudice* (1813), from this standpoint:

It is a truth universally acknowledged, that a single man in possession of a good fortune, must be in want of a wife.

However little known the feelings or views of such a man may be on his first entering a neighbourhood, this truth is so well fixed in the minds of the surrounding families, that he is considered as the rightful property of some one or other of their daughters.[49]

In these paragraphs, the narrator of the novel invites the reader to join her in the omniscient position: 'It is a truth universally acknowledged, that . . . ' and 'of such a man . . . first entering a neighbourhood . . . this truth is so well fixed . . . that he is considered . . . ' The narrator makes statements that Austen presents as universal and invites the reader to perceive the novel's characters and reality from this generally applicable level as if from up to down. The irony in the first paragraph ('It is a truth universally acknowledged . . . ') does not shake this arrangement of looking at things from up to down, but rather reinforces it, since the narrator can be thought of as ironizing one of the novel's central characters, Mrs Bennet, to whom the narration indeed transfers immediately after our quotation.

However, the irony can be thought to hoist the narrator by her own petard. Even though she ironizes Mrs Bennet in the first paragraph, the views she brings forth in the second one can be understood as her own opinions ('such a man . . . '). In this, it is the narrator herself who succumbs to exactly such universalizing for which she ironizes the objects of her narration in the first paragraph. This universalizing is linked to an attempt to seek one solid meaning. The narrator strives for that not only by producing a narrative hierarchy (the discourse of the narrator above the discourse of the characters), but also by naturalizing a certain viewpoint of the narrative. To get a grip on this viewpoint, the reader can ask: of whom do these paragraphs tell? Who are 'the surrounding families'? The narrator hardly means all the families of Hertfordshire, where the novel takes place, but only those who have daughters that 'an unmarried wealthy man' could possibly consider marrying in the England of the time.

However, here the narrator's attempt to produce one solid meaning is driven out to sea. The narrator starts out by universalizing, but in order to universalize she must embrace a certain limited perspective to the narration (in the novel, only people who are well enough off or otherwise noteworthy in their social status – clergy, for example – belong to 'real' Hertfordshire). Thus, *Pride and Prejudice*, which is considered a paragon of a classic realist novel, does not get further than the first two paragraphs before it becomes obvious that the universality and omniscience of its narrator are in fact restricted and narrow-minded.

Plurality of meanings

In his essay, 'From Work to Text' Barthes discusses text as the implementer of the real plurality of meanings, 'explosion and dissemination'.[50]

Mikhail Bakhtin summarized this in his time, in the following way:

> No living word relates to its object in a singular way: between the word and its object, between the word and the speaking subject, there exists an elastic environment of other, alien words about the same object, the same theme. . . . Indeed, any concrete discourse (utterance) finds the object at which it was directed already as it were overlain with qualifications, open to dispute, charged with value, already enveloped in an obscuring mist – or, on the contrary, by the 'light' of alien words that have already been spoken about it. It is entangled, shot through with shared thoughts, points of view, alien value judgements and accents. The word, directed toward its object, enters a dialogically agitated and tension-filled environment of alien words, value judgements and accents, weaves in and out of complex interrelationships, merges with some, recoils from others, intersects with yet a third group: and all this may crucially shape discourse, may leave a trace in all its semantic layers, may complicate its expression and influence its entire stylistic profile.[51]

Every uttered or written word therefore collides with innumerable other words. Equivalently, every auditory or visual symbol encounters other auditory and visual symbols. What these other symbols are determines in a significant way, how we read the symbols we meet. This notion that Bakhtin calls *heteroglossia* (which was briefly discussed in Chapter 3) emphasizes the relationship of context in the formation of meanings. At all times, texts acquire meanings in contexts of other texts.

Hence, the plurality of meanings signifies that all texts are perpetually open to new readings, to other ways of reading. It also signifies that texts can never be read as if *per se*, torn apart from their contexts. All texts contain material that refers outside of themselves.

Text and context

According to British cultural researcher Tony Bennett, it is never possible to say anything very significant about the 'text itself': discussing it only becomes an option when it is decided in what context some text is made into the object of analysis – is it the author's supposed intentions, the horizons of the author's contemporary audience or something other that is selected as the point of departure?[52] Elsewhere Bennett remarks that as a matter of fact texts do not even exist outside their contexts. According to him, we can never find a 'pure text' or 'text in itself'. Texts are always shaped by the contextual adjuncts with which they are joined.[53] Bennett clarifies the notion as follows:

Texts exist only as always-already organised or activated to be read in certain ways just as readers exist as always-already activated to read in certain ways: neither can be granted a virtual identity that is separable from the determinate ways in which they are gridded onto one another within different reading formations.[54]

Correspondingly, Ross Chambers has also stressed the point that the 'text itself' cannot exist: 'the text *an sich*, the text appreciated "in terms of itself" is an impossibility, since there is always a context, whether recognized or not, in which it is read.'[55]

The comments by Bennett and Chambers seem sensible in that hardly anybody ever reads a 'text in itself'. There are always reasons 'outside of the text' to read it, whether they are connected to seeking pleasure, killing time, research interests or anything else. Besides, an attempt to read a 'text in itself' is already a certain kind of reading with a specific intention: the attempt to dig out the 'text itself'. In this respect, text can never be read entirely without a specific interest 'in its own terms'.

Though different symbolic forms do contain the possibility of a practically unlimited formation of meanings, to mean something they still need to condense into utterances or expressions, which in turn are understood in certain contexts. Language and other symbolic systems are ambiguous in principle, but in practice they are realized in utterances or expressions directed towards some contexts.

All the while writers are producing texts, they have a number of intended readers in mind. For example, I obviously do not belong to the number of intended readers of Balzac's above-mentioned novel, since I lack the cultural knowledge about what 'the last opera ball' is: I do not know whether it was a question of the last opera ball of the season, or perhaps the very last opera ball of all time, during which season of the year it was organized, who was invited, and so forth. In this case, the context by no means illustrates the meaning but in fact demolishes it.

The reader of each text can only seize a certain, quite limited number of reading options. For myself, the stated reference to 'the last ball' does not produce any very clear connotations. As I begin to read the novel, I can certainly presume that the question is of a social event, but even then I do not grasp a distinct vision of who the 'maskers' might be. Nevertheless, I can try – as readers generally do – to fill these kinds of 'gaps' in texts to the best of my ability and produce a relatively coherent meaning for myself from the text.

Texts indeed require certain kinds of knowledge, values and conceptions of their readers. For readers of texts, the amount of positions is not infinite. This is well manifested, for example, when reading guides to dieting, which address readers who all appear to be leading unhealthy lives, are obese adults totally unable to control their desires, seem to have eaten too much at Christmas, Easter and during their vacation, and obviously drink too much all the time. In these guides, the positioning of the reader is often taken all the way to the end and this unbridled being is addressed with the familiar term 'you'.[56]

However, it is worth noticing that positioning the reader never works solely on the basis of the text. Let us think, if we can, of a culture where a substantial body is taken as a sign of wealth and self-restraint is considered straitlacedness. In this kind of a culture, the common way dieting books address their readers would appear as sheer lunacy or an unbearable attempt to patronize the readers and persuade them to adopt weird eating habits.

Moreover, nothing automatically guarantees that readers will take the positions they are offered in texts. A reader addressed by a text can embrace the position s/he is offered, but also reject it. Hence, people who are not thin but feel comfortable in their lifestyle of not too much fussing over weight or waistlines do not need to give a hoot about dieting books and wish them to go to blazes.

Examples of rejecting the intended position of the reader can also be found in the world of fiction. Astrid Lindgren's protagonist, Pippi Longstocking, in the children's novel, *Pippi Goes on Board*, will not accept the position of an advertising text in a perfume shop:

> The children came to a perfume shop. In the show window was a large jar of freckle salve, and beside the jar was a sign which read: DO YOU SUFFER FROM FRECKLES?
>
> 'What does the sign say?' asked Pippi. She couldn't read very well because she didn't want to go to school as other children did.
>
> 'It says, "Do you suffer from freckles?"' said Annika.
>
> 'Does it indeed?' said Pippi thoughtfully. 'Well, a civil question deserves a civil answer. Let's go in.'
>
> She opened the door and entered the shop, closely followed by Tommy and Annika. An elderly lady stood back of the counter. Pippi went right up to her. 'No!', she said decidedly.
>
> 'I don't understand what you mean,' said the lady.
>
> 'No, I don't suffer from freckles,' said Pippi.
>
> Then the lady understood, but she took one look at Pippi and burst out, 'But my dear child, your whole face is covered with freckles!'
>
> 'I know it,' said Pippi, 'but I don't suffer from them. I love them. Good morning.'[57]

Pippi refuses to take the position the skin cream advertisement offers her in which freckles cause a problem to those who have them. Instead, she adopts a position of her own making, in which the matter others perceive as a problem is made the pillar of her own identity and a source of pride. As such, Pippi's manoeuvre resembles the way many marginalized groups aim to reverse the ways of speaking that marginalize them to work for their own benefit.

Texts – totally open?

So are readers then free to produce any meanings whatsoever from texts? Or do texts set certain limits to the ways of reading to which readers can subject them?

If texts were studied as if totally open and free to be read in any way at all, it would, among other things, shut out of sight the exercise of power that is always present in connection with texts. In our culture, producers of texts have more power than their readers. Besides, producers do not produce 'texts in general', but at all times envision a certain function for them, be it propagating a viewpoint, making a profit or creating pleasure. Seriously speaking, we hardly ever read texts as totally open. It is highly unlikely that anyone would approach Jane Austen's *Pride and Prejudice* as a descriptive history of the relationship between Prince Charles and Camilla Parker-Bowles. Readers of *Pride and Prejudice* possess the contextual knowledge that prevents them from mixing up the match-making of the nineteenth century with the complex human relationships of celebrities nearly 200 years later.

A notion of texts being totally open would lead to as absurd conclusions as formerly was the case with respect to the idea of texts determining their own readings to the very end. If texts had all the power, readers would involuntarily have to yield to everything that is written into texts. Again, if readers held all the power, texts would be mere empty spaces into which readers could read anything they fancied. The central problem in both views is that they are extremely reductionist: in both, an attempt is made to return reading back to either the reader or the text as a whole. These entities, the reader and the text, are assumed to have existed 'in themselves' as such, before their mutual meeting, and remain so during the reading. Instead of these kinds of views that essentialize meanings, however, it is fruitful to strive to study the formation of meanings expressly through *the interaction of texts, contexts and readers.*

From text to textuality

Instead of the reductionist and essentializing views (texts have all power versus texts have no power) we can seize a view in which meaning is emphasized as *a relationship* between texts, contexts and readers and the share of each one of them is studied in the formation of meanings.

From the latter point of view, texts *do* have significance in the formation of meanings. They attempt to position their readers in various ways, which readers can either accept or resist. Texts strive to provide their readers with certain ways of reading, certain interpretations of them that take priority over others. (There are naturally great differences between texts: there are also texts that intentionally attempt to exploit the polysemy of language and undermine readers' attempts to construct consistent meanings in them. However, even then readers can reach a consensus on the fact that it is a question of an undermining, that is, subversive text, and hence adjust their reading to this point of departure.)

Even texts that aim at 'total openness' are not completely open. We would not be able to debate the meaning of some text if we did not, at least to some extent, agree with the fact that we are talking about the same text. There could not be disagreement were there not an agreement about the existence of something to disagree about.

In the late Antony Easthope's words:

> the text . . . has a fixed identity at the level of the signifier. Whether as writing or print a text occurs always as these signifiers (and not others) in *this* linear order, and so a text is able to persist when it is not being read. Of course, at this level the text has no signifieds attached to it, but it has a 'silent identity' which makes possible certain meanings and not others when it is read, meanings determined within the semantic system of language. . . . the identity of a text is not fixed by the system of meanings in a language because the text must also be construed according to a context if it is to produce coherent meaning.[58]

However, it is important to recognize, as Easthope does, that text's identity is situated expressly on the level of *signifier*. Text is identical with itself, that is, it remains the same on this material level. This level does not equal the meaning of the text, but is only the material basis for the meaning: it is these very signifiers in this very linear order. On the level of *signified*, on the other hand, text is not able to remain identical with itself, since contextual and textual matters now enter the scene.

If the pluralism of texts results in relatively stable readings, the stability does not originate only in the qualities of the text itself, but also in the contexts in which texts are read. Tony Bennett thus writes:

> the text is not the place where the business of culture is conducted. Culture is not a thing but a process and a system of relationships within which the production of meaning takes place. Within that process, the rituals and artifacts which constitute the visible surface of culture – books, paintings, rituals of consumption – are constantly rearticulated in relation to one another. The self-same objects and practices are constantly placed within different contexts and put to different uses as the relationships between them are constantly reshuffled.[59]

Ultimately it is not possible to finalize a text, to restrict it to only one context. It is more profitable to think of texts as travellers who have once been sent on the road and who can meet most different contexts on their way, where they can appear in most manifold forms.

In *The Satanic Verses* Salman Rushdie talks about exiles in a way that well describes the material being of texts outside their actual readings.

Rushdie writes (I ask the readers to replace the word 'exile' with the word 'text'):

> Exile . . . is an endless paradox: looking forward by always looking back. The exile is a ball hurled high into the air. He hangs there. Frozen in time. Translated into a photograph; denied motion. Suspended impossibly above his native earth. He awaits the inevitable moment at which the photograph must begin to move, and the earth reclaim its own.[60]

As physical beings, texts are paradoxical beings. Materially they exist as if ready, finalized. Their 'readiness' is merely a readiness to act as the raw material for meanings. As raw material, however, texts are similar to balls hurled in the air which await their fall back to the world of meanings. Yet, as exiles never return to the same land they once left (their leaving alone has changed the land to a different stage of being), neither do texts fall back into the same context in which they were produced (their appearance changes the context, places fellow texts in a new constellation).

Texts' ability to transfer from context to context shatters the attempts to finalize their meanings. As semiotic beings, texts are like living beings with their manifold meanings and effects. Reading them always means simultaneously rewriting them.

The multiplicity of ways to receive texts, the multiplicity of the contexts in which texts can position themselves, as well as the multiplicity of the cultural systems to which their meanings can connect signify that the formation of meanings cannot be adequately understood if texts are studied through the notions of uniformity and consistency. Instead, they must be approached via the notions of plurality and difference. Texts are not ready or final, but obtain their meaning in interaction with contexts.

When speaking about meaning potentials contained in different texts, it may be better to use the concept of 'textuality' as the point of departure instead of 'text'.[61] The problem with the concept of 'text' is that, like all nouns, it easily brings to mind the notion of some object that already exists, that is complete and stagnant in itself. Certainly, texts exist physically prior to their reading – as books, videos, recordings, newspapers and magazines and so on – but the notion of texts as objects leads us perilously close to thinking that *meanings* would exist as 'complete' in an equivalent way. When studied in respect to their meanings, texts are not objects in the same way as chairs or tables are, but are just a sphere of potentiality, the raw material for meanings.[62] 'Textuality' does not refer to something already existing but to potentiality, something that is always on its way and that is not a final state but in continuous production. As such, the principle of textuality makes indistinct the borders between the internal and external, the symbolic and real. The notion of textuality underlines the point that texts as such are always incomplete and on the move, and that in order for them to obtain meanings they must be read.

Despite this, the polysemy of texts does not mean that they are anarchically open. The multiplicity of meanings does not denote that any meaning whatsoever can be read in or into texts. Polysemy does not equal infinite multiplicity of meanings. The number of potential meanings is staked out by readers' textual competence, as well as by the text being read. David Morley aptly outlines the matter when he speaks about television texts:

> The analysis of the text or message remains, of course, a fundamental necessity, for the polysemy of the message is not without its own structure. Audiences do not see only what they want to see, since a message (or programme) is not simply a window on the world, but a construction. While the message is not an object with one real meaning, there are within it signifying mechanisms which promote certain meanings, even one privileged meaning, and suppress others: these are the directive closures encoded in the message.[63]

Therefore, texts themselves have significance in the formation of meanings. Though, as Morley continues, these mechanisms and instructions that texts contain are just potentials, which must be connected to some reading contexts for actualization: 'The message is capable of different interpretations depending on the context of association.'

Each text opens up a non-predestined but relatively limited area of potential meanings. The notion in the concept of 'textuality' about the potential openness of meanings thus must be complemented by studying how potential meanings become actual. Provided that texts are catalysts which set potential meanings in motion, the study cannot come to a halt at the level of texts but it must proceed on to 'other ingredients' of the formation of meanings; factors connected to contextual and cultural practices.

As a matter of fact, this notion is also applicable to the current cultural circumstances where texts are read. For example, in the Roman Catholic culture of the Middle Ages it was probably thought that texts had a relatively established place and identity. The number of texts was more limited in those times, and they served certain clearly institutional purposes. In current culture, which is characterized by an infinite multiplicity of texts and mingling of traditional cultural categories, texts are issued into circulation, so to speak, and they obtain meanings in connection to other texts that are most dissimilar and in extraordinary ways that are difficult to predict.

Towards contexts

In the *Phaedrus* dialogue by Plato, Socrates assures Phaedrus that there is 'a great error' in written texts:

S: In a way, Phaedrus, writing has a strange character, which is similar to that of painting, actually. Painting's creations stand there as though they were alive, but if you ask them anything, they maintain a quite solemn silence. Speeches are the same way. You might expect them to speak like intelligent beings, but if you question them with the intention of learning something about what they're saying, they always just continue saying the same thing. Every speech, once it's in writing, is bandied about everywhere equally among those who understand it and those who've no business hearing it. It doesn't know to whom it ought to speak and to whom not. When it's ill-treated and unfairly abused, it always needs its father to help it, since it isn't able to help or defend itself by itself.[64]

Socrates' point of departure – the notion of texts as 'dead' beyond their frames of reference – is quite correct. However, in this chapter I have attempted to explain why Socrates' conclusion, according to which text consequently can only 'always just continue saying the same thing', is way out.

Even though texts as physical beings can be identical with themselves regardless of time and place, as meaningful objects they still are not one and the same always and everywhere. On the contrary, we cannot even read one single text twice in the same way. In the second reading, the first reading already directs the way we re-read the text. The first reading has become part of the second reading's context! A reader of Agatha Christie's *Ten Little Indians*, for example, or a spectator of Alfred Hitchcock's *Vertigo* pays attention to quite different things the second time around than in the first reading or viewing of the text.

Earlier I remarked that in the formation of meanings 'other ingredients' must also be studied in addition to texts. Strictly speaking, talk about 'other ingredients' is misleading in the sense that the ingredients in question are not necessarily located on the outside of texts, but can often be seized expressly by reading texts. The beginning of the novel *A Harlot High and Low* illustrates the point splendidly. From the first two sentences we were already able to read out plenty of the stated 'other ingredients', contextual factors that participate in the formation of meaning to different degrees depending on the reader. So the border between 'text' and 'context' is like the famed line drawn in sand. In practice it is often impossible to tell where 'text' ends and 'context' starts.

All in all, the temporary separation of 'texts' and 'contexts' for analytical purposes makes its own sense. If it indeed is true that meanings change as texts meet with other texts and readers, there is reason to examine all of the parties involved in this process. Next on our expedition we will proceed into the world of contexts.

Notes

1. See Graddol 1994, 41–2.
2. See ibid., 49.
3. See Fornäs 1995, 147–8.
4. See Saussure 1974, 67.
5. Ibid., 72.
6. Barthes 1981, 33–5.
7. Ibid., 37.
8. Berger 1995, 84.
9. Barthes 1986a, 52–3.
10. Høeg 1997, 305.
11. See Palmer 1991, 52–3.
12. Barthes 1981, 36.
13. See Baynham 1995, 189–90.
14. Barthes 1988, 95 and 130.
15. See Talbot 1995, 3–5.
16. See Branigan 1992, 3.
17. Todorov 1980, 80.
18. Chambers 1984, 50.
19. Culler 1980, 50.
20. See Long 1994, 201.
21. In connection to this, Stuart Hall talks about employing different texts as kinds of exercise fields or test laboratories. He characterizes a certain television soap opera in years past as a kind of fictional training field where people could contemplate questions that perplex them – questions of how to live one's life, how to understand the changes in society and so on. Hall remarks that by this, he does not mean that people do not understand the fictional character of fiction. Instead, he sees that fiction like soaps – and, one could add, fiction in general – can function and frequently also does function as a certain kind of imaginary scenario as to what can happen to people and how they can react to different events and circumstances. In front of their TV sets, the viewers of the series Hall refers to (*Coronation Street*) have, for example, had the opportunity to consider such matters as what happens in a case of divorce, how the different parties involved experience it, and other such questions (Hall 1984, 9–10).
22. Ibid., 7.
23. Labov 1972, 366.
24. Chambers 1984, 51.
25. See Williams 1981a (see 'fiction'), and Williams 1977, 163–8.
26. Balzac 1970, 17.
27. Such background knowledge the linguist Norman Fairclough has termed 'members' resources', by which he refers to the different interpretational frames that a reader is expected to have, and which limit the readership of the text (see Fairclough 1989, 141–5).
28. Saussure 1974, 122–4.
29. Cohan and Shires 1988, 12–13.
30. Ibid., 14.
31. Ibid.
32. Ibid., 15.

33. See Lemke 1995, 42.
34. Cohan and Shires 1988, 21.
35. Ibid.
36. Barthes 1986a, 57–8; Barthes 1981, 39–40.
37. Barthes 1986a, 59.
38. See Lewis 1995, 3.
39. See, for example, Baldick 1990, 'metaphor'.
40. See Culler 1975, 118.
41. Ibid., 115.
42. In this quite traditional way, the poem is read by – perhaps a little surprisingly, considering that the person in question is a cultural studies researcher – Andrew Ross: see Ross 1989, 65–6.
43. See Perloff 1977, 181.
44. See the corresponding reading of Ezra Pound's poem 'In a Station of the Metro' in Cohan and Shires 1988, 26–30.
45. Eagleton 1996a, 6.
46. Hutcheon 1995, 17.
47. Belsey 1980, 70.
48. Belsey 1980, 70–84.
49. Austen 1990, 1.
50. Barthes 1971/1986b, 59.
51. Bakhtin 1981, 276.
52. Bennett 1984, 122.
53. Bennett 1982, 234–5.
54. Bennett 1987, 71.
55. Chambers 1979, 167.
56. See Barton 1994, 60–1.
57. Lindgren 1977,18–19.
58. Easthope 1988, 59.
59. Bennett 1979, 174.
60. Rushdie 1988, 213–14.
61. Likewise, it is reasonable to speak about 'constructuration' and 'structuration' instead of 'construction' and 'structure' to indicate that texts are not so much finalized structures as they are producers of certain structurations of meanings.
62. See here, for example, Meinhof and Richardson 1994, 17.
63. Morley 1992, 21.
64. Plato 1993, 133

CHAPTER 6

THE WORLD OF CONTEXTS

O ur journey to the world of contexts begins with the guidance of Lewis Carroll: the duck in *Alice's Adventures in Wonderland* was well aware of the context-bound nature of texts. When Alice's company, which consists of the duck, as well as a lory, a mouse, a dodo, and an eaglet among others is soaked, the mouse attempts to dry the party off by presenting 'the driest thing I know'. This means a tedious account of the era of William the Conquerer. A dialogue between the mouse and the duck follows:

> 'I proceed. "Edwin and Morcar, the earls of Mercia and Northumbria, declared for him: and even Stigand, the patriotic archbishop of Canterbury, found it advisable —"'
>
> 'Found *what?*' said the Duck.
>
> 'Found *it*,' the Mouse replied rather crossly: 'of course you know what "it" means.'
>
> 'I know what "it" means well enough, when *I* find a thing,' said the Duck: 'it's generally a frog or a worm. The question is, what did the archbishop find?'[1]

Unlike the mouse giving the monologue, the duck well understands the context-bound nature of pronouns. 'I', 'you', 'she' and 'he', 'it', 'this' and 'that' and other pronouns are empty signs as such, which are fulfilled by referentiality only in their contexts. However, the duck's realization can also be extended further. Metaphorically, it is possible to speak about all texts as kinds of pronouns, which obtain actual meanings according to their contexts.

Each text always has its context which surrounds and penetrates it both temporally and locally and links it with other texts, as well as with other human practices. As much as the meanings of linguistic signs depend on their position in relation to other signs, the meanings of texts are ultimately impossible to study detached from their contexts, since texts as *semiotic* beings do not exist without the readers, intertexts, situations and functions that at all times are connected to them.

In traditional notions of texts and contexts, contexts are seen as separate 'backgrounds' of texts, which in the role of a certain kind of additional information can be an aid in understanding the texts themselves. In this kind of notion of contexts, it falls to the reader's lot to be a passive recipient. S/he is the decoder of notions included in the text who exploits his/her possible contextual knowledge to reveal the meanings that are fixed and final already in advance. Text resembles a crossword puzzle with one and only one solution, and context in turn is a number of reference books that the solver of the puzzle consults in order to find the right solution.

However, earlier I attempted to argue that texts in fact are not at all like this kind of puzzle to be solved. Moreover, readers never encounter the text they are reading on its own: there are always a number of other texts and factors present in the interaction of text and reader. This matter can be illustrated by an experiment the French discourse analyst Michel Pêcheux had his students conduct at the beginning of the 1980s. Pêcheux made two groups of students read the same text that dealt with economic science, but told one of the groups that the text in question had leftist tendencies in it, while he told the other group that the text was written by a conservative. The two groups interpreted the text in totally opposite ways, since they approached it with different conceptual frameworks and with contrary expectations.[2] In the light of this example, we can see that we never meet texts without certain hypotheses and conceptual frameworks with the aid of which we produce some sense in the text.

Contexts as co-texts

The notion I have outlined about contexts categorically departs from the traditional model concerning the relationship between text and context. In fact, the entire nature of the concept of 'context' must be thoroughly re-evaluated. *Context does not exist before the author or the text, neither does it exist outside of them.* True to their literal meaning, 'con-texts' are fellow texts which always exist *together* with the texts for which they are contexts. Moreover, this togetherness often means being *inside* the text, as *part* of it (as I attempted to point out with the help of the Balzac excerpt in the previous chapter). As such, texts are the raw material of meanings, which activate (and also produce) readers' contextual resources: linguistic resources, conceptions of reality, values, beliefs and so on.[3] Additionally, contexts are present in both writing and reading. They are not 'backgrounds', some kind of static assemblies of ideals and values, but actively affect the conventions writers have at their disposal, and how readers meet texts.

Quite often in texts, particularly in those that present themselves as scientific, one can detect an attempt to obscure all traces of their 'original' circumstances, the writing process, as well as the people who produced them. As a technology, writing makes this possible; doesn't it indeed detach texts from the time and place of their production? Guy Cook characterizes this situation in the following way:

> You, the reader, do not see me, the writer, as you read this book, or know anything about the circumstances in which I am writing. You do not know what changes I have made in this sentence, when I added it to the manuscript, or whether I paused to have a cup of coffee between these dots . . . or these . . . And by the conventions of our culture you do not care. You read this

book for the information or ideas it carries, not to communicate with me as an individual physical presence. Writing makes this language no longer dependent on me and my situation in any way. You can read this book in any order, when and how you want: and I will not even know. I may even be dead.[4]

Cook's taunting demonstrates how in texts – particularly, though not solely in scientific ones – the contextual factors concerning their production and reception are used to banish the reader's range of vision. In the light of this convention, it is not surprising that context is frequently understood as some element external to the text, especially that historical and social background where the text is produced.

Contrary to this notion that is so deeply embedded in our culture, not a single text comes to us without a context that has been connected to it. From this standpoint, let us study a science fiction novel by Philip K. Dick, *Do Androids Dream of Electric Sheep?* (1968), and to be precise, the paperback version of it published by HarperCollins in 1993. The name of the novel is certainly printed on the cover of the paperback, but otherwise the appearance of the publication is far more strikingly tied to the *Blade Runner* movie made on the basis of the book in 1982. The name of the leading actor, Harrison Ford, is emblazoned on the cover in nearly as large print as the name of Philip K. Dick, who after all wrote the novel. Additionally, the movie's logo and the figures of its central characters link the text with the movie in the style of 'you saw the flick, now read the book'. The same goings-on continue on the back cover. The time period of the novel's events is claimed to be the twenty-first century (as it is in the movie), though Dick's novel takes place in 1992.

Hence, HarperCollins offers Dick's novel to be read in an intertextual (as well as intermedial) connection with the movie *Blade Runner*. However, the situation is complicated by the fact that on the page preceding the title page of the book (the so-called bastard or mock title) information concerning the life of Philip K. Dick is presented, and on the other side of it all his other novels and short story collections are listed. Thus, the publisher simultaneously also links the novel to other intertexts which are formed of the life of a person called 'Philip K. Dick' during the years 1928–1982 and his works, which consist of 40 novels (of which two were written with a co-writer), six short story collections and five volumes of collected short stories.

After the title page, just to be on the safe side, we are provided with a note from the publisher in which all these contexts – the movie, the life of the author and his works – are linked to each other:

In 1968, Philip K. Dick wrote a book called *Do Androids Dream of Electric Sheep?* A scintillating science fiction novel which later became the inspiration for the movie *Blade Runner*. Though the characters and the background of the novel differ somewhat from their counterparts in the movie, readers who enjoyed the film can reach renewed depths in their experience by conversing with the original work. HarperCollins is indeed satisfied in being able to bring this classic novel once again to the reach of its readers.

In fact, all of these contextual elements are embedded inside the text. They actually do not differ in any way from those contextualizing elements that Dick himself has left in the text: the dedication (to Maren Augusta Bergrud, who died in 1967), the epigraph (a quote from Yeats) or the news reported in 1966 by Reuters which tells of the death of the turtle that Captain James Cook gave as a gift to the king of Tonga in 1777. These contextual matters participate in the process of the formation of meanings that is initiated by the text of Philip K. Dick's novel.

Changes in contextual matters may have quite a strong effect on how we read a text. A dramatic example of this is the Finnish translation of the work *Titanic* written by the renowned Estonian poet and essayist Jaan Kaplinski in 1993, that is, before the sinking of the car ferry *Estonia* with its hundreds of passengers that took place in September 1994 in an autumn storm. In fact, the text in question would not be available in Finnish at all but for the *Estonia* shipwreck, since its Finnish publisher did not accept it for publication until after the tragedy, macabre decision though it was. Kaplinski himself describes the new context of his text in the epilogue he wrote for the Finnish language edition of the work, dated November 1994, in the following way:

> The word Estonia no longer means what it meant before September 28th. Moreover, this story of ice and the *Titanic*, the earthquake of San Francisco, the redwoods, and the white ships of the Baltic Sea which are as unsinkable as the *Titanic* was, also this story that I completed already a year ago now means something totally different than at the time it was first finished.[6]

On the back cover text by the Finnish publisher this explicit linking of the book with the *Titanic* and the sinking of the *Estonia* ferry was unnecessary: contextual matters immediately after the sinking of the *Estonia* had such an impact on readers that whether they wanted to or not, they placed the word 'Estonia' next to, or even instead of, the word 'Titanic'. Hence, the function of the text can be seen to have changed. It was no longer read as universal ponderings about how people blindly surrender to technology, but also as a statement of the causes behind the *Estonia* catastrophe and of how we can survive on the shores of the Baltic in a future that appeared less safe than ever after the accident.

The study of both Dick's and Kaplinski's texts highlights the fact that texts and contexts are in an interactive relationship. Contexts are co-texts to texts, but texts alone do not have an effect on what other co-texts are linked to them as they are read.

'Text' and 'context'

Context can mean – depending on the context – such a variety of things that the faint-hearted may shudder at the very thought. Contexts of texts can be, for example, certain global social structures (in Dick's novel it was the already fought World War III), an immediate situation (the sinking of the *Estonia* as a reference for the Finnish edition of Kaplinski's *Titanic*) or the co-texts of the text (let us say, the film *Blade Runner* directed by Ridley Scott). Contexts include all such factors that writers and readers bring into the process of the formation of meanings, especially their discursive competence and framework of value judgement.

Guy Cook gives one possible list of the different dimensions of 'context' in his book that deals with advertisements:

> Context includes all the following:
> 1 substance: the physical material which carries or relays text
> 2 music and pictures
> 3 paralanguage: meaningful behaviour accompanying language, such as voice quality, gestures, facial expressions and touch (in speed), and choice of typeface and letter sizes (in writing)
> 4 situation: the properties and relations of objects and people in the vicinity of the text, as perceived by the participants
> 5 co-text: text which precedes or follows that under analysis, and which participants judge to belong to the same discourse
> 6 intertext: text which participants perceive as belonging to other discourse, but which they associate with the text under consideration, and which affects their interpretation
> 7 participants: their intentions and interpretations, knowledge and beliefs, interpersonal attitudes, affiliations and feelings . . .
> 8 function: what the text is intended to do by the senders and addressers, or perceived to do by the receivers and addressees.[7]

Cook's notion of context is quite practical. 'Factors external to the text' – situations, readers and functions intended for the text – are strongly on display in it next to the textual matters that are customarily counted among context.

As matters participating in the formation of meanings (both as non-textual and as textual), it is most fertile to consider contexts variable and special cultural *resources*, with the assistance of which readers produce meanings in texts. Textual meanings are potentials which actualize according to what kinds of contextual resources readers have at their use and how they produce sense in the texts they read relying on these resources.

Therefore, in practice, it is impossible to separate texts and contexts from each other (separating them temporarily for analytical purposes is a different matter). Let us consider, for instance, discourses which as reference frameworks are one of the most central of contextual factors in the formation of meanings. Discourses act as a kind of cultural resource battalion, within the limits of which readers produce meanings out of texts. They set limits not only to what can be said but also to how the said can be understood. Whatever else texts are, they are also always realizations of discourses. However, the notion of discourses questions the separation of text and context as if they were the interior and exterior. According to the above-mentioned division, discourses would belong in the exterior of texts, but as defining the potential of saying and understanding they are most firmly located in the interior of texts.

Hence, discourses – like many other textual and contextual factors – in fact pull down the barrier between text and context. The border between the two is not ready-made, but takes shape in the negotiation readers have with texts. The border between text and context is thus changing and unstable, and to top it all, works on several different levels.[8]

It is not possible to make conclusive determinations about the border between text and context at the beginning of their study; these types of definition can be reached only during the study and as its outcome. The contextual study of texts in fact problematizes the starting point that the traditional study of texts has rather unproblematically set itself: text as a relatively clearly limited and definable entity. *Now, the point of departure becomes a problem, the explainer becomes the one to be explained.* The situation is further complicated by the fact that texts are always co-produced by some contexts, but simultaneously themselves reshape and rearrange their contexts.[9] In this way, texts and contexts in fact do not exist at all as meaningful entities before they enter into a mutual interaction: each text in a way produces an adequate context for itself, and similarly each context produces an adequate reading of each text. Jaan Kaplinski's *Titanic* produced a certain context for itself which included other texts (literary, aesthetic, scientific, journalistic, movie or television texts) in which the relationship between nature and humankind is treated, as well as the role of technology in this relationship. In this context, Kaplinski's text was read as one address in relationship to other texts dealing with similar subjects. However, along with the tragedy of the *Estonia* this context changed. The new context produced a new text: now Kaplinski's essay appeared to readers as a prophetic warning about the (fatal) consequences of blind faith in technology.

Texts as processual non-beings

Contexts play an essential role in what has traditionally been described as the 'understanding' of texts. If we start reading a novel previously unknown to us, for example the novel by Balzac that was mentioned earlier, how are we able to produce sensible interpretations from what we read? Naturally, it does not occur on the basis that we have already read the entire novel and so are able to evaluate one part of it based on our knowledge of the whole. Instead, in our interpretative attempts we must rely on our previous knowledge of texts similar to the one under analysis. This kind of shuttling between micro and macro levels means exploiting contextual knowledge in order to form sensible meanings.

The concept of 'context' can be thought to contain a strong emphasis on readers' activity. 'Context' refers to the fact that meanings are created not only in activities traditionally considered as producing meanings – bringing about spoken, written, audiovisual and other texts – but also in receiving texts. The reading of texts equals actively giving meanings to the meaning potentials they contain, interaction with texts. This is the case also when reading means exerting oneself to understand the special quality of a 'strange' text. So it could be said that all reading is always re-reading, re-production of the text through the reading process.

At times the term 'consuming' is used about reading. 'Consuming' can be thought of as a fossilized metaphor. When I 'consume' something, it 'wears', and therefore is no longer as good as new. 'Consuming' is the opposite of everything the word 'producing' represents. 'Consuming' a text adds nothing to it, but rather takes something away from it. From this viewpoint, 'consuming' is an extremely poor metaphor for what happens when text and reader meet.

The pair of opposites of consuming and producing is misleading. Is consuming not also directly producing? For instance, as a person consumes food, s/he simultaneously reproduces his/her own body. Hence, consumption is immediate production, and correspondingly, production is consumption. At the same time, mediating motion can be thought to take place between the two. Production mediates consumption since it creates an object for it. Equally, consumption mediates production since it is consumption alone that creates a subject for products – it creates a need for production.[10]

These views on production and consumption that are borrowed from a certain Karl Marx can be applied to texts and reading. Texts transmit reading, since they produce an object for it. Correspondingly, reading transmits texts since it is only reading that creates a subject for texts.

In the light of these notions, the term 'reception' does not necessarily describe the meeting of readers and texts any better than 'consumption', since 'reception' has its problems, too. 'Receiving' can be understood as 'receiving as such', without taking anything away from the text (at which point it favourably differs from 'consumption') but on the other hand, without adding anything to the text.

The meeting of a text and a reader is better characterized by the word 'reading' – also from the viewpoint of cultural text theory – than 'consumption' (in its everyday meaning) and 'receiving'. The word in question refers to readers' activity as well as to the fact that the activity contains learned, cultural ingredients.[11] 'Reading' is signification of the world, practical consciousness of readers. The word 'practical' is apt in this connection, since signification is solely a question of the more or less abstract level of consciousness but also, and above all, of the activity which operates with certain materials (signs and media) and practices (discourses, genres, conventions, etc.).

In this respect, we should be quite careful not to take the metaphor of reading too literally. Though different technologies and sign systems do not determine how meanings are made from texts produced with their assistance, reading, for example, a novel, a newspaper or television are quite different activities from one another and require very different resources from their readers.

So along with reading we could also talk about 'textual interaction' where not only the text and reader, but also a fair number of other influential parties are simultaneously present. Textual interaction is a process of producing meanings where the polysemy of signs and discourses meets the questioning nature of reading which strives to expand beyond text.[12]

However, producing meanings in the interaction of texts and readers is not arbitrary or purely idiosyncratic, namely relating only to an individual or group, but takes place under certain preconditions. These preconditions, in turn, are social, cultural and textual. Social and cultural preconditions have an effect on the subjectivity of the people producing meanings, whereas textual preconditions affect the texts read. The difference is naturally solely analytical, since in practice subjectivity and textuality are in close interaction.[13]

Textual interaction does not produce solid, predetermined and everlastingly immutable meanings. Interaction is a production in which the meaning potentials contained by texts meet the cultural resources of readers. In this production, texts obtain meanings, certain identities; even if they are temporary and vulnerable.

Tony Bennett characterizes meaning as 'a transitive phenomenon'. It is not a being that texts can possess, but an object that can only be produced.[14] To continue Bennett's line of thinking, it could be said that texts do not *have* meanings, they *obtain* them. In other words, reading is not receiving meanings of texts, since texts in a certain sense have no meanings before they are read, but reading meanings *into* texts. Talking about 'reading texts' though does not describe the interactive event in question as well as 'reading with texts'.

This does not mean that meanings (even relatively stable meanings) do not exist at all, but it does mean that meanings are always temporary, bound to a certain time, place and context. This is also the case when meanings *appear* stable, or even eternal, to those who use language. However, here it is only that the meanings in question are so stable in the time and place in question that they manage to appear indisputable to a certain extent.

On the theory of meanings, I have developed a point of departure in which *meanings have no guarantee of permanence in advance*. Not one single meaning in a text is warranted beforehand. Certain ways of reading can in a certain time and in a certain place be considered more valuable than others, but readings are only different ways of activating texts' meaning potentials.

Texts are no islands

Relationships between texts and their readers can be examined in many ways. Roughly, these ways can be divided into two: firstly, there are approaches to them where those formal mechanisms by which texts produce certain positions for readers are studied. It is then usually asked what a text's internal reader, model reader or preferred reader is like. The terms vary, but the basic notion remains the same: a text implicitly produces its own reading. Attention is then paid to those *intratextual* factors that have an effect on reading. The fact that these approaches do not take into account the possibility of divergent ways of reading presents a problem. What really guarantees that texts are read in the way they 'intend' themselves to be read? Nothing, naturally. As Stephen Heath writes of movies:

> It is possible, with regard to a film or group of films, to analyse a discursive organisation, a system of address, a placing – a construction – of the spectator. This is not to say, however, that any and every spectator – and for instance, man or woman, of this class or that – will be completely and equally in the given construction, completely and equally there in the film; and nor then is it to say that the discursive organisation and its production can exhaust – be taken as equivalent to – the effectivity, the potential effects of a film.[15]

In the second way of studying the relationships between texts and readers those *extratextual* factors, particularly cultural and ideological ones, that affect reading are stressed. Whereas the problem in the first way is that it imagines the text itself to be capable of producing meanings regardless of extratextual factors, the second approach pays little attention to the text itself but explains different readings, considering readers alone as the starting point.

The problem of both approaches is, as Tony Bennett and Janet Woollacott remark, that the formation of meanings is studied normatively: in practice, the meaning of a text is determined either by the text or its reader alone.[16] Another problem is that intratextual and extratextual active factors are studied separately from each other, as if there was some 'text in itself' with its own unchanging qualities totally regardless of the readings to which it is subjected.[17]

However, texts cannot, as already stated, guarantee the readings they are subjected to, since not one text is – as I attempted to show in the previous chapter – ever a watertight entity. Moreover, texts can also be consciously read against the grain. No text is an island; neither is any reader a newborn. So instead of studying an encounter between a 'bare' text and a 'qualified' reader, the actual signification and reading should be studied, which in turn cannot be detached from those cultural practices and relationships where the producers and readers of texts are active human beings. This notion of textual meanings follows the same lines as the earlier-discussed notion of linguistic meanings. If words and sentences acquire meanings through differences – that is, through not equalling something else – they do not have a meaning 'in themselves'. As Michel Pêcheux summarizes:

> the meaning of a word, expression, proposition, etc., does not exist 'in itself' (i.e., in its transparent relation to the literal character of the signifier), but is determined by the ideological positions brought into play in the socio-historical process in which words, expressions and propositions are produced (i.e., reproduced). This thesis could be summed up in the statement: words, expressions, propositions, etc., change their meaning according to the positions held by those who use them, which signifies that they find their meanings by reference to those positions.[18]

If words are multi-accented, it means that words do not have one and only one natural meaning. Since one and the same signifier can function in different ways in different discursive formations, it is impossible to find a linguistic stage where it could be said to have one true meaning, compared to which all other meanings are distortions.[19] However, if this applies to individual words, it must also apply to more complex and multi-dimensional texts. Hence, Tony Bennett proposes studying reading in a new way:

> The study of reading, as it has been developed, has been characterized by a marked one-sidedness. It has placed the reader into the melting pot of variability whilst retaining the text as a fixed pole of reference within the analysis. It is necessary, and high time, to place the text into the melting pot of variability, too; to recognize that the history of reading is not one in which different readers encounter 'the same text' but one in which the text readers encounter is already 'over-worked', 'over-coded', productively activated in a particular way as a result of its inscription within the social, material, ideological and institutional relationships which distinguish specific reading relations.[20]

As material beings texts are real and relatively distinct, whereas as semiotic beings the borders of texts are set in motion. According to Tony Bennett and Janet Woollacott, texts in fact should not be thought to exist at all before, or regardless of, their different readings. It is not until their readings that texts are produced as 'readable objects'. However, texts are not passive objects. Bennett and Woollacott indeed call them 'culturally constructed objects' and readers 'culturally constructed subjects'. The interaction of the two, in turn, according to Bennett and Woollacott , is always culturally, ideologically and inter-textually organized in such a way that their separation into a subject and an object is questionable.[21]

By the hyphen, Bennett and Woollacott want to distinguish inter-textuality from the more traditional concept of intertextuality. According to them, the latter means references to other texts that can be found in some texts, whereas 'inter-textuality' refers to a broader organization of relationships between texts in actual readings. These readings they describe by the term 'reading formation', with which they indicate special conditions between texts, that is, inter-textual and discursive conditions which shape and limit the interaction of a text and a reader. They emphasize that this is not a question of reducing a text to its context, but an attempt to consider the notion of context in such a way that ultimately text and context would not be studied separately. They write:

> The concept of reading formation . . . is an attempt to think contexts of reception as sets of discursive and inter-textual determinations which, in operating on both texts and readers, mediate the relations between them and provide the mechanisms through which they can productively interact.[22]

In an actual reading situation, there are in fact several factors present other than the mere text which is being read. As was stated in Chapter 4, readers at all times have a number of expectations concerning a text. Reading begins well before the first word of the text is read. For instance, the medium of the text, its appearance or its belonging to a certain genre already communicates meanings contained in the text. A reader's expectations are quite different if the text that is being read is an editorial in a daily newspaper, a menu of a restaurant or a serial in a magazine. Familiarity with text types enables the anticipation of meanings. Readers are prepared to expect each text type to activate its distinctive meanings, which are distinguishable from other text types.

There is no 'text in itself'

The dimensions of reading do not remain only on this textual level. Reading a cook book is an illustrative example of all the kinds of requirements there are for a reader when s/he attempts to produce some sense in the text. First of all, a reader must know quite a bit about cooking (provided s/he is not reading the book more or less masochistically, without any intention to satisfy the culinary desires raised as the reading proceeds). S/he must be familiar with all kinds of gadgets and thingamabobs in the kitchen, foodstuffs, supplies provided by the local stores and other such things. Furthermore, the reader must have a certain rudimentary mathematical knowledge and some tools to measure and estimate amounts of ingredients. S/he also must be capable of turning the oven on to the correct temperature (which is quite a mathematical challenge, if the oven is marked with degrees in Celsius but the cook book insists on Fahrenheit, or vice versa), selecting the correct size and form of pots and pans, and solving numerous other such puzzles. The reader is also required to be able to decode the jargon in which the recipes are written. S/he needs to know what 'a pinch' is, what it means to let something 'simmer' and how to 'beat egg whites until hard'. Finally, the reader must transform the activities described in the recipes into his/her activities in reality.[23]

Certainly, it can now be claimed that cook books demand more of their readers than many other texts, and that's why they are not a particularly presentable example of reading. I agree with this view, but for contrary reasons: in fact the number of skills and amount of knowledge required by cook books – their context – is relatively limited in comparison with many other texts. With regard to texts that aim at the less practical, it is markedly more complicated to define their context. Cook books are usually read in certain kinds of situations for certain purposes. Moreover, there is a certain hierarchical relationship between the text and its reader: the reader expects the book to know something 'more', and consequently is susceptible to taking its content at face value without easily problematizing it. In the case of many other texts – novels, TV soaps, etc. – the situation is different. Their potential contexts are more complex and readers often consider themselves experts able to assess how well they realize the expectations earlier evoked.

Nevertheless, in regard to novels or soap operas it is possible to attempt to clarify their actual contexts. Bennett and Woollacott's notion of 'reading formation' represents one attempt to bring out those definitions that, while affecting both texts and readers, convey relationships between text and context, link them with each other and provide mechanisms through which they can be in productive interaction. Here context does not introduce itself as extratextual, but as intertextual and discursive relationships which produce readers to texts and texts to readers. From these points of departure, the study of texts would be 'reading texts as they have been constructed into readable objects in different reading formations, which have shaped their existence as historically active, culturally received texts', that is 'reading texts in the light of their readings and studying readings in the light of their texts'.[24]

According to Bennett and Woollacott, discursive and intertextual definitions do not affect texts only from outside, but also from within, shaping texts into those historically concrete forms in which they are available as readable texts. For example, readers' expectations concerning genre have an effect on how they position themselves in regard to the text and how the text consequently becomes shaped. There is no fixed border between the extratextual and intratextual determinations of a text which would prevent the external ones from having an effect on the internal ones. 'Intratextual' is a product of certain intertextual relationships.[25]

Bennett and Woollacott's notion has a critical relationship to the traditional view according to which texts, readers and contexts are separate elements that already exist before getting involved with each other.

In Tony Bennett's view, texts cannot exist in general as anything other than mutable. He compares texts to pieces in a game that change in the processes in which their content is struggled for. Texts survive along with their claims and counter-claims concerning them. However, this survival takes place at the cost that they never equal 'just themselves', but are always something else as a result of the struggles concerning their meanings and location.[26]

Together with Janet Woollacott, Bennett surpasses even himself. According to them, 'text in itself' is an impossible object of knowledge. There is no such thing as 'text in itself' as a semiotic being. Instead, texts exist within different reading formations which shape their being. By this, Bennett and Woollacott do not mean to deny the objective, *material* being of texts. Texts in use most definitely exist as material sign systems which acquire concrete, sensory forms and are recycled as part of social and cultural relationships. Instead, they want to question the notion of there being an 'ideal text which is the source of true meaning' somewhere.[27] The rejection of 'text in itself', however, does not need to be seen as a rejection of texts in use; on the contrary it can be thought to enable the seizure of their full meaning potential.

Reading

As already discussed in Chapter 5, readers approach texts actively, equipped with certain expectations. Already the texts' material qualities raise certain expectations of what readers are reading, as stated in Chapter 4. Similarly, knowledge of the genre of the text awakens a number of expectations about what is ahead, and participates in the formation of meanings in reading. As readers then meet the text and begin to read it – words and sentences in written texts; pictures, colours, forms, spatial dimensions and such in visual texts; in audiovisual texts primarily sounds and images, and narratives in all these – they are looking for familiar elements and construct hypotheses concerning the meanings of the text. Simultaneously, readers reach conclusions on implicit meanings and fill the text's gaps. As part of all this, they also position the text in relationship to certain places, times and other texts, which is further affected by the allusions present in the text.

In presenting the theory of reception, Terry Eagleton has described this activity of the reader in the following way:

> Although we rarely notice it, we are all the time engaged in constructing hypotheses about the meaning of the text. The reader makes implicit connections, fills in gaps, draws inferences and tests out hunches; and to do this means drawing on a tacit knowledge of the world in general and of literary conventions in particular. The text itself is really no more than a

series of 'cues' to the reader, invitations to construct a piece of language into meaning.[28]

Only in exceptional cases do readers meet texts in such a way that they do not have any information whatsoever about them in advance which would direct their reading. The mass media infinitely manufacture secondary texts out of primary ones – new novels, movies, TV programmes and recordings. In addition to reviews in papers, we can read gossip about the private lives of the makers, interviews with them, advertisements and commercials about their products, and so forth. As we consider our relationship to primary texts, we have at our disposal an abundance of information which helps us to weigh whether the texts are worth our while. Moreover, there is often a third level present: the readings of texts by other people who are close to us. It is not at all unusual for the recommendation by a friend to make us take up a certain text. These secondary texts – public or private – can have a great impact on the way we read the primary text in question.[29]

The poetics of texts and the hermeneutics of contexts

Previously, I used the term *the poetics of texts* to describe the study of texts as meaning potentials. Poetics has several different meanings. The poetics of texts studies how a text is made and how it can obtain different meanings. However, this 'poetic' study of texts alone is not enough. In addition to meaning potentials, which of many potential readings are actualized when texts are read must also be studied. This study can be called *the hermeneutics of contexts*.

Just as the term 'poetics' has numerous meanings, so does the term 'hermeneutics' . Usually a theory concerning interpretation which is occupied with universal matters concerning the understanding of texts is called hermeneutics. Originally, 'hermeneutics' meant explaining the Bible, but since the nineteenth century its meaning has expanded to include broader questions of philosophy and the study of texts. As such, hermeneutics is often connected with the German tradition that was initiated by Friedrich Schleiermacher and Wilhelm Dilthey in the nineteenth century. Its most well-known representatives in the twentieth century have been Martin Heidegger (1898–1976) and Hans-Georg Gadamer (1900—). Within this tradition, interpretation is thought to take place in the so-called hermeneutical circle: attempts are made to understand a text by proportioning its parts to the entirety and the entirety to parts. Hermeneuticians particularly concern themselves with such questions as producing certain meanings from a text, the role of the author's intentions in the formation of meanings, historical variability and the reader's part in the creation of textual meanings.

In this book, I use the term 'hermeneutics' in its limited and practical meaning. As the poetics of texts studies what different meaning potentials texts contain, the hermeneutics of contexts sets off by asking which of these potential meanings actualize to any given reader in a respective context.

The border between the poetics of texts and the hermeneutics of contexts is anything but unambiguous. The questions they present about the activity of the text (the level of the signifier) and its meaning (the level of the signified) are not distinguishable in practice, but only analytically. On the other hand, there is sense in distinguishing them from each other which directs us to ask certain questions concerning texts. By means of the poetics of texts we can ask: *what can all this text mean?* whereas the hermeneutics of contexts attempts to give an answer to the question: *which of these meanings are actualized in different contextually constructed reading situations?*

Texts are sites where a struggle for producing meanings goes on. They do not contain 'fixed codes', neither do they have pre-defined meanings. In the formation of meanings, texts are not 'primary' determiners in relation to others. Rather, texts are open fields the meanings of which are principally determined by how they are interpreted, adopted and positioned in a larger textual, cultural and practical field; that is, in contexts.

The concept of 'a preferred reading' refers to the notion that texts can invite their readers to study them from certain positions. This takes place in such a way that texts contain discursive positions from which their discourses seem 'natural', transparently attached to 'reality' and plausible. As an example of this we can take a look at the novel by Jane Austen that was under discussion in the previous chapter. Its narrator invites readers to examine the world it has created from her own viewpoint. But, as David Morley remarks, a preferred reading is not the only reader position written in the text, and in no case is it the one and only reading that the readers can produce from the text:

> Even in the case of the 'classic realist text', the subject positions inscribed by the text, as a condition of its intelligibility, may be inhabited differently by subjects who, in the past (as the result of interpellations by other texts/ discourses/institutions) or in the present, are already positioned in an interdiscursive space. . . . The text may be contradicted by the subject's position(s) in relation to other texts, problematics, institutions, discursive formations.[30]

A text and a reader do not exist regardless of each other, but produce each other as the text of the respective reader, and as the reader of the respective text. As Tony Bennett and Janet Woollacott write:

> The text that is read . . . is an always-already culturally activated object just as . . . the reader is an always-already culturally activated subject. The encounter between them is always culturally, ideologically and – which is to say the same thing – inter-textually organised in such a way that their separation as subject and object is called into question. The reader is

conceived not as a subject who stands outside the text and interprets it any more than the text is regarded as an object the reader encounters. Rather, text and reader are conceived as being co-produced within a reading-formation, gridded on to one another in a determinate compact unity.[31]

Where to begin?

As texts are not predetermined, neither do contexts exist ready-made but take shape according to the circumstances. Lawrence Grossberg has thus remarked that 'Contexts are not entirely empirically available because they are not already completed, stable configurations, passively waiting to receive another element. They are not guaranteed in advance but are rather the site of contradictions, conflicts, and struggles.'[32] Correspondingly, a researcher's task as an interpreter, according to Grossberg, is expressly the construction of valid contexts: 'any interpretation . . . is an articulation, an active insertion of a practice into a set of contextual relations that determines the identity and the effects of both the text and the context. Articulation is the continuous deconstruction and reconstruction of contexts.'[33]

In the light of Grossberg's views, textual meanings can firstly be thought of as *interactive*: meanings are created in interaction between texts and their contexts. Secondly, meanings appear in Grossberg's conceptions as *conjunctural*: texts obtain meanings always in some conjunction, in their connection with contextual and broader socio-cultural factors. Readers do not produce textual meanings arbitrarily, but expressly in the encounter between their own socio-cultural history and the meaning potentials structured by the text.

Hence, the relationship between texts, contexts and readers can be the point of departure in the search for the formation of meanings. Texts are determined by a great number of factors related to their production and reading. Contexts of production are, among other things, the available language and the discursive limitations it contains, literary and other conventions of signification, current trends, commitments of the writer (national commitments, commitments related to the writer's genre, 'race' and social class, etc.), pressures created by publishing machinery and other cultural institutions and, finally, the writer of the text. The contexts of reading in turn include the intended audience of the text, the reader addressed within the text, pressures created by publishing and distributory institutions and also the actual readers of the text, with their qualities.[34]

Intertexts

One of the central methods with which the relationships between texts and contexts has been explored in recent decades is the theory of inter-textuality.[35] In the theory of intertextuality, it is emphasized that every text must be read in connection with other texts.[36] Similarly, as our conception of extratextual reality is produced linguistically (see Chapter 3), texts also do not primarily refer to 'reality' according to this concept, but to all of the other texts in the culture. As Roland Barthes stresses, 'reality' exists to us through how culture has attired it in spoken and written words, as well as images.[37] However, this does not mean that meanings are totally unreal. On the contrary, intertextual relationships participate in a significant way in the temporary stabilization of texts, in certain readings produced by certain audiences.

The theory of intertextuality emphasizes that texts do not exist as hermetic and self-supporting entities. Therefore, they do not act as closed systems. Firstly, writers are always the first readers of texts before they become the producers of texts. For this reason, texts are inevitably filled with references to other texts, as well as quotations and the influences of other texts. Secondly, texts are only available through the means of reading them. What is produced in reading is influenced by all of the other texts that the reader brings into the reading.[38] In this the question is not necessarily, or even primarily, of direct references to other texts contained in texts. Rather, intertextual knowledge directs readers to use texts in certain ways, to read some meanings rather than others into them.[39] As John Frow remarks, it is not central in this process to recognize some intertextual source but to track down the more general discursive structures (genres, discursive formations of ideologies) that the text belongs to.[40]

The traditional study of meanings has also at times been interested in the relationships between texts. More commonly, however, the question has concerned the study of which texts have had an impact on a certain writer. These influences have then been tracked down by seeking allusions in the writer's texts to other texts. A person conducting this kind of study would without doubt pay attention, for example, to the fact that the title of Chapter 1 in this book has a certain reverse relationship to the title of the film *Stop the World – I Want to Get Off* (Great Britain, 1966) directed by Philip Saville.

The notion of intertextuality, however, reaches far beyond the hunt for direct references. All use of language can be thought to be inevitably intertextual for several different reasons. Firstly, individuals do not invent language: language precedes individuals. Secondly, signification could not exist without pre-existing forms, conventions and codes.[41] Therefore, the concept of intertextuality can be seen as referring to how relationships between texts are organized in reading a certain text under certain circumstances.

John Fiske has made a distinction between two dimensions of inter-textual relationships. *Horizontal* relationships are between primary texts, more or less explicit relationships which are usually established through genre, characters or contents. *Vertical* intertextuality, on the other hand, prevails between a primary text and other, different texts which explicitly refer to the primary text. For instance, in TV programmes these secondary texts can be the reactions of studio audiences, newspaper articles, reviews or texts produced by spectators themselves, such as letters to editors or chattering about programmes. Secondary texts activate certain meanings of primary texts and have an influence on which relatively stable readings are produced from their polysemy.[42]

In the concept of intertextuality it is not only a question of the internal relationships of some genre or medium. For instance, a murder shown in a TV detective series obtains meanings in connection with the crime reports in newspapers and other representations concerning murders in novels, movies, the theatre, and so forth. Intertextuality understood in this sense is not so much extracting meanings from one text through looking for references to other texts in it; rather it refers to those meaning potentials that exist in the states between texts; to the resource of cultural meanings which both texts and readers can rely on as they produce meanings.[43]

Hence, there is reason to complement the notion of intertextuality with the idea of *intermediality*. Our cultural resources do not originate in a sphere of only one medium. None of us is a member of only one audience, a TV viewer or a reader of novels. We also bring those resources into our reading or watching texts that we have gained as radio listeners, users of a computer, and readers of newspapers and magazines.

Genres

John Fiske considers genre the most influential element of intertextual factors. He defines it as follows: 'Genre is a cultural practice that attempts to structure some order into the wide range of texts and meanings that circulate in our culture for the convenience of producers and audiences.'[44] According to Fiske, genres are inter- or even pre-textual, since they form a network of certain conventions which directs both the production of texts and the reading of them.[45] Stephen Neale describes this activity in mainstream movies in the following way:

> Genres institutionalise, guarantee coherence by institutional conventions, i.e. sets of expectations with respect to narrative process and narrative closure which may be subject to variation, but which are never exceeded or broken. The existence of genres means that the spectator, precisely, will always know that everything will be 'made right at the end', that everything will cohere, that any threat or any danger in narrative process itself will always be contained.[46]

Neale remarks that genres affect the production of text on the level of narrative. A form of narrative characteristic of the genres of mainstream movies, for instance, is one in which events are organized in such a way that the disturbance of balance that launches the narrative, and the following reorganization of the relationships ultimately produce a new balance, the reaching of which is a prerequisite for the closure of the narrative. Genres are forms of these kinds of narrative systems which regulate the potentials of the narrative and have an impact on how the signifiers and discourses are shaped, organized and varied in narrative processes.[47]

Usually the term 'genre' refers to a species or a type of text, to whether the text is classified as a poem, a horror movie, a commercial or some other kind of text. 'Genre' comes from the Latin noun *genus* (descent, family, class, species, group). However, the term is problematic in several senses. Is there a limited number of text types? And what is it that defines a genre? Is it a question of some formal qualities of the text itself, or merely of the categorizer's own suppositions? How can we know that certain movies, let us say the movies of the *Die Hard* series, belong to a certain genre, for example action films? What formal features of the *Die Hard* films as texts would designate them as belonging to the genre of action films? Or, is there, perhaps, one specific factor which automatically places these films in the genre of action films? Maybe it is possible to distinguish some common means through which the *Die Hard* films and other action films address their audiences and which act as the basis of a common genre for these films?

Perhaps it would be better to examine other films which are commonly considered to belong to the genre of action films. Hence it would not be a question of definitions concerning the text and its reception, but of certain conventions. Certain films are action films because people regard them as such. These conventions, in turn, are affected by certain expectations and prototypes. Texts do not necessarily have to have all generic features to be categorized as a member of some genre. Mel Brooks' *Young Frankenstein*, for example, could be a horror film even though it inspired more laughter than horror, as long as it otherwise followed the genre's conventions.

The example of Mel Brooks' parody also brings forth the fact that genres are not solid and unvariable. Content can change and new genres can be born. Generic convention is continually shaped by the production and dissemination of texts as well as the reactions of audiences.[48] With regard to genres the question is of both repetition and difference.[49] In fact, repetition and difference are not unconnected, but function in a mutual relationship. We do not meet a repetition *and* a difference, but repetition in differences or differences in repetitions. Genres are two-dimensional: both their regulated and irregular sides are of great importance.

Genre is not something that exists outside of its manifestations, finalized and unchanging. Rather, genres are abstracts, classifications made by the examiners of a number of certain kinds of texts, which exist operationally as they define, on their part, textual production and reading. In this respect, genres are a certain kind of more or less wordless knowledge which the producers and readers of texts exploit in their activities.[50]

Genres do not consist only of texts, but also in an equally important way of different expectation systems and hypotheses which readers bring to texts, and which influence the texts themselves during the reading process.[51] These expectations and hypotheses can function on several levels. One is the level of an individual text: what actually is the text in question and what kind of pleasure is one permitted to expect from it? Another level is the level of the writer. A certain amount of repetition and a certain amount of difference can be anticipated in the texts of an individual writer.

Hence, genre refers simultaneously to both a number of texts and a relatively systematic number of expectations.[52] As such, the concept of genre highlights the fact that attention must be paid to reading in addition to text. Genres produce expectations which in turn affect how the text is read and understood. In this respect, genres are the largely wordless knowledge of expectations and techniques that direct reading and are utilized in reading. Genres are similar to trade descriptions which assist people in orienteering in an open sea of texts searching for experiences which they know from former experiences to give them pleasure. John Hartley has summarized the notion regarding TV programmes:

> Audiences' different potential pleasures are channeled and disciplined by genres, which operate by producing recognition of already known sets of responses and rules of engagement. Audiences aren't supposed to judge a western for not being musical enough, a musical for not being very horrific, or a sitcom for not being sufficiently erotic.
>
> Such is the 'contract' of the genre. It entails a loss of freedom of desire and demand in order to achieve efficiency and properly labeled packaging.[53]

From our viewpoint, one central dimension of the notion concerning genre is that it helps to dismantle the differentiation between text and context. We never find ourselves in situations where a pure text first exists and only later settles within different contexts. On the contrary, contexts – in this case, generic conventions – are always already within texts. Producing texts is never purely or even primarily creating anew, but always exploiting already existing models. This becomes apparent even on the level of individual sentences: words and sentence structures already exist and new ones are hardly ever invented, let alone introduced into general use. This exploitation also applies to the level of discourses: themes, comparisons, coordinations and distinctions are primarily based on the resources of cultural conventions in the culture in question. And ultimately, it applies to the level of genre; that label which is attached to the text.

The processuality of texts

Interaction of texts and readers is not an encounter between two pre-constructed, completed instances. In studying the formation of meanings one must abandon the point of departure in which people adopt already existing, qualitatively pre-defined texts according to their own pre-defined social status, experience and needs. Instead the formation of meanings takes place in a process that Lawrence Grossberg has described in the following way:

> In fact, both audiences and texts are continuously remade – their identity and effectiveness reconstructed – by relocating their place within different contexts. The audience is always caught up in the continuous reconstruction of cultural contexts which enable them to consume, interpret and use texts in specific ways.[54]

An encounter between a text, a context and a reader is essentially negotiation. It is negotiation that is directed not only towards the meaning to be produced, but also towards the identity of each party involved. The meeting of the aforementioned three parties produces not only meanings but also a new identity for each one of them. Therefore, contexts do not exist as totalities that are complete, let alone without contradictions, but are reconstructed in their specificity time and again.

One essential contextual matter that in this book has not yet been discussed is the so-called context of usage of texts. The concept refers to those immediate circumstances in which texts are read. For instance, reading literature quietly on one's own and connecting it to the dominant literary conceptions of the subjectivity and individuality of each reader has made the reading of modern poetry, short stories and novels largely a private activity. It was common in the bourgeois families of the nineteenth century for the whole family – which with its several generations living under the same roof, as well as aunts and uncles, rather resembled an entire clan rather than a nuclear family – to gather together in the evenings in the drawing room to listen to reading aloud, while at the end of the twentieth century reading to anybody else but oneself rarely takes place beyond children's bedtime stories. These different ways of use also produce different meanings for the read texts. When the whole family was reading, the meanings formed were above all regulated by the oldest members, whereas a reader on his/her own is more free to form his/her own meanings.

Questions about the interpretation of texts and different uses of texts have traditionally been separated from each other. Questions concerning interpretation have generally been studied in literary studies, whereas the use of texts has primarily been approached through sociology or cultural studies. Strictly speaking, however, these two questions should not be separated, since interpretation directs the ways of use, and vice versa. The study of contexts must be expanded by including readers as objects of study. Indeed, the reader is the hero of the next chapter.

Notes

1. Carroll 1994, 22.
2. Sara Mills explains the experiment. See Mills 1995, 66.
3. See ibid., 31, and Fairclough 1989, 24.
4. Cook 1992, 72.
5. Dick 1993, 4.
6. Kaplinski 1995, 141–2.
7. Cook 1992, 1–2.
8. See e.g. Meinhof and Richardson 1994, 19.
9. See Soon 1994, 77.
10. See Marx 1973, 93–4.
11. Cf. Fiske 1992, 62. However, in its everyday meaning 'reading' still does not necessarily appear to be a very prompt activity. In the *Concise Oxford Dictionary* of the 1950s some of the primary meanings that were provided for the verb 'read' are as follows:

    > [To be able to] convert into the intended words or meaning (written or printed or other symbols or things expressed by their means.)
    > To reproduce mentally or vocally, while following their symbols with eyes or fingers, the words of (author, book, tale, letter, etc.)

    The meanings of 'reading' stated here are quite passive. In this light, 'reading' would be 'converting symbols into their intended meanings' or the 'vocal reproduction of the words of an author'. All power would be held by the text, which the reader must obey.

    However, in all fairness the same dictionary offers the following as the primary meaning of 'read': To interpret mentally, declare interpretation or the coming development of something. The word 'interpret' provides the reader with more room for manoeuvre, but is not free from problems, as will be seen below.

12. See Morley 1980b, 167. An attentive reader must have taken a note of the fact that I have carefully avoided the term 'interpretation' in connection with reading. There are several reasons for this. The word comes from the Latin *interpretatio*, which means 'explaining', and *interpres*, which is intermediary, interpreter or courier. In the light of its etymology, 'interpretation' is a certain kind of explaining that is positioned between a 'sender' and a 'receiver'. The matter is further complicated by the much-used division between 'understanding' and 'interpreting'. Roughly speaking, this division means that someone can understand the plot of a James Bond film even if the hidden mythical, ideological or sexual levels of meaning did not open up to him/her. However, the talk about 'hidden' meanings, 'levels' of meanings and their 'opening' contains a view according to which a text would be a kind of a container into which the writer has put meanings for the interpreter to excavate. Therefore, the use of the term 'interpretation' easily obscures the fact that what there is to interpret does not lie in the given text, but is created only in the interaction of the text and the reader. This is why I thought it best not to use the term at all in this connection. (On the term, see Bordwell 1989, 1–3.)
13. See Fiske 1989b, 57

14. Bennett 1983, 218.
15. Heath 1978, 105–6.
16. See Bennett and Woollacott 1987, 61–2.
17. Ibid., 261.
18. Pêcheux 1982, 111.
19. See also Bennett 1983, 223.
20. Ibid., 224.
21. Bennett and Woollacott 1987, 64.
22. Ibid., 263.
23. See Baynham 1995, 174–5.
24. Bennett 1987, 74.
25. Bennett and Woollacott 1987, 263.
26. Bennett 1987, 76.
27. Bennett and Woollacott 1987, 264–5. Elsewhere, Tony Bennett characterizes the attempts to define 'text in itself' as metaphysical for the reason that such attempts are based on the presumption that the discursive wrappings entwined around texts could be peeled away, and thus the ultimate nucleus of texts could be seized (Bennett 1987, 75–6).
28. Eagleton 1996a, 66.
29. See Fiske 1987, 66.
30. Morley 1980b, 167.
31. Bennett and Woollacott 1987, 64.
32. Grossberg 1988, 168.
33. Ibid., 168–9.
34. See Mills 1995, 31–43.
35. A good introduction to the field is Worton and Still 1990.
36. See Still and Worton 1990, 1.
37. See Barthes 1974, 20–1.
38. See Still and Worton 1990, 1–2.
39. Fiske 1987, 108.
40. Frow 1990, 46.
41. See Montgomery et al. 1992, 164.
42. Fiske 1987, 64–5.
43. See Fiske 1987, 109.
44. Ibid.
45. Ibid., 111.
46. Neale 1980, 28.
47. Ibid., 20.
48. See e.g. Montgomery et al. 1992, 169–74.
49. Neale 1980, 48.
50. Ibid., 49.
51. Neale 1990, 46.
52. Neale 1980, 54–5.
53. Quoted by Fiske 1987, 114.
54. Grossberg 1992b, 54.

Chapter 7

The World of Readers

In the previous chapter I discussed the notion that texts and readers never exist independently of each other, but in fact produce one another. Texts do not semiotically exist without readers, but neither do readers exist without texts. John Fiske compresses the notion into a provocatively clear form when he examines television texts and their audiences:

> There is no such thing as 'the television audience', defined as an empirically accessible object, for there can be no meaningful categories beyond its boundaries – what on earth is 'not the television audience'? The 'television audience' is not a social category like class, race, or gender – everyone slips in or out of it in a way that makes nonsense of any categorical boundaries: similarly when in 'it' people constitute themselves quite differently as audience members at different times – I am a different television 'audience' when watching my football team from when watching *The A-Team* with my son or *Days of our Lives* with my wife. Categories focus our thinking on similarities: people watching television are best modeled according to a multitude of differences.[1]

Provided that we take Fiske's argument at face value, in practice each one of us constitutes him/herself as a reader of television and other texts in innumerable different ways, which in turn are dependent on what texts we read at a given time. At the same time, Fiske's way of taking readers, who are made of flesh and blood, as the objects of his study, strongly brings forth the notion that the intertextuality of the formation of meanings can only be realized through people bringing their own histories and subjectivities into the reading process.

Readers simultaneously live in several overlapping times and places which, however, do not necessarily determine each other. They live simultaneously as if they have several lives – personal lives, family lives, possible working lives, recreational lives, the lives of their nations, the lives of different texts and so on. Even as they remain stable physically, they are in motion as subjects. However, 'subject' can be understood in two different ways, as is well known: either in the passive or active. Traditionally, readers' subjectivity has been understood as a passive quality: they have been thought merely to fulfil the position the text has pre-created for them. In this case, the notion of texts as being able to determine the ways of reading for which they have been intended lurks in the background. If, however, there is any validity to the views presented in the two previous chapters, contrary to traditional views there is reason to stress the activity of readers, their agency, their ability to create their own meanings rather than simply adapt to given meanings.

By this I certainly do not wish to claim that people always automatically read against the grain. Activity can also mean an active yielding to a text – an interactive production of the meanings that the texts themselves attempt to give priority to.

However, reading even in these cases is never a mere passive selection of meanings from texts by acknowledging the meanings of words and joining them together according to the rules of grammar. Reading includes choosing what to read, organizing and linking them together in order to form meanings, as well as bringing the reader's own knowledge into texts.

Subjects and language

The notion of the co-dependency of texts and readers is not surprising in so far as it recapitulates the idea of the intense link between language and subjectivity, which essentially belongs to the 'linguistic turn' of the humanities and social sciences. As already discussed in Chapter 3, we are constituted as subjects expressly within language. Let us now examine this notion more closely in order to get a grip on what kinds of subjectivities the reading of different texts produces and how those subjectivities in turn participate in the formation of meanings in reading texts.

In recent decades, quite a 'discursive explosion'[2] has been experienced where the 'subject' has been of concern. At the same time, the concept has been a target of strong criticism. Stuart Hall has summarized some of the most important aspects of the critique as follows:

> The deconstruction has been conducted within a variety of disciplinary areas, all of them, in one way or another critical of the notion of an integral, originary and unified identity. The critique of the self-sustaining subject at the centre of post-Cartesian western metaphysics has been comprehensively advanced in philosophy. The question of subjectivity and its unconscious processes of formation has been developed within the discourse of a psychoanalytically influenced feminism and cultural criticism. The endlessly performative self has been advanced in celebratory variants of post-modernism. With the anti-essentialist critique of ethnic, racial and national conceptions of cultural identity and the 'politics of location' some adventurous theoretical conceptions of cultural identity have been sketched in their most grounded forms.[3]

On the basis of Hall's remarks we can therefore ask: why speak about the 'subject' at all any more? Who needs it? Hall himself replies by saying that deconstructive approaches do not attempt to seek for 'more true' concepts to replace failed ones; the key concepts are placed as if 'under erasure'. Bracketing, in turn, demonstrates the fact that the concepts are no longer viable in their original and undeconstructed forms. Since they have not been totally displaced, or toppled over by brand new concepts that replace them, we simply have to continue thinking with their deconstructed forms.

'Subject' can be seen as this kind of a concept used in brackets: it can no longer be considered in the previous way, but without it certain key questions could not be considered at all.

Subjectivities are not simple and individual, but always disintegrated, fragmented and multidimensional. Becoming a subject is a complex process of separation and unification which takes place under the influence of such biological, social and cultural factors as age, gender and elements of cultural identity. Subjects are real, but their identity is not predetermined. As the Swedish cultural researcher Johan Fornäs concludes: 'We know we are, but not who or how we are.' Fornäs also links subjectivity and texts: 'To understand our identities is a task that forces us to reflect on what we do, to interpret the texts we produce.'[4] He continues:

> All understanding of subjectivity is a combination of self-understanding and interpretation of others, or of the Other. All self-reflection is mediated by texts. By narrating itself in the works, texts and discourses of symbolic modes, the subject reconstructs itself in intelligible form. Subjective experience becomes meaningful when it can be narrated or 'emplotted' – given a temporal structure with direction, beginning and end.[5]

The identities of subjects are stories presented by the person him/herself or other people, they are tales, histories. They are something that is produced, made, told; by no means are they something to be found ready-made. Identities are always built on memories, fantasies, stories and myths. As such, all identities are adopted.

The close connection of subjects and language has significant consequences for the subjectivities themselves. Provided that the identities of subjects are born as an outcome of narration, it indicates that the speaking subject splits in two. In stories we tell about the identity of a subject, the speaking subject and the subject under discussion are never identical, never precisely in the same place. However, this does not overturn the basis of the 'reality' of the identity. As Stuart Hall summarizes:

> Identities are . . . constituted within, not outside representation. . . . They arise from the narrativization of the self, but the necessary fictional nature of this process in no way undermines its discursive, material or political effectivity.[6]

On the basis of the statement above, Hall emphasizes that since subjectivities are produced within discourse, how they are produced in special historical and institutional places as a part of special discursive formations and practices by using certain strategies of utterances must be studied. 'Discourse' and 'utterances' in turn refer to the fact that different texts in different media have a central role in the birth of subjectivities.

However, the question is not of simple determinations where subjects are forced to reiterate the same thing they meet in already existing discourses and utterances. Subjects are not absolutely enslaved in forming meanings, and, through them, also themselves – but they are not utterly free either.

The simultaneous freedom to some degree and non-freedom to some degree of a subject are already demonstrated in the different meaning dimensions of the word 'subject'. In 'subject', agency and submissiveness mix historically. 'Subject' originates from the Latin expression *subiectus* (*sub* = under, *iacio* = throw, toss). (This meaning is still apparent in the way of speaking about the 'subjects' of the Queen of Great Britain). However, in the 17th century the set of coordinates of thinking shifted position. Since a human being was no longer seen as being positioned in his/her set place in the cosmic order, human actors were no longer examined as parts of a broader, significant entity; the meaning of human existence had to be found in the person him/herself. The thinking self became the first essential terrain of knowledge. The autonomous existence of all other beings, now called 'objects', had to be argued through the subject.

Subjects and meanings

Subjects always exist through signification. However, signification cannot be separated from subjects who utilize signification and have self-determination apart from it. 'Signification', 'subject' and 'symbolic order' are all closely connected, as the semiotician Kaja Silverman has noted.[7] In fact, it is only language that makes it at all possible that subject and subjectivity can exist. Every 'I' is inevitably a subject. No one can be 'I' unless s/he has a proper name which, in turn, is given long before the named learns to say 'I'.

Therefore, language is as fundamental to subjectivity as subjectivity is to language. Without language there would be no subjectivity, but the subject also equally determines language. 'I', 'you', 'this' and other equivalent pronouns have no established meaning: they gain one only in relationship to the subject that utters them. In this, the subject is relational. It does not exist by its own virtue.

As with the signs of language, the meaning and value of subjects also rely on other terms. 'I' does not exist wihout 'you'. Thus, the subject is not an essential being, but a number of relationships. Different cultural factors have a significant role in the kinds of groups of relationships subjects constitute. Yet, correspondingly, different subjectivities participate in defining how the meaning potentials of texts are actualized.

Even though cultural texts do not have predetermined meanings, they do have real, actual meanings. These meanings are not causally warranted, but nevertheless they do exist. As real, linked to a certain time and place as well as to certain readers, meanings are not born previous to the reading of texts, but are constituted as texts are read. Texts themselves do not define in advance how and for what purposes they are used. The same text can have several functions.[8] It can mean different things to different people – or mean nothing at all – according to the circumstances and readers. (The rejection of a text, leaving it unread, is also interpretation.)

Texts are part of our daily lives. Studying them is also studying our everyday lives. From this viewpoint, the cultural study of texts could be characterized as placing a new object of analysis under inspection. This object is how texts are contained in or become linked with 'the ever-changing kaleidoscope of daily life'.[9]

One of the earliest studies conducted from this point of view was Dorothy Hobson's 1982 presentation on the female audience of the British soap opera, *Crossroads*. When Hobson visited the home of a female spectator, she prepared supper for her family, fed her five- and three-year-old daughters and simultaneously attempted to follow the programme in question on a black-and-white TV set placed on top of the fridge opposite the kitchen table.[10] In the light of this description, it is hardly surprising that Hobson wound up studying the watching of TV particularly as part of the spectators' daily lives. Following the soap was not an activity separate and isolated from other activities, but rather a part of the women spectators' daily routines and duties. Hobson's study pointed out that readers' relationships to texts are defined not only by the text itself, but also by readers' own position: their entire resources of (textual and non-textual) knowledge and experience.

Therefore, texts can indeed have other than just textual effects and their meanings can connect with other than just representational relationships. An example of this could be, for instance, how daily soap operas such as *The Bold and the Beautiful* affect their viewers' daily use of time.

Janice Radway bumped into the non-textual effects of texts as she studied American women who read popular romantic novels. Radway perceived that many women combined their reading with those rare moments of privacy they managed to sneak in between the demands of work and family. Her interviewees seemed to regard the moments they spent with romantic entertainment nearly as declarations of an independence of sorts. Taking a book in hand signified building a wall between the reader and the unwashed dishes, laundry and unmade beds. Radway concludes:

> romance reading functions for the women as a kind of tacit, minimal protest against the patriarchal constitution of women: it enabled them to mark off a space where they could temporarily deny the selflessness usually demanded of them.[11]

Thus, non-textual dimensions can indeed connect with reading. In regard to this, Lawrence Grossberg has discussed the potential *multifunctionality* of cultural texts: texts can also have effects which are not connected with their meaning.[12] However, despite the studies of Radway, Grossberg and others, the interpretations of texts and their uses have not often been studied in connection with each other.

Readers as social and semiotic beings

Reading can be many different kinds of activity. A reader can read a text word by word or leap back and forth in the text according to what interests him/her most at the time. S/he might have keenly darted off to purchase a certain text as soon as it was delivered to the local bookseller, or a text may be force-fed to a reluctant reader as part of a study programme. A reader can muse upon a text's relationship to the incidents in the life of its writer or seek for constellations of certain words in it. Each of these ways of reading produces different meanings.

It is not enough in studying readers to emphasize that they are active participants in the formation of meanings. The terms 'active reader' or 'active audience' are, on closer inspection, tautologies. Aren't all readers somewhat active according to this definition? Roger Silverstone indeed remarks that the key question is not whether readers are active or not, but does their active quality have a certain meaning, does it matter, does it provide them with an opportunity for critical or creative reading?[13]

Only in exceptional cases regarding reading is it a question of readers attempting to produce a 'correct' meaning from a text. Though in our culture texts are easily understood as independent entities outside of reading situations, not many readers assume (unless perhaps under the coercion of literary or other studies) that a text is some loose object separate from everything else, of which a reader then as a subject attempts to produce an 'objective interpretation'.

In studying readers, there is reason to keep at hand viewpoints that are generally separated from each other and see readers simultaneously as 'social' and 'textual' beings. According to John Fiske, a social subject has a history which includes class, social gender, age, living environment, etc. This is constructed along with a complex social history which is both social and textual in nature. The subjectivity of a social subject is the outcome of both 'real' social experiences and indirect or textual experiences. In Fiske's opinion, readers of texts are first and foremost social subjects. Social subjectivity, according to Fiske, has a greater impact on the formation of meanings than the subject produced textually, which exists only at the very moment of reading.[14] Subjects are always already social subjects as they meet texts. They have their place in different social practices and formations. Reading in this respect is anything but a solitary activity. The meanings readers produce from texts and their pleasure in doing so are largely determined also by those social contexts in which texts are recycled and consumed.

Hence, the meanings produced by the interaction of readers and texts can never be read out directly from 'textual features' or discursive strategies. In addition to them, one must also take into account how a text is used, to what kind of conjuncture it is connected, into what institutionalized dimensions it steps, and in what kinds of relationships it is with any given audience.[15]

As she studied the romantic reading of women, Janice Radway perceived that readers constructed the characters of texts, their deeds, the causes and effects of the events described, as well as their own interpretations concerning the course of the narrative according to their own previous experiences and value judgements. These experiences and value judgements, however, were not according to Radway idiosyncratic, characteristic only of the readers in question. Radway emphasizes that readers had adopted the dominant strategies and interpretational conventions in their reading expressly as members of 'interpretive communities'.[16]

There are several of these 'interpretive communities' in relation to each text. The culture described as late capitalist or late modern is characterized by great multiplicity. The culture is abundant in subcultures and groups which have very different types of relationship with texts. In this kind of situation, each person is in varying positions in his/her relationships with different texts. People enter the culture through differently organized and varying social formations and relationships. Every reader can be a different reading subject at different times, and in various relationships with different texts. The question is of a situation which is aptly described by the metaphor of the nomadic subject – 'nomadic subject' indeed means a moving, tentative subject that, according to its position, can acquire different identities.[17]

Ien Ang describes the multiple relationship between readers and texts with respect to TV audiences in the following way:

> It is often said . . . that the television audience is becoming increasingly fragmented, individualized, dispersed, no longer addressable as a mass or as a single market, no longer comprehensible as a social entity, collectively engaged and involved in a well-defined act of viewing. Indeed, television's proliferation has made it painfully clear that it does not make sense to speak about the 'television audience' as a neatly demarcated object of study.[18]

According to Ang, the proliferation of televisual texts has signified the fragmentation of television audiences. However, Ang's observations also characterize the rest of the field of textuality. Are not, for instance, the audiences of novels already fragmented in quite the same way as television audiences? In the circle of readers of novels, we may meet not only the connoisseurs of the classic or modernistic novel but also the fans of detective, popular, science fiction and horror novels. Moreover, the audience of sci-fi or the horror novel may consist largely of the same people as the spectatorship of science fiction and horror films, when the unifying factor between the audiences is no longer the same medium (the printed word) or genre (novel) but rather their membership of the intermedial science fiction or horror audiences.

The many uses of texts

In several paintings and novels the readers of literary texts are portrayed as people who have withdrawn from the world to read in seclusion. In these presentations, reading is positioned in the sphere of the private. It has been removed from its cultural determinants and seen as an encounter between an isolated reader and an isolated text. (In portraying movie audiences, collective watching situations also come forward, but with regard to TV, videos and personal computers, the focus is again transferred to the privacy of homes.) Hence, the inevitability that the reader must have learned to read at one time or another (which could not have happened in absolute solitude), and the fact that people frequently select their reading material according to the views of other people or parties of significance to them, has not been taken into account.[19]

Reading or watching, contrary to entrenched conceptions, is not merely a bargain between two parties, that is, a text and its reader. Since neither a text as a significant unit, nor a reader as an agent producing meanings would exist without linguistic and cultural contexts, there must be many more than two parties involved in their mutual encounter. For instance, television sets are recreational centres which offer something to everyone from tots to grannies. They can provide the background din in the local pub, kindle an animated discussion, ease loneliness, provide information, reinforce family ties ('let's watch *Forrest Gump* on video all together!'), establish rituals (the Queen's Christmas Speech or the Wimbledon Tennis Tournament), provide behavioural role models, be a teaching aid, babysitter, or act as an instrument of personal distinction from the masses ('Me? I *never* watch the telly! What IS *Ally McBeal*, anyhow?').

Consequently, television and watching it cannot be studied in isolation but as part of a larger context which includes recreational activities both complementary to and competing with it. The context in question is not merely textual, but consists of pretty much all possible ways of spending free time from wild mushroom hunting to tormenting oneself at the gym. Television watching can only be understood in this larger context, which covers one's whole lifestyle all the way up to one's occupation.[20] Television watching is a complex and multifaceted activity, which is generally interwoven with other simultaneous activities.

Roger Silverstone notes that television watching does not have a singular meaning or function for its audience. All of us watch TV from time to time, but our attentiveness to it – let alone our commitment – may vary greatly from one situation and programme to another.

Television watching is thus in many senses interaction between many parties. Yet, likewise we may think that all of the factors concerning TV mentioned above can just as well, more or less, concern any other cultural text form: neither are their uses predetermined, nor are their contexts of use pre-arranged. Yesterday's newspaper makes today's fish wrapper.

The *way of usage* is one of the central contextual factors in the formation of meaning. It determines the intensity of reading, the reader's expectations and direction of attention, as well as his/her attitude towards the text being read (whether the question is of studying, being together or killing time). Reading also includes those *situations* in which texts are read. Reading a text in a café, on a trip abroad, in the bedroom when down with the flu or on the beach not only produces different concrete contexts to reading, but also links the reading experience into different reader identities (a bohemian, a cosmopolitan, a killer of time, a devourer of books). If one watches *Love Story* amidst a divorce crisis or when madly in love, the life situation most probably affects reading of the text in different ways.

The reading of novels, for instance, can be thought to serve various kinds of function. Novels by Jane Austen have been in the limelight since the cinematization and TV versions of many of her novels in the mid-1990s. Those who have seen the movies and TV series based on *Pride and Prejudice* may open the Austen novel with expectations of finding in its pages more of the pleasure given by the film and series. They and other readers can also employ the novel and its characters to reflect their own life experiences – as does the writing subject of *Bridget Jones' Diary* (1996) by Helen Fielding in her perpetual hunt for her own Mr Darcy. There might be readers who select an Austen from a bookseller's or the library for the reason that these novels are considered so-called 'page turners', in which one can completely absorb oneself. Furthermore, one reader type can delve into Austen's texts to satisfy an interest in anything taking place in the Napoleonic era, another because of the author's gender. And so forth.

Texts' forms also have their own effects on the uses of texts. There is a good chance that watching a movie in a cinema and absentmindedly eyeing the same one on a home video produce two quite different texts. When we step into a traditional cinema with its art deco interior and other refer-ences to the golden age of the cinema, there are probably rather different streams of expectations flowing in our veins than in the circumstances of entrenching oneself on the couch on a rainy afternoon with a bag of crisps to half-heartedly stare at a random film picked up from the local video shop. Going to the cinema often contains more elements than a mere watching of the actual film – the first date, for example. It may be a question of going out with friends, relaxing or maybe even making it a small-scale celebration of something. We rarely go out just to see a certain film, but do generally go 'to the cinema'. In this case, the meanings of the film we watch also connect with the meanings of the entire cinematic institution: to be able to enter the womb of a dark, warm cinema with a bag of popcorn or candy, to experience the titillating expectation that the beginning of the film signifies, to absorb oneself in the world of sounds, images and colours without intruding factors, and to discuss the film afterwards with our companions.

John Ellis has noted that regarding their ways of use, television and movies differ markedly. A viewer of television is approached as if s/he had accidentally turned on the set without paying much attention to it but eyeing the programmes absentmindedly while puttering about. Television coaxes this inattentive putterer to drop all other things and concentrate only on the offerings of television. According to Ellis, this takes place through the means of the constant reiteration of the channel's signature tune or by directly addressing the viewer. Part of the attempt to capture the viewer is the use of sound: 'Sound draws the attention of the look when it has wandered away,' Ellis writes.[21] In the cinema, spectators would not experience these kinds of gimmicks and would probably find them completely ridiculous or infuriating.

The material form does indeed have its impact on textual qualities. Movie-makers have started with the notion that viewers come to the uterine atmosphere of cinemas prepared to submerge themselves in the magic realm of imagery and sounds, whereas watching TV can mean just about anything from absolute fascination to utter apathy (though in the production of movies currently the possible future video distribution must also be taken into account).

Through their material forms, texts are also connected with quite a number of cultural practices of readers concerning them, which participate in the production of meanings. Janice Radway writes with regard to romantic entertainment:

> A good cultural analysis of the romance ought to specify not only how the women understand the novels themselves but also how they comprehend the very act of picking up a book in the first place. The analytic focus must shift from the text itself, taken in isolation, to the complex social event of reading where a woman actively attributes sense to lexical signs in a silent process carried on in the context of her ordinary life.[22]

TV audiences never consist only of people who watch a certain programme, but also of people who watch television 'at large'. These viewers' readings of texts are also affected also by their general habits of watching television.

As Lawrence Grossberg has remarked, the effect and influence of each medium (TV, for instance) changes significantly when it is transferred from one context to another (to a pub, theatre, sitting room, bedroom, beach or rock concert). People rarely concentrate on merely listening to the radio, watching TV or even only on going to the cinema any more – they simultaneously study, have a date or keep company with someone, perform other tasks, celebrate and so forth. 'The same' text is not only different in different contexts, but its multiple manifestations also influence one another in a complex way.[23] In reading texts it is never a question of interpretation only, but also of different uses. Texts settle as part of their readers' life practices in different ways. Even when a text is being read with total concentration and keen dedication, the process involves a great number of extratextual questions springing from the reader's life practices and intertextual knowledge. Reading in order to solve the 'great questions' of life in one's *Weltschmerz*-ridden youth or employing reading as an aid in living through a grieving process are clear examples of this.[24]

Ethnography as studying the meanings of the everyday

All of this brings a new aspect to the study of the formation of meanings: ethnography. The object of ethnographic study is the study of how people live out their own culture. Through participatory observation, the use of informants and deep interviews, ethnographers attempt to understand the everyday world of different social groups, their mutual communication and the use of media.[25] The term 'ethnography,' though, includes certain problematic connotations and presumptions. An ethnographic study is usually aimed at a different group than the one the conductor of the study belongs to him/herself. Therefore, from an ethnographic viewpoint, reading has been studied expressly as an activity of 'some other people'. Moreover, the texts studied have mainly been those of popular culture.

Ethnographic studies of readers have so far largely focused on how meanings are formed in the private circles of the home. This is due to the fact that the objects of study have principally been women who read popular romantic novels or watch soap operas. However, reading and forming meanings do not take place solely inside the home. Hence, studies should also take into account the institutional, occupational, industrial, educational and recreational venues where meanings of texts are produced.[26]

Nevertheless, ethnographic viewpoints have their justification in the sense that they remind us in a healthy fashion of the fact that people are not so much 'recipients' or 'consumers' of texts as producers of them. As emphasized in the previous chapter, the 'consumption' of cultural texts is in fact semiotic production. The notion can now be continued by stating that this semiotic production consists of the formation of meanings concerning readers' social experiences and identities with the assistance of available cultural material.[27]

Furthermore, ethnographical approaches remind us of the fact that readers are not atomistic subjects, but at all times belong to, on the one hand, broader cultures and, on the other hand, more limited groups (men or women, young, middle-aged or elderly people, work and student communities, families, circles of friends and acquaintances, enthusiasts of different hobbies and activities, inhabitants of municipalities, neighbour-hoods and so on), which have their own effects on ways of reading.

Reading as bricolage

As we saw earlier, we ask texts different things according to the circumstances we read them in, and the purposes we read them for. One and the same person can produce a great variety of meanings from one and the same text if the contexts are different. This is quite possible since none of us as readers is one, solid subject but each of us is split by a number of different discourses.

Next to the questions asked by the poetics of texts ('how does this text work?') and the hermeneutic of contexts ('which of the text's meanings are actualized in special reading situations?'), a third question must be raised: 'what kinds of meanings and why do people produce them from this text (or in this text) in this historical time and place?' And 'What possible effects does this text have on the practices of people's lives?'

In this light, reading is aptly described by the term 'bricolage'. This means improvising or arbitrary handiwork. It is also used in the meaning of 'collage' when speaking about works of art. Here it signifies a collection rigged up from materials that happened to be handy. It can also mean modifying materials found by chance by adding them to the work as part of it. Bricolage has been characterized as 'a science of the concrete'. As such it refers to the means that so-called 'primitive' peoples (which, naturally, are primitive only from the perspective of those who call them so) use as they attempt to produce sense in the surrounding world. The question requires careful analysis and categorizing the complex world according to the logic characteristic of the people in question. This kind of 'improvised,' so to speak *ad hoc*, categorization – created expressly for the situation at hand – produces connections between different phenomena, 'explains' reality and enables people to live in it.[28]

The metaphor of bricolage refers to us producing meanings out of what at a given time is at hand, which we do through the interpretive frameworks that are characteristic of us.[29] A *bricoleur*, the producer of these combinations, is a sampler of meanings; s/he connects meanings with each other and thus makes reality meaningful to him/ herself. Different samplers produce different meanings from the same texts, always according to what they have at hand. Studying the formation of meanings as bricolages emphasizes their processual and stratified quality. In this respect, the primary task of researchers is not to place meanings in general categories. Rather, it is a task of studying meanings in their concrete specificity – how and of what ingredients they have taken shape.

The *bricoleur*'s limitations of freedom

The metaphorical concept of 'bricolage' also reminds us that in the process of forming meanings we are dependent on the ingredients at hand. Hence, the freedom of a *bricoleur* is always limited. S/he cannot choose materials of which to form combinations. Neither are the interpretive frameworks of a *bricoleur* of his/her own making only: they are an outcome of those multiple addresses to which s/he has been subjected.

In this connection, it is useful to recall the dual meaning of the term 'subject' as both an agent and as subservient to something. As subjects, we are in fact both: responsible agents of our deeds and servants subjugated to authorities. How can that be?

According to the French Marxist philosopher, Louis Althusser (1918–1990), who utilized the structuralist and the Lacanian psychoanalytical framework, the question is of a so-called ideological effect. In his essay 'Ideology and Ideological State Apparatuses' (1971), Althusser asked why and how human subjects frequently submit themselves to the dominant ideologies of their time. According to Althusser, it is expressly ideology that enables us to experience ourselves as free, complete, autonomous and self-governing individuals. Subjects are shaped in an ideology in such a way that they see themselves as free agents. Althusser writes:

> The category of the subject is a primary 'obviousness' . . . : it is clear that you and I are subjects (free, ethical etc . . .). Like all obviousnesses . . . the 'obviousness' that you and I are subjects . . . is an ideological effect. . . . It is indeed a peculiarity of ideology that it imposes (without appearing to do so, since these are 'obviousnesses') obviousnesses as obviousnesses, which we cannot fail to recognize and before which we have the inevitable and natural reaction of crying out (aloud or in the 'still small voice of conscience'): 'That's obvious! That's right! That's true!'[30]

However, in what way is this obviousness created? And how come it is a mere ideological effect and not a real perception of our true being? In this respect, Althusser's central thesis is that '*ideology hails or interpellates concrete individuals as concrete subjects*, by the functioning of the category of the subject'.[31] By this, Althusser means that ideology acts or works by 'recruiting' or 'inviting' subjects from amidst individuals, or 'modifies' individuals into subjects through this recruiting operation. As a token of the operation, Althusser presents the following everyday incident:

> There are individuals walking along. Somewhere (usually behind them) the hail rings out: 'Hey, you there!' One individual (nine times out of ten it is the right one) turns round, believing/suspecting/knowing that it is for him, i.e. recognizing that 'it really is he' who is meant by the hailing.[32]

Althusser presents his anecdote to demonstrate how all ideology invites individuals into their positions and gives them their identities through the means of this identification mechanism. So it is not so much a question of an ideology being forced upon its supporters as it is of them becoming subjects of their own free will, an outcome of their own conversion. Terry Eagleton summarizes Althusser's argumentation in this respect:

I come to feel, not exactly as though the world exists for me alone, but as though it is significantly 'centred' on me, and I in turn am significantly 'centred' on it. Ideology, for Althusser, is the set of beliefs and practices which does this centring. It is far more subtle, pervasive and unconscious than a set of explicit doctrines: it is the very medium in which I 'live out' my relation to society. The realm of signs and social practices which binds me to the social structure and lends me a sense of coherent purpose and identity.[33]

The nucleus of Althusser's argumentation embraces the notion that we cannot get beyond ideology. Our consciousness takes shape under the imaginary process of becoming a subject. We are always as if already inside ideology. This notion has destructive consequences with regard to traditional bourgeois humanism. Provided that our consciousness is always pre-constructed and we are not free centres of activity and initiative, the traditional conception of the central role of 'subject' in history must be an illusion. Even the freedom of a *bricoleur* is always limited.

'Ideology' from Althusser's point of view is not some banner or slogan with which some class or other group of people manifests its own rights; by ideology he refers first and foremost to the way in which an individual actively lives his/her role in a social entity. For this reason, ideology participates in the forming of an individual, and enables him/her to function. Ideology includes all the activities, practices, rituals and similar participation which cultivate an identity in us such that we truly are concrete, individual, distinct and irreplaceable subjects. This is connected to the fact that ideology confirms – even if only temporarily or in opposition to other confirmations – a certain identity of all the possible identities in which an individual could participate. This confirmation, in turn, occurs on the basis that ideology makes one or more certain identities appear natural and obvious.

However, Althusser's critique is left unfinished in that it only presents one generally applicable identification mechanism with which we become subjects. 'Hailing' refers to a one-sided process in which the 'hailed' has no option but to listen. So from Althusser's viewpoint, simplified for pedagogical purposes, it is too easy to draw the conclusion that we all automatically become subjects, and resistance and change are not possible. Nevertheless, there is reason to seize the fire, though leave the ashes, from Althusser's views. The critique he gives is indeed a healthy reminder of the fact that the contributions readers make to texts have their own limitations, and that texts do attempt to address readers and call them subjects, meaning that readers' activeness can also mean yielding to already existing ideologies. Ideologies make many matters in texts, as well as outside of them, appear very 'commonsense' universal necessities in the eyes of readers. This is particularly so concerning certain text types such as realistic fiction or scientific writing, which Terry Eagleton depicts as follows:

In some literary works, in particular realist fiction, our attention as readers is drawn not to the 'act of enunciating', to *how* something is said, from what kind of position and with what end in view, but simply to *what* is said, to the enunciation itself.[34]

According to Eagleton, these kinds of text, such as legal documents or scientific textbooks, do not offer their readers information on how the facts they contain are selected, what was left out, how come these certain facts have been arranged in just this certain way, which hypotheses dominate this process, what kinds of working methods have been utilized in preparing these texts and in what way everything could have been done differently. As an example of these kinds of text, Eagleton also mentions the Hollywood movie, in which as we are watching it, it is easy to forget that what takes place on the screen is not just something taking place but an extremely complex product constructed of the activities and views of a large number of different people.[35] These texts hold within themselves the above-mentioned ideological attempts to set limits to how readers understand them.

Subcultures and fans

The metaphor of bricolage is quite useful when discussing the formation of different subcultures. Subcultures are meaning systems in which groups of different kinds develop as they attempt to cope with the conflicts related to their members' social positioning.[36] A subculture does not just 'be', but expressly does and acts. They strive to stand out from the mainstream culture, employ different cultural products for their own purposes, conquer their own space (quite a lot of subcultures have literally conquered a territory of their own).[37] Mods, for instance, used to wear a certain kind of dress and ride scooters, the combination of which manifested their feeling of togetherness.

Bricoleurs wage (in Umberto Eco's terms) a semiotic guerrilla war. They produce collages, combine what has not previously belonged together. Where surrealists combined an umbrella with a sewing machine, punk rockers linked together heavy make-up and safety pins and hip-hoppers, bell bottoms and anti-racism.[38] Moreover, the so-called scratch video that blossomed at the end of the 1980s operates with media images, TV commercials, TV series and current affairs programmes. Its tactics were to use the techniques of montage and 'fixing' to turn the images of dominant power systems and mainstream media into subjects of ridicule.

Subcultures also frequently consist of powerful elements of fandom. The term 'fan' is an abbreviated form of the word 'fanatic,' the roots of which go back to the Latin word *fanaticus*. In its time, *fanaticus* literally meant a person who is a member or a servant of a temple or dedicated to one. However, even in Latin, the word acquired negative connotations. It also meant a person who was enthusiastic about orgiastic rites and ferociously ecstatic. From this origin, the word's meaning expanded to cover all excessive forms of faith, the worship of gods, and later on actual insanity ('such as might result from possession by a deity or a demon').[39] The abbreviated form of the word, 'fan', was first introduced into the English language at the end of the nineteenth century in connection with the followers of football teams. Soon the use expanded to other groups as well, such as female theatre-goers, who according to male critics came to the theatre to worship the romantic leads rather than enjoying the plays.[40]

From the perspective of studying the formation of meanings, fans are important first and foremost because they often attempt to use texts for their own purposes, which can greatly differ from those intended. This activity has been described by the term 'poaching'. Michel de Certeau depicts the activity in the following way:

> Far from being writers . . . readers are travellers; they move across land belonging to someone else, like nomads poaching their way across the fields they did not write, despoyling the wealth of Egypt to enjoy it themselves.[41]

Comparing readers with poachers or hunters presents the relationship between producers and consumers as an ongoing struggle for control over texts and the monitoring of their meanings. De Certeau talks about 'the scriptural economy', which is controlled by the producers of texts and interpreters employed by institutions, and which strives for the regulation of production and distribution of meanings. He portrays popular readings as a group of 'advances and retreats, tactics and games played with the text'. Popular readings are kinds of cultural bricolage, through which readers break the text into pieces and then reassemble it in the way it best suits their own purposes, to produce sense out of their own experiences.[42] Moreover, these readings are not a matter of just dismantling and reassembling individual texts; nomadic readers can also build connections between texts and thus construct new meanings.[43]

With reference to Michel de Certeau's views, the Australian Meaghan Morris speaks about popular culture not as a group of texts, a marketing category, a reflection of social status or even as a battlefield, but as *a course of operation and action*. According to Morris, reading is not writing or rewriting but travelling through a system pushed along by oneself, be it a text, a street, a mall or a state celebration. As such, reading borrows something from what it meets, but does not produce its own stable 'place'.[44]

Fans have no immediate access to the sphere of textual production. From this point of view, their nomadism manifests the urge to be in motion, an inability to conquer a place of their own and to settle.[45] On the other hand, fans' ability to use the texts they read for their own purposes also manifests a certain kind of autonomy. Fans are capable of exploiting the fact that texts can never predetermine the readings they are objects of. However, this does not mean that fans' readings are automatically contradictory to the meanings intended by the producers. The selection of the texts that are objects of fandom from the infinite abundance of texts available already contains an identification to a certain extent with the world of the texts. The chosen texts must be at least to some degree linked with the already existing social commitments and cultural interests of fans. In similar fashion, the meanings produced by fans must have some relation to the read text.[46]

'Fandom' is usually linked with cultural forms which in the dominant social hierarchy are sneered at – pop music, romantic readers, comic strips, Hollywood stars and other such items. Fans are discernible from other consumers of culture by the fact that they form communities where the special meanings they produce out of cultural texts are, so to speak, in circulation. John Fiske has called this reciprocal recycling of meanings between fans 'the shadow economy of culture'.[47]

Apt as Fiske's notion of a shadow economy is, we can nevertheless ask: do fans actually differ so very much from other readers in producing new meanings from the texts produced by others? After all, are not all of the above-mentioned features associated with fans' ways of reading – perhaps not counting the intensity of commitment – and do they not also apply to those readers that cannot be called fans? Moreover, do they not also apply to the producers of texts?

There may be some grounds for this juxtaposition that may at first glance appear surprising. Provided that fans are poachers and hunters, are not writers those very things as well? What else is this book, for instance, than a new entity put together out of ideas and excerpts gathered from here and there, thus gaining new meanings? Writers' words do not appear as if from nowhere, but from the 'mouths of others'. As Mikhail Bakhtin reminds us:

> The word in language is half someone else's. It becomes 'one's own' only when the speaker populates it with his [sic] own intention, his own accent, when he appropriates the word, adapting it to his own semantic and expressive intention.[48]

Even when readers fill the words of language with their own tones of voice, the meanings thus created are temporary and transient. They are made in motion as readers transfer in their nomadic fashion from one place and context to another.[49]

Texts are largely read for the reason that they provide their readers with pleasure and empowerment. Noting this, though, does not take one very far, since the meanings and pleasure can vary greatly even in respect of one and the same text. Ien Ang, who in the 1980s studied Dutch viewers of the then-popular TV series *Dallas*, met Marxist *Dallas* enthusiasts who watched it as a splendid critique of capitalism, but also others who experienced pleasure in identifying with the praise of Americanism and the modern lifestyle.[50] Hence it could be thought that this kind of ambiguity to a certain degree is a precondition for popularity of texts.[51]

The identity of texts

The attempts of producers of texts to regulate texts' heteroglottic nature are ultimately doomed to failure. Producers can never control in advance how their texts are going to be read. Texts themselves do not contain elements that would warrant specific predetermined reading of them. Hence, Stuart Hall has remarked that

> Almost *all* cultural forms will be contradictory in this sense, composed of antagonistic and unstable elements. The meaning of a cultural form and its place or position in the cultural field is *not* inscribed inside its form. Nor is its position fixed once and forever. . . . The meaning of a cultural symbol is given in part by the social field into which it is incorporated, the practices with which it articulates and is made to resonate. What matters is *not* the intrinsic or historically fixed objects of culture, but the state of play in cultural relations.[52]

Hall uses the concepts of 'a field', 'a practice' and 'a play'. All of them link the formation of meanings to the struggle people wage to form their own identification and identities. Texts with which we have an active relationship tell us about where, how and with what intensity we can cling to the world and find a possible nest for our identities.[53]

Hence people not only build meanings into texts but also build meanings for their lives from texts by defining what is important to them, among other things. Texts may become instruments with which they contribute to the world, mould their identities, become discernible from 'others'. However, there is no need for a great gap to exist between the social and the textual. On the contrary, producing meanings from texts and producing meanings from social life closely resemble each other. John Fiske has noted that social experiences are like texts: they can be signified only by social subjects applying their discursive competence in them. Fiske compares daily life with intertextuality: it is an enormous potential of intertwined elements which can be activated and mobilized in uncountable ways. 'Making sense of social experience is an almost identical process to making sense of a text,' Fiske writes.[54]

The identities of readers

Each one of us has several simultaneous identities as readers. Different texts can activate different readers in us. Moreover, as subjects we are discursive constructions full of contradictions and gaps. As texts and readers meet, the question is not of two complete and uniform beings taking the measure of one another, but of an encounter between two incomplete and contradictory parties, in which the polysemy of meanings and the multiplicity of readings in part arises expressly from these deficiencies and contradictions.[55]

However, the deficiencies and inconsistencies of readers do not mean that they are doomed to remain prisoners of texts. TV viewers are not often considered critical readers. They are thought to either accept or reject what they see, but have not usually been studied as beings who use their own senses. Contrary to these views, however, viewers are quite capable of critically evaluating what they see on a relatively coherent basis as well as to see the 'constructed' nature of the programmes.[56] When Tamar Liebes and Elihu Katz studied the viewers of *Dallas* in different cultures (Russian, American, Israeli, Arabian and Moroccan), they perceived that the viewers reacted to what they saw in two different ways, either referentially or critically. In referential readings, the viewers perceived the characters of the series as if they were real people, and related them to the real people in their living environments; whereas in critical readings, the series was watched as a fictional construction with its own aesthetic rules.[57]

Liebes and Katz divide the critical readings further into semantic and syntactic readings. According to them, in semantic readings, attention was particularly paid to such things as the themes of the programme and the possible didactic intentions of the makers. The makers were often suspected of gimmickry by semantic readers and the archetypes behind the characters were recognized, or the extent to which the series reflected reality was debated. Syntactic readings, on the other hand, connected to the viewers' awareness of the genre's conventions, the commercial pressure upon the production of the series and the contemplation of the viewers' own reactions.[58]

Naturally, referential and syntactic critical readings produce different meanings. The former make the viewers attach themselves more intensely to the programme, whereas the latter make them more detached from it. All in all, the study by Liebes and Katz demonstrates that the audiences of popular culture are quite conscious of the preconditions of the production of the texts they read, as well as the basic features of the genres they represent.

Conjunctural study of texts

Earlier I outlined the reader-oriented approach to the study of texts with the aid of the following questions: 'What kinds of meanings do people produce from this text (or in this text) in this historical time and place, and why?' Or: 'What effects does this text have in the life practices of people?' The point of departure in these questions is that though there are not *predetermined* meanings, there are always *real* meanings. The meaning and effects of certain texts – that is, their identity – are never guaranteed causally, from their origin. Yet texts have meanings and effects – and, therefore, identities. In this conception of text, which Lawrence Grossberg called 'conjuncturalistic', post-structuralism is followed in the sense that it emphasizes differences and the deconstruction of identities (by denying essentiality and necessity of identity). Simultaneously, however, conjuncturalism attempts to critically study the historical formation of a certain identity.

The meaning of texts is bound to the given conjuncture. Etymologically, 'conjuncture' is literally 'joining together'; it springs from the Latin words *con* 'together', and *iungo*, to join. As 'connection', it is also close to the concept of 'articulation'.

Here it is useful to recall the double meaning of the concept 'articulation'. On the one hand, it signifies speaking, pronouncing, expressing one's thought clearly. (As such, articulation is close to the concept of 'discourse' in its traditional meaning.) On the other hand, articulation also signifies joining together and uniting by joints. Hence, articulation makes two or more elementary pieces a unity.[59] A well-known example of articulation is the stereotype of the 'dumb blonde', which still is in cultural circulation. Even though hair colour and intelligence have little to do with each other, they have been articulated, joined together, in blonde jokes. However, articulation can at any time be dismantled or rearticulated. Hence, in Norway, prior to the EU referendum, a women's group 'Blondes Against the EU' was created.

This example shows how articulation knows no limits. Just about anything can be articulated with anything else, and thus new meanings can be formed. When, for instance, the word 'world' is linked to the word 'literature', an articulation is created in its Goethean meaning which refers to 'time after time valuable European art of literature.' With respect to 'world', this 'world literature' is quite limited and in fact anything but 'worldly'. When 'world' is articulated with 'music', the 'world music' that is created explodes all aspirations of European cultural centres and raises the infinite spectrum of marginal groups, from Cameroonian Pygmy music via Bulgarian women singers to the Sami Wimme abreast with the canons of classical music, jazz and nowadays even rock 'n' roll. Hence, the word 'world' has two rather opposite meanings according to whether it is articulated with 'literature' or 'music'.

Articulation theory denies texts' essential identity without giving up the notion that texts can have functioning identities. In different conjunctures, texts can be articulated in different ways. They can be articulated with different meanings, experiences, interests and identities. So texts are, besides being the objects of ongoing struggles and articulations, also fields of battle and articulation.

Conjuncturalism is interested in the 'object side' from the viewpoint of how 'certain texts, practices and identities always seem as if already interpreted, how their politics seems already predetermined'.[61] Hence, in the case of 'the dumb blonde' a conjuncturalist is interested in how the articulation has come to be part of cultural common sense. However, conjuncturalism is also interested in the 'subject side', of how people always struggle against pre-constructed articulations looking for a way out, for leeway to mould texts and practices to suit their own lives. Hence, a conjuncturalist is also interested in how 'blondeism' can be turned into a positive quality, as it is when linked to resisting the EU.

From the point of view of articulation theory, readers have an important role in the formation of meanings. But how do readers produce meanings from the raw materials offered by texts and contexts? This is the topic of the last chapter of this book.

Notes

1. Fiske 1989b, 56.
2. The term is from Stuart Hall. See Hall 1996a, 1.
3. Ibid.
4. Fornäs 1995, 225.
5. Ibid., 229.
6. Hall 1996a, 4.
7. Silverman 1983, 3.
8. Grossberg 1992b.
9. Cf. Radway 1988, 366.
10. Hobson 1982, 112.
11. Radway 1984b, 68.
12. Grossberg 1992a, 45.
13. Silverstone 1994, 153–4.
14. Fiske 1987, 62.
15. Morley 1980b, 171–2.
16. Radway 1984a, 11.
17. Fiske 1989b, 57.
18. Ang 1996, 67.
19. See Long 1994.
20. From this point of view, the way to contextualize watching TV (of which see, e.g., Silverstone 1994) seen in more current TV studies seems like impoverishing the object. Taking the nuclear family as the point of departure is also problematic because increasingly few TV watchers live in a nuclear family. For instance, in Great Britain at the beginning of the 1990s, single parent families formed more than one quarter of all households, and in several cities nearly half of all households consisted of a single person (Hobsbawm 1995, 332).
21. Ellis 1992, 162.
22. Radway 1984a, 8.
23. Grossberg 1992b.
24. Herta Herzog, who studied listeners of radio's daily series as early as the beginning of the 1940s, obtained results leaning in this direction. According to Herzog, the series offered their listeners the opportunity to unload the tensions in their emotional lives and for daydreaming, as well as a large amount of advice and guidance. Out of the 2,500 listeners, 41 per cent declared that they received help in their everyday problems from the series (Herzog 1954).
25. See, for example, Lull 1990, 31.

26. See Tulloch 1990, 20–1.
27. See Fiske 1992, 37–8.
28. See Hawkes 1977, 51.
29. Jenkins 1992, 2.
30. Althusser 1971, 161.
31. Ibid., 162.
32. Ibid., 163.
33. Eagleton 1996a, 149.
34. Eagleton 1996a, 147.
35. Eagleton 1996a, 148.
36. See Morley 1980a, 14.
37. See Hall and Jefferson 1976, 14.
38. On subcultures as formers of meanings, see Hebdige 1979.
39. *Oxford Latin Dictionary*, see 'fanaticus', and the *Oxford English Dictionary*, see 'fanatic'. See also Jenkins 1992, 12.
40. See Jenkins 1992, 12.
41. Certeau 1984, 17.
42. Ibid., 175.
43. Ibid., 174.
44. Morris 1990, 30.
45. See Budd et al. 1990, 176.
46. See Jenkins 1992, 34.
47. See Fiske 1992, 30.
48. Bakhtin 1981, 293.
49. See Jenkins 1992, 44.
50. See Ang 1985.
51. Fiske 1989a, 31.
52. Hall 1981, 235.
53. See Grossberg 1992b, 42.
54. Fiske 1989b, 58–9.
55. Fiske 1987, 67.
56. See Livingstone and Lunt 1994, 71.
57. Liebes and Katz 1990, 100.
58. Ibid., 116.
59. Hall 1996b, 141.

CHAPTER 8

THE WORLD OF ARTICULATIONS

This book is nearing its end, but – as Brezhnev's brows were in relation to Stalin's moustache – on a new, higher level. I started this book off with the everyday. To end it, we return to the same everyday, but hopefully equipped with analytical tools with which we can grasp how the meanings of the world are formed.

In this book, I have attempted to show how complex the matters of the formation and forming of meanings are. A great number of factors participate in and contribute to the formation of meanings, the role and effects of which cannot be known in advance. The identities of texts, contexts and readers are not predetermined – and neither are meanings which are created as they are articulated with one another.

Due to their worldliness, producing and reading texts are infinitely multiple activities. All this in turn complicates the tasks of study: if meanings are not solid and distinct units but temporary arrangements of complex relationships, the question in the study of meanings cannot be of solidifying the passing but of examining unstable situations, in which – except for the temporal – it is not possible to discern the borders and units they supposedly produce except for analytical purposes. There are no solidified beings, there is only an uncountable amount of relationships which are in the 'process of their becoming'.

The world of meanings does not consist of clear objects but of hybrids which perpetually alter their form.[1] In this respect, meanings are not so much completed products as intermittent production determined by multiple factors. Even though we could temporarily stabilize certain meanings, they are by no means final but have their own meanings and effects, which in turn have their own effects and meanings and so on for ever.

Thus, the central concepts of the book – 'text', 'context', 'reader' and 'meaning' – are ultimately indefinable categories. It is impossible to list in advance what possible meanings and qualities each category has in the various specific situations in which people produce meanings.[2]

In order to get a grasp of the actual formation of meanings, we must develop a model of analysis which goes beyond the horizon of mere text and also takes into account the contextual and reader-related matters that participate in the formation of meanings. In this type of analysis, one must move as necessary on all of the three levels of texts, contexts and readers, and exploit the methodology of the poetics of text and the hermeneutics of context, as well as studying reading and readers. Here the point of departure is the notion that texts working as raw material of meanings gain actual meanings as they encounter contexts and readers. The varying position of texts, contexts and readers in cultural time and space becomes an essential factor with respect to what meanings are concocted when they meet. Actual meanings, for their part, are studied in their singularity and positivity. Meanings in this respect are both practices and outcomes of practices.

To illustrate this complex entity I have constructed the following graph. To be on the safe side let it be said that I do not attempt to claim that it is possible to clearly discern three separate aspects in real processes of the formation of meanings. In actual reading situations, all matters separated from each other in the graph for the purpose of analysis have an intertwined impact on one another. Nevertheless, the reading situations can be schematically presented in the following way:

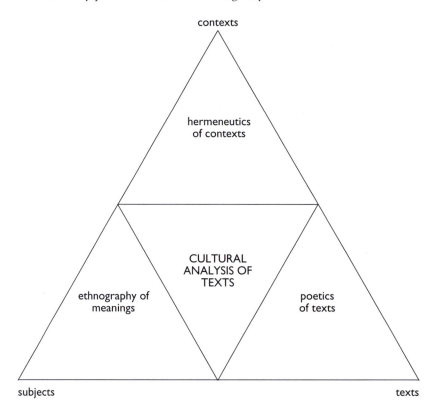

The graph is inevitably roughly sketched. It does not even attempt to be a comprehensive description of the formation of meanings, but instead sets out a certain approach. Its aim is to raise questions, to chart a certain area. I do not propose that the model be used as such, but think that it may function as a tool for *radical contextualism*, which itself is further developed during the research work.

Examining the chart, the reader may wonder why I have ignored the context of production and the producer. There are contextual reasons for my decision – first and foremost the fact that there is markedly more written material available on the matters in question than there is on contexts of reading and readers. Yet, in the background of this exclusion there also lurks the conviction that reception is a much more central and complex activity than often imagined. Both the producers of texts and their readers are active agents and formers of textual meanings. The production of signifying artefacts is still important, but the nucleus of signification ultimately lies in the formation of meanings in reading.[3]

Articulation

Valentin Voloshinov characterizes the birth of meanings in the following way:

> Meaning does not reside in the word or in the soul of the speaker or in the soul of the listener. Meaning is the effect of interaction between speaker and listener produced via the material of a particular sound complex. It is like an electric spark that occurs only when two different terminals are hooked together. Those who . . . in attemping to define the meaning of a word, approach its lower, stable, self-identical limit, want, in effect, to turn on a light bulb after having switched off the current. Only the current of verbal intercourse endows a word with the light of a meaning.[4]

Meaning is a spark that is kindled in the interaction between the producer of the text and its reader (Voloshinov's speaker and listener). In this interaction there are other parties present besides its producer and reader. If one wants to get a grip on the formation of meanings, tools must be developed with which to examine how each of the parties in each given case participates in the process of the formation of meanings. In this respect, the concept of articulation is useful in seeking for the connection of each level to the others in the formation of meanings (the levels, naturally, can only be separated from each other analytically, and therefore do not form 'levels' in the real world). From the viewpoint of the formation of meanings, the theory of articulation directs us to ask how the levels produced for analytical purposes articulate with each other as certain readers read certain texts in certain contexts.

Hence, articulation can be defined as by Lawrence Grossberg as follows:

> Articulation is the production of identity on top of difference, of unities out of fragments, of structures across practices. Articulation links this practice to that effect, this text to that meaning, this meaning to that reality, this experience to those politics. And these links are themselves articulated into larger structures, etc.[5]

And further:

> Articulation offers a theory of contexts. It dictates that one can only deal with, and from within, specific contexts, for it is only there that practices have

specific effects, that identities and relations exist. Understanding a practice involves theoretically and historically (re)constructing this context.[6]

Hence we could think that the concept of 'articulation' provides us with tools to study the formation of meanings simultaneously in their individuality and their generality. Articulation is not some solidified mass of relationships or connections, but consists of processual, shape-taking connections.[7] From the viewpoint of the theory of articulation, texts articulate with contexts and the articulated texts and contexts further articulate with subjects and cultural practices. The formation of meanings, for its part, can be traced, with regard to its central parts, expressly from these articulations. Hence, articulation can be conceived as recontextualizing, as loosening the relationship between text and its previous context (at times even as detaching the text totally from its previous context) and bringing new contextual elements along, or even linking the text totally with a new context.

As such, the study of the formation of meanings seeks out the terrain in between essentialism ('texts necessarily have certain meanings') and anti-essentialism ('texts can mean just about anything'). It aims at both the deconstructing of textual meaning (the poetics of text) and its reconstructing (the hermeneutics of context), as well as linking it with its broader connections (the study of readers and their cultural practices). In this work one must be aware of the fact that the designated separations are abstractions, that the borders between these three framings of the question are drawn in sand, that they really are analytical separations with which something, which in real cultural practice is actualized as one and the same process, is sorted into different matters.

An essential part of this study method is to question the conception that the participants in the formation of meanings (text, context, readers' practices) are individual or identical entities, which exist before they enter the processes of the formation of meanings. They exist only as part of the process of the formation of meanings – and even then only for a fleeting moment.

All in all, it is meanings that are subjected to study in their singularity and positivity. The formation of meanings is approached by constructing contexts of meanings, by describing the complex articulations that give meanings their singular identity.

Radical contextuality

There is a certain dilemma contained in the notion of the radical contextuality of meanings: it threatens to create a position for researchers that is impossible in practice. Provided that 'every context is a piece of other contexts', as Lawrence Grossberg says, contextuality expands

THE WORLD OF ARTICULATION **159**

boundlessly.[8] There is reason to ask if a researcher must henceforth be present everywhere at once in some mystical way. Must s/he not continuously hunt for an ever-expanding number of specific realities determined contextually? Researchers cannot be present simultaneously everywhere. They must always speak and write from a certain position. Stuart Hall describes this in an interesting way:

> It may be true that the self is always, in a sense, a fiction, just as the kinds of 'closures' which are required to create communities of identification – nation, ethnic group, families, sexualities, etc. – are arbitrary closures . . . I believe it is an immensely important gain when one recognizes that all identity is constructed across difference and begins to live with the politics of difference. But doesn't the acceptance of the fictional or narrative status of identity in relation to the world also require as a necessity, its opposite – the moment of arbitrary closure? . . . Potentially, discourse is endless: the infinite semiosis of meaning. But to say anything at all in particular, you do have to stop talking. Of course, every full stop is provisional. The next sentence will take nearly all of it back. So what is this 'ending'? It's a kind of a stake, a kind of wager. It says, 'I need to say something, something, just now.' It is not forever, not universally true. It is not underpinned by any infinite guarantees. But just now, this is what I mean; this is who I am.[9]

The artificial closure of Hall's is close to the notion of positional subject developed within the circles of feminism.[10] According to the notion of arbitrary closure, identities are necessarily fictional, but there is also the necessary fiction of arbitrary closure which does not equal final closure but which in any case makes identity possible.

However, we should bear in mind that even the interpretations of researchers equipped with the three above-mentioned analytical tools are only interpretations. They do not reconstruct some 'ultimate' meanings, but construct certain real meanings. As readers, researchers too are positioned in the fields of their research, they are part of the process of the formation of meanings. Hence, a central part of the research and its claims is the position of researchers, for instance their own interests of knowledge.

The study of meanings does not reach its objects by standing outside of the research field. In order to perceive multidimensional objects, several approaches from the research field itself are demanded. David Morley writes:

> The world of everyday life is not one which can be satisfactorily viewed through a single pair of spectacles, or from a single position. It requires varieties of distance, magnification and position.[11]

A subject that is located in the field s/he studies can also better see how his/her own locatedness affects how the objects studied appear for him/her. It is not a question of one, final perspective but of a moving, feeling researcher. A moving and feeling subject can unveil more sides of his/her object than can one who merely stares at his/her object from a single vantage point. The research object no longer appears final, but as something else which I call 'a coyote' in Donna Haraway's words.[12]

> The coyote, which appears in the mythology of the Hopi and Navajo people of America, personifies the notion of the world being perpetually problematic, never completed, capable of always meaning something other than what we conceived it could mean. In the stories of the Hopi and the Navajo, the coyote is never an immutable and stable object, but a trickster and a conniver capable of appearing now as a god, then as a fool.

To match this 'coyote' a nomadic researcher is needed whose knowledge is local and who critically analyses his/her own construction, who in short as a researcher is a participant in the reality s/he studies. Being a participant signifies the realization of the notion that cultural products are not in fact 'objects' at all in the sense of passive objects, obtaining meanings only as the researchers appear on the site; instead the cultural products subjected to research would be agents, active subjects, which at all times influence, for instance, who the researchers themselves are. So the research is not a question of mimesis, imitating the objects, but always of constructing and reconstructing reality from some position and point of view.

The creativity of the everyday

In reading and writing the question is at all times of our being in the world, the subjectivity of each one of us. Often enough reading and writing reinforce the reader's and writer's already existing concept of their own identity. At times, however, it can happen that a reader does not experience him/herself as the same self who opened a book or turned on a TV set to watch a certain TV programme, or went to the movies. A new world has unfolded, a new vocabulary has introduced itself.

Along with romanticism, the myth of the exceptional individual became fashionable – those geniuses who, in some way unfathomable to us mortals, managed to create the new from the bottomless riches in the depths of their souls. The myth is popular even today. It is based on dichotomy, in which the genius and creativity of exceptional individuals is one pole, the opposite of which is the routine unindividual everyday of us mortals. In the fashion of other equivalent dichotomies, this also has no basis – and, moreover, is harmful. That is, it prohibits us from seeing the vast extent to which our everyday life contains elements of creativity. Daily life, with its human interaction and events, has its own dramaturgy and poetics.[13] Without the creativity of the everyday there would be no linguistic and textual creation of the new.

I began the study of the formation of meanings from language seen as practical consciousness which is born in interaction with other people.

According to the definition I presented, language and its meanings are seizing reality, people's practical consciousness, dynamic and articulated *presence* in the world. Through this, language is a central part of the symbolic creativity of the everyday. Symbolic work and creativity also produce new meanings and identities, and therefore have important empowering potentials.[14]

As I have proceeded, I have attempted to show what creativity-demanding exertion an activity as common as reading requires. All textual interaction in fact contains an abundance of human creativity. Not even the simplest note can be read without the activation of a great amount of knowledge and skills, which are needed in the formation of meanings.

Interaction with texts means opening oneself up to others, predisposing oneself to the influence of others, the first step in communication, that is, community. At best, texts take readers somewhere they have not been to before, somewhere that perhaps has not existed before as a place to be in. As the discovery of the new, reading is simultaneously a reader's submergence into him/herself, and expansion far beyond his/her own boundaries. Perhaps it is precisely this multidimensional quality of reading that it is so hard to describe except through the aid of different metaphors. One thing is certain regarding reading, though: it is a physical and affective activity. For myself, a sign of finding the new is the sensation of tremors going down my spine as I finish a book, a movie or another kind of text. My body is actively participating in the formation of meanings.

When textual interaction is at its best, it signifies not only the expansion of the pleasure of writers and readers, but also their ability to act. As the writer of this book there is no way for me to know all the ways that it is read, and all the contexts in which it is articulated. The book is similar to the ball tossed up in the air to which Salman Rushdie compares an exile. If this book provides its readers with the tools to cast new kinds of amazed gazes at the world of meanings, it has more than fulfilled the task its writer has set it. For the world of meanings is also, and above all, the world of change. The central dimension of the theory of articulation is to offer the tools for altering the world of meanings, for rearticulating it.

Yet, there are no ultimate guarantees in the world of meanings. As an unexpected process it is described by Peter Høeg, who will have the last word:

> As soon as we lay eyes on the world it starts to change. And we with it. Viewing reality doesn't mean making sense of a setup. It means surrendering oneself and triggering an unfathomable transformation.[15]

Notes

1. See, for example, Baker 1994, 183–6.
2. See, on television, Ang 1996, 70.
3. See also Fornäs 1995, 191.
4. Voloshinov 1971, 102–3.
5. Grossberg 1992a, 54.
6. Ibid., 56. In the light of this and the previous quotation, it is also possible to perceive that 'articulation' is retheorizing what earlier in cultural studies was examined through the concept of 'determination'. On 'determination', see Williams 1977, 100–6; on relationships between 'articulation' and 'determination' see Slack 1996, 118–21.
7. See Slack 1996, 114.
8. Grossberg 1992a, 58.
9. Hall 1988b.
10. See, for example, Braidotti 1991 and Haraway 1991.
11. Morley 1992, 184.
12. See Haraway 1991.
13. Willis 1990, 22.
14. Ibid.
15. Hoeg 1997, 335.

Althusser, Louis (1971) *Lenin and Philosophy*. Translated by Ben Brewster. London: New Left Books.

Ang, Ien (1985) *Watching Dallas. Soap Opera and Melodramatic Imagination*. London: Methuen.

Ang, Ien (1996) *Living Room Wars. Rethinking Media Audiences for a Postmodern World*. London: Routledge.

Austen, Jane (1990) *Pride and Prejudice* (1813). Edited by James Kinsley. Oxford: Oxford University Press.

Austin, J.L. (1975) *How to Do Things with Words* (1962), 2nd edition. Cambridge, MA: Harvard University Press.

Baker, Houston A. Jr (1994) 'Beyond Artifacts: Cultural Studies and the New Hybridity of Rap' in Margaret J.M. Ezell and Katherine O'Brien O'Keefe (eds) *Cultural Artifacts and the Production of Meaning*. Ann Arbor: The University of Michigan Press.

Bakhtin, M.M. (1981) *The Dialogic Imagination. Four Essays*. Edited by Michael Holquist. Translated by Caryl Emerson and Michael Holquist. Austin: University of Texas Press.

Baldick, Chris (1990) *The Concise Oxford Dictionary of Literary Terms*. Oxford: Oxford University Press.

Balzac, Honoré de (1970) *A Harlot High and Low*. Translated by Rayner Heffenstahl. Harmondsworth: Penguin.

Barthes, Roland (1974) *S/Z*. Translated by Richard Miller. London: Jonathan Cape.

Barthes, Roland (1981) 'Theory of Text', in Robert M. Young (ed.) *Untying the Text. A Post-structuralist Reader*. London: Routledge & Kegan Paul.

Barthes, Roland (1986a) 'The Death of the Author' (1968), in Roland Barthes (1986) *The Rustle of Language*. Translated by Richard Howard. Oxford: Basil Blackwell.

Barthes, Roland (1986b) 'From Work to Text' (1971), in Roland Barthes (1986) *The Rustle of Language*. Translated by Richard Howard. Oxford: Basil Blackwell.

Barthes, Roland (1988) 'Introduction to the Structural Analysis of Narratives', in *The Semiotic Challenge*. Translated by Richard Howard. Oxford: Basil Blackwell.

Barton, David (1994) *Literacy. An Introduction to the Ecology of Written Language*. Oxford: Basil Blackwell.

Barwise, Patrick and Hammond, Kathy (1998) *Media*. London: Phoenix.

Baynham, Mike (1995) *Literacy Practices: Investigating Literacy in Social Contexts*. London: Longman.

Belsey, Catherine (1980) *Critical Practice*. London: Routledge.

Bennett, Tony (1979) *Formalism and Marxism*. London: Methuen.

Bennett, Tony (1982) 'Text and History', in Peter Widdowson (ed.) *Re-reading English*. London: Methuen.

Bennett, Tony (1983) 'Text, Readers, Reading Formations', *Literature and History*, 9 (2).

Bennett, Tony (1984) 'The Text in Question', *Southern Review*, 17 (July).

Bennett, Tony (1987) 'Texts in History', in Derek Attridge, Geoff Bennington and Robert Young (eds) *Post-structuralism and the Question of History*. Cambridge: Cambridge University Press.

Bennett, Tony (1990) *Outside Literature*. London: Routledge.

Bennett, Tony and Woollacott, Janet (1987) *Bond and Beyond*. Houndmills: Macmillan.

Berger, Arthur Asa (1995) *Cultural Criticism. A Primer of Key Concepts*. Thousand Oaks, CA: Sage.

Berger, Peter L. and Luckmann, Thomas (1981) *The Social Construction of Reality: a Treatise in the Sociology of Knowledge* (1971). Harmondsworth: Penguin.

Bordwell, David (1989) *Making Meaning. Inference and Rhetoric in the Interpretation of Cinema*. Cambridge, MA: Harvard University Press.

Braidotti, Rosi (1991) *Patterns of Dissonance. A Study of Women in Contemporary Philosophy*. Cambridge: Polity Press.

Branigan, Edward (1992) *Narrative Comprehension and Film*. London: Routledge.

Budd, Mike, Entman, Robert M. and Steinman, Clay (1990) 'The Affirmative Character of US Cultural Studies', *Critical Studies in Mass Communication 7*.

Burke, Peter (1993) *The Art of Conversation*. Cambridge: Polity Press.

Carroll, Lewis (1994) *Alice's Adventures in Wonderland* (1865). London: Puffin Books.

Certeau, Michel de (1984) *The Practice of Everyday Life*. Berkeley: University of California Press.

Chambers, Ross (1979) *Meaning and Meaningfulness. Studies in the Analysis and Interpretation of Texts*. Lexington: French Forum Publishers.

Chambers, Ross (1984) *Story and Situation: Narrative Seduction and the Power of Fiction*. Manchester: Manchester University Press.

Cohan, Steven and Shires, Linda M. (1988) *Telling Stories. A Theoretical Analysis of Narrative Fiction*. New York: Routledge.

Cook, Guy (1992) *The Discourse of Advertising*. London: Routledge.

Couturier, Maurice (1991) *Textual Communication. A Print-based Theory of the Novel*. London: Routledge.

Crane, Diana (1992) *The Production of Culture. Media and the Urban Arts*. Newbury Park, CA: Sage.

Culler, Jonathan (1975) *Structuralist Poetics. Structuralism, Linguistics and the Study of Literature*. London: Routledge & Kegan Paul.

Culler, Jonathan (1980) 'Prolegomena to a Theory of Reading', in Susan R. Suleiman and Inge Crosman (eds) *The Reader in the Text. Essays on Audience and Interpretation*. Princeton, NJ: Princeton University Press.

Culler, Jonathan (1990) *Ferdinand de Saussure* (1976). London: Fontana Press.

Dick, Philip K. (1993) *Do Androids Dream of Electric Sheep?* (1968) (filmed as *Blade Runner*) 1982, London: HarperCollins.

Docherty, Thomas (1987) *On Modern Authority*. Brighton: Harvester Press.

Duby, Georges and Braunstein, Philippe (1988) 'The Emergence of the Individual', in Georges Duby (ed.) *A History of Private Life. II: Revelations of the Medieval World*. Cambridge, MA: The Belknap Press of Harvard University Press.

Durant, Alan and Fabb, Nigel (1990) *Literary Studies in Action*. London: Routledge.

Dyer, Richard (1993) *The Matter of Images. Essays on Representations*. London: Routledge.

Eagleton, Terry (1991) *Ideology. An Introduction*. London: Verso.

Eagleton, Terry (1992) 'Crisis in Contemporary Culture', *New Left Review*, 196.

Eagleton, Terry (1996a) *Literary Theory. An Introduction*, 2nd edition. Oxford: Blackwell.

Eagleton, Terry (1996b) *The Illusions of Postmodernism*. Oxford: Blackwell.

Easthope, Antony (1988) 'Same Text, Different Readings: Shakespeare's Sonnet 94', in Colin MacCabe (ed.) *Futures for English*. Manchester: Manchester University Press.

Ellis, John (1992) *Visible Fictions. Cinema: Television: Video*, revised edition. London: Routledge.

Fairclough, Norman (1989) *Language and Power*. London: Longman.

Fiske, John (1987) *Television Culture*. London: Routledge.

Fiske, John (1989a) 'Popular Television and Commercial Culture: Beyond Political Economy', in Gary Burns and Robert J. Thompson (eds) *Television Studies. Textual Analysis*. New York: Praeger.

Fiske, John (1989b) 'Moments of Television: Neither the Text nor the Audience', in Ellen Seiter, Hans Borchers, Gabriele Kreutzner and Eva-Maria Warth (eds) *Remote Control. Television, Audiences, and Cultural Power*. London: Routledge.

Fiske, John (1992) 'The Cultural Economy of Fandom', in Lisa A. Lewis (ed.) *The Adoring Audience. Fan Culture and Popular Media*. London: Routledge.

Fornäs, Johan (1995) *Cultural Theory and Late Modernity*. London: Sage.

Foucault, Michel (1972) *The Archaeology of Knowledge*. Translated by A.M. Sheridan Smith. London: Routledge.

Foucault, Michel (1979) 'What Is an Author?' in José V. Harari (ed.) *Textual Strategies. Perspectives in Post-Structuralist Criticism*. Ithaca, NY: Cornell University Press.

Fowler, H.W. and Fowler, F.G. (eds) (1956) *The Concise Oxford English Dictionary of Current English*. Fourth edition (revised by E. McIntosh) Oxford: Oxford Unversity Press.

Fowler, Roger (1996) *Linguistic Criticism*, 2nd edition. Oxford: Oxford University Press.

Frow, John (1990) 'Intertextuality and Ontology', in Michael Worton and Judith Still (eds) *Intertextuality. Theories and Practices*. Manchester: Manchester University Press.

Gaur, Albertine (1992) *A History of Writing*, revised edition. London: The British Library.

George, Susan (1992) *The Debt Boomerang*. London: Pluto Press.

Goody, Jack (1981) 'Alphabets and Writing', in Raymond Williams (ed.) *Contact: Human Communication and its History*. London: Thames & Hudson.

Graddol, David (1994) 'What Is a Text?' In David Graddol and Oliver Boyd-Barrett (eds) *Media Texts: Authors and Readers*. Clevedon: Multilingual Matters Ltd in association with Open University Press.

Grillo, R.D. (1989) *Dominant Languages. Language and Hierarchy in Britain and France*. Cambridge: Cambridge University Press.

Grossberg, Lawrence (1988) 'Putting the Pop Back into Postmodernism', in Andrew Ross (ed.) *Universal Abandon? The Politics of Postmodernism*. Minneapolis: University of Minnesota Press.

Grossberg, Lawrence (1992a) *We Gotta Get Out of This Place. Popular Conservatism and Postmodern Culture*. New York: Routledge.

Grossberg, Lawrence (1992b) 'Is There a Fan in the House?: The Affective Sensibility of Fandom', in Lisa A. Lewis (ed.) *The Adoring Audience. Fan Culture and Popular Media*. London: Routledge.

Hall, Stuart (1980) 'Cultural Studies: Two Paradigms', *Media, Culture and Society* 1/1980.

Hall, Stuart (1981) 'Notes on Deconstructing "the Popular"', in Raphael Samuel (ed.) *People's History and Socialist Theory*. London: Routledge & Kegan Paul.

Hall, Stuart (1982) 'The Rediscovery of "Ideology": Return of the Repressed in Media Studies', in Michael Gurevitch, Tony Bennett, James Curran and Janet Woollacott (eds) *Culture, Society and the Media*. London: Methuen.

Hall, Stuart (1984) 'The Narrative Construction of Reality', *Southern Review*, 17 (March).

Hall, Stuart (1988a) 'The Toad in the Garden: Thatcherism among the Theorists', in Cary Nelson and Lawrence Grossberg (eds) *Marxism and the Interpretation of Culture*. Houndmills: Macmillan.

Hall, Stuart (1988b) 'Minimal Selves', in *Identity* (ICA Document 6). London: ICA.

Hall, Stuart (1992a) 'The West and the Rest: Discourse and Power', in Stuart Hall and Bram Gieben (eds) *Formations of Modernity*. Cambridge: Polity Press.

Hall, Stuart (1992b) 'The Question of Cultural Identity', in Stuart Hall, David Held and Tony McGrew (eds) *Modernity and Its Futures*. Cambridge: Polity Press.

Hall, Stuart (1994) 'Reflections upon the Encoding/Decoding Model: An Interview with Stuart Hall', in Jon Cruz and Justin Lewis (eds) *Weaving, Reading, Listening. Audiences and Cultural Reception*. Boulder, CO: Westview Press.

Hall, Stuart (1996a) 'Who Needs Identity?' In Stuart Hall and Paul du Gay (eds) *Questions of Cultural Identity*. London: Sage.

Hall, Stuart (1996b) 'On Postmodernism and Articulation', in David Morley and Kuan-Hsing Chen (eds) *Stuart Hall: Critical Dialogues in Cultural Studies*. London: Routledge.

Hall, Stuart and Jefferson, Tony (eds) (1976) *Resistance through Rituals: Youth Subcultures in Postwar-Britain*. London: Hutchinson.

Halliday, M.A.K. (1978) *Language as Social Semiotic. The Social Interpretation of Language and Meaning*. London: Edward Arnold.

Haraway, Donna (1991) *Simians, Cyborgs, and Women. The Reinvention of Nature*. New York: Routledge.

Harris, Roy (1980) *The Language-Makers*. London: Duckworth.

Hawkes, Terence (1977) *Structuralism and Semiotics*. London: Methuen.

Heath, Stephen (1978) 'Difference', *Screen*, 19 (3) Autumn.

Hebdige, Dick (1979) *Subculture. The Meaning of Style*. London: Routledge.

Herzog, Herta (1954) 'The Motivations and Gratifications of Daily Serial Listeners', in Wilbur Schramm (ed.) *The Process and Effects of Mass Communication*. Urbana: University of Illinois Press.

Hobsbawm, Eric (1995) *The Age of Extremes. The Short Twentieth Century, 1914–1991*. London: Abacus.

Hobson, Dorothy (1982) *'Crossroads': The Drama of Soap Opera*. London: Methuen.

Høeg, Peter (1997) *Tales of the Night*. Translated from Danish by Barbara Haveland. London: Harvill Press.

Hunter, J. Paul (1994) 'From Typology to Type: Agents of Change in Eighteenth-Century English Texts', in Margaret J.M. Ezell and Katherine O'Brien O'Keeffe (eds) *Cultural Artifacts and the Production of Meaning*. Ann Arbor: University of Michigan Press.

Hutcheon, Linda (1995) *Irony's Edge. The Theory and Politics of Irony*. London: Routledge.

Jenkins, Henry (1992) *Textual Poachers. Television Fans & Participatory Culture*. New York: Routledge.

Kaplinski, Jaan (1995) *Titanic*. Translated from Estonian into Finnish by Anja Salokannel. Helsinki: Otava.

Kress, Gunther (1979) 'The Social Values of Speech and Writing', in Roger Fowler et al. (eds) *Language and Control*. London: Routledge & Kegan Paul.

Kress, Gunther and van Leeuwen, Theo (1996) *Reading Images: The Grammar of Visual Design*. London: Routledge.

Labov, William (1972) *Language in the Inner City*. University Park: University of Pennsylvania Press.

Lakoff, George (1980) *Metaphors We Live By*. Chicago: University of Chicago Press.

Leach, Edmund (1964) 'Anthropological Aspects of Language: Animal Categories and Verbal Abuse', in E.H. Lenneberg (ed.) *New Directions in the Study of Language*. Cambridge, MA: MIT Press.

Lee, David (1992) *Competing Discourses. Perspective and Ideology in Language*. London: Longman.

Lemke, Andy L. (1995) *Textual Politics. Discourse and Social Dynamics*. London: Taylor & Francis.

Lewis, Nigel (1995) *The Book of Babel. Words and the Way We See Things*. London: Penguin Books.

Liebes, Tamar and Katz, Elihu (1990) *The Export of Meaning*. Oxford: Oxford University Press.

Lindgren, Astrid (1977) *Pippi Goes on Board*. Translated by Florence Lambord. Harmondsworth: Puffin Books.

Livingstone, Sonia and Lunt, Peter (1994) *Talk on Television. Audience Participation and Public Debate*. London: Routledge.

Long, Elizabeth (1994) 'Textual Interpretation as Collective Action', in Jon Cruz and Justin Lewis (eds) *Weaving, Reading, Listening. Audiences and Cultural Reception*. Boulder, CO: Westview Press.

Lull, James (1990) *Inside Family Viewing. Ethnographic Research on Television's Audiences*. London: Comedia/Routledge.

Lury, Celia (1993) *Cultural Rights. Technology, Legality, and Personality*. London: Routledge.

McCloskey, Donald N. (1990) 'Storytelling in Economics', in Christopher Nash (ed.) *Narrative in Culture. The Uses of Storytelling in the Sciences, Philosophy, and Literature*. London: Routledge.

MacKenzie, Donald and Wajcman, Judy (1985) 'Introductory Essay', in Donald

Mackenzie and Judy Wajcman (eds) *The Social Shaping of Technology: How the Refrigerator Got its Hum*. Milton Keynes: Open University Press.

Martin, Henri-Jean (1981) 'Printing', in Raymond Williams (ed.) *Contact: Human Communication and its History*. London: Thames & Hudson.

Marx, Karl (1857–1858) (1973) *Grundrisse: Foundations of the Critique of Political Economy*. Translated with a Foreword by Martin Nikolaus. Harmondsworth: Penguin.

Meinhof, Ulrike and Richardson, Kay (1994) 'Introduction', in Ulrike Meinhof and Kay Richardson (eds) *Text, Discourse and Context. Representations of Poverty in Britain*. London: Longman.

Mengham, Rod (1995) *Language*. London: Fontana Press.

Mills, Sara (1995) *Feminist Stylistics*. London: Routledge.

Mitchell, W.J.T. (1994) *Picture Theory. Essays on Verbal and Visual Representation*. Chicago: University of Chicago Press.

Montgomery, Martin (1986) *An Introduction to Language and Society*. London: Methuen.

Montgomery, Martin, Durant, Alan, Fabb, Nigel, Furniss, Tom and Mills, Sara (1992) *Ways of Reading: Advanced Reading Skills for Students of English Literature*. London: Routledge.

Morley, David (1980a) *The 'Nationwide' Audience: Structure and Decoding*. London: British Film Institute.

Morley, David (1980b) 'Texts, Readers, Subjects', in Stuart Hall, Dorothy Hobson, Andrew Lowe and Paul Willis (eds) *Culture, Media, Language. Working Papers in Cultural Studies, 1972–1979*. London: Hutchinson.

Morley, David (1992) *Television, Audiences and Cultural Studies*. London: Routledge.

Morris, Meaghan (1990) 'Banality in Cultural Studies', in Patricia Mellencamp (ed.) *The Logics of Television*. Bloomington: Indiana University Press.

Murdock, Graham, Hartmann, Paul and Gray, Peggy (1992) 'Contextualizing Home Computing: Resources and Practices', in Roger Silverstone and Eric Hirsch (eds) *Consuming Technologies: Media and Information in Domestic Spaces*. London: Routledge.

Neale, Stephen (1980) *Genre*. London: BFI Publishing.

Neale, Stephen (1990) 'Question of Genre', *Screen*, 31(1) Spring.

Norman, Donald A. (1993) *Things That Make Us Smart: Defending Human Attributes in the Age of the Machine*. Reading, MA: Addison-Wesley.

Oxford English Dictionary (1956) Oxford: Clarendon Press.

Oxford English Dictionary (1989) Oxford: Clarendon Press.

Oxford Latin Dictionary (1968) Oxford: Clarendon Press.

Palmer, Jerry (1991) *Potboilers. Methods, Concepts and Case Studies in Popular Fiction*. London: Routledge.

Pêcheux, Michel (1982) *Language, Semantics and Ideology. Stating the Obvious*. Translated by Harbans Nagpal. London: Macmillan.

Perloff, Marjorie (1977) *Frank O'Hara: Poet among Painters*. New York: Braziller.

Plato (1993) *Erotic Dialogues*. Translated by William S. Cobb. New York: State University of New York Press.

Porter, Roy (1991) 'Introduction', in Peter Burke and Roy Porter (eds) *Language, Self, and Society. A Social History of Language*. Cambridge: Polity Press.

Radway, Janice (1984a) *Reading the Romance. Women, Patriarchy, and Popular Literature*. Chapel Hill: University of North Carolina Press.

Radway, Janice (1984b) 'Interpretative Communities and Variable Literacies: The Functions of Romance Reading', *Daedalus*, Summer.

Radway, Janice (1988) 'Reception Study: Ethnography and the Problem of Dispersed Audiences and Nomadic Subjects', *Cultural Studies*, 2(3).

Régnier-Bohler, Danielle (1988) 'Imagining the Self', in Georges Duby (ed.) *A History of Private Life. II: Revelations of the Medieval World*. Cambridge, MA: The Belknap Press of Harvard University Press.

Rich, Adrienne (1972) 'When We Dead Awaken: Writing as Re-Vision', *College English*, 3.

Ross, Andrew (1989) *No Respect. Intellectuals and Popular Culture*. New York: Routledge.

Rossi-Landi, Ferruccio and Pesaresi, Massimo (1981) 'Language', in Raymond Williams (ed.) *Contact: Human Communication and its History*. London: Thames & Hudson.

Rushdie, Salman (1988) *The Satanic Verses*. London: Viking.

Saint-Martin, Fernande (1990) *Semiotics of Visual Language*. Bloomington: Indiana University Press.

Saussure, Ferdinand de (1974) *Course in General Linguistics*. Edited by Charles Bally and Albert Sechehaye in collaboration with Albert Reidlinger. Translated by Wade Baskin. Fontana/Collins.

Schiach, Morag (1989) *Discourse on Popular Culture*. Oxford: Polity Press.

Schutz, Alfred (1973) 'On Multiple Realities', in *Collected Papers*, Vol. 1. The Hague: Martinus Nijhoff.

Silverman, Kaja (1983) *The Subject of Semiotics*. New York: Oxford University Press.

Silverstone, Roger (1994) *Television and Everyday Life*. London: Routledge.

Slack, Jennifer Daryl (1996) 'The Theory and Method of Articulation', in David Morley and Kuan-Hsing Chen (eds) *Stuart Hall: Critical Dialogues in Cultural Studies*. London: Routledge.

Smith, Anthony (1991) *The Age of Behemoths: the Globalization of Mass Media Firms*. New York: Priority Press.

Smith, Olivia (1984) *The Politics of Language 1791–1819*. Oxford: Clarendon Press.

Soon Peng Su, (1994) *Lexical Ambiguity in Poetry*. London: Longman.

Stallybrass, Peter and White, Allon (1986) *The Politics and Poetics of Transgression*. London: Methuen.

Steen, Gerard (1994) *Understanding Metaphor in Literature. An Empirical Approach*. London: Longman.

Still, Judith and Worton, Michael (1990) 'Introduction', in Michael Worton and Judith Still (eds) *Intertextuality. Theories and Practices*. Manchester: Manchester University Press.

Still, Judith and Worton, Michael (1993) 'Introduction', in Judith Still and Michael Worton (eds) *Textuality and Sexuality. Reading Theories and Practices*. Manchester: Manchester University Press.

Swann, Cal (1991) *Language and Typography*. London: Lund Humphries.

Talbot, Mary M. (1995) *Fictions at Work. Language and Social Practice in Fiction*. London: Longman.

Tiffin, Chris and Lawson, Alan (1994) 'Introduction: The Textuality of Empire', in Chris Tiffin and Alan Lawson (eds) *De-Scribing Empire. Post-colonialism and Textuality*. London: Routledge.

Todorov, Tzvetan (1980) 'Reading as Construction', in Susan R. Suleiman and Inge Crosman (eds) *The Reader in the Text. Essays on Audience and Interpretation*. Princeton, NJ: Princeton University Press.

Tulloch, John (1990) *Television Drama. Agency, Audience and Myth*. London: Routledge.

Voloshinov, Valentin (1971) *Marxism and the Philosophy of Language*. Translated by Ladislav Matejka and I.R. Titunik. Cambridge, MA: Harvard University Press.

Voloshinov, Valentin (1976) *Freudianism: a Marxist Critique*. Translated by I.R. Titunik. New York: Academic Press.

Weedon, Chris (1987) *Feminist Practice and Poststructuralist Theory*. Oxford: Blackwell.

Williams, Raymond (1961) *The Long Revolution*. London: Chatto & Windus.

Williams, Raymond (1977) *Marxism and Literature*. Oxford: Oxford University Press.

Williams, Raymond (1981a) *Keywords. A Vocabulary of Culture and Society*. London: Fontana Paperbacks.

Williams, Raymond (1981b) *Culture*. London: Fontana Paperbacks.

Williams, Raymond (1983) *Towards 2000*. London: Chatto & Windus.

Williams, Raymond (1990) *Television. Technology and Cultural Form*. Second Edition. Edited by Ederyn Williams. London: Routledge.

Willis, Paul (1990) *Common Culture. Symbolic Work at Play in the Everyday Cultures of the Young*. Milton Keynes: Open University Press.

Worton, Michael and Still, Judith (eds) (1990) *Intertextuality, Theories and Practices*. Manchester: Manchester University Press.